THE GOSPELS

ACCORDING TO MATTHEW, MARK, LUKE AND JOHN

NRSV

Bible Society

Cover design by Patrick Knowles
Colour section design by Colin Hall
Typesetting and production management by Bible Society Resources Ltd, a
wholly-owned subsidiary of The British and Foreign Bible Society

BSRL/NRSV530/2019/5M
Printed in Italy

biblesociety.org.uk

CONTENTS

Foreword

Welcome to this special edition of the gospels. These four accounts of the life, death and resurrection of Jesus Christ represent the heart of the Christian story – a story which describes the gift of new life, offered to each one of us.

Through the lenses of these four accounts, we perceive a rich and compelling depiction of Jesus. We see him in the vulnerability of a baby, the inquisitiveness of a child, the gentleness of a healer, the force of a prophet, the determination of an activist and the humility of a servant. We encounter Jesus – fully God, fully man.

The words of these gospels echo through the centuries precisely because they speak afresh in every generation. Ever ancient, ever new, this story of transformation invites us to be transformed and gradually conformed to the likeness of the one who was the gift to others. Not dead words on a page, but a living message addressed to each of us personally.

I invite you now to prayerfully discover again the gift of Christ through this sacred book. Allow yourself to be challenged and persuaded. Permit yourself to be refreshed and surprised.

My prayer for you is that in reading these accounts, you will once again discover the joy of the gospel, and – renewed in your faith – you will live that gospel message aloud in the world around you as a gift to all those whom you encounter.

The Rt Revd Peter M Brignall
Bishop of Wrexham

Beginning to Read the Gospels

> The Bible is the most read book in the history of the world.

> It has influenced the lives of people as diverse as Kaká and Rembrandt, Mumford & Sons and Mother Teresa, Rihanna and Winston Churchill.

> It has inspired revolutions of change and is at the heart of the way our own society works.

Yet, for many of us, it's a challenge to get to grips with the scriptures. So to make it easier, we offer these four gospels, taken from the New Testament, with some helpful information about their background and meaning. Through these gospels we hope you will discover more about the person of Christ, who is at the centre of our faith, and who is always with us on our own journey through life.

What is a 'gospel'?

'Gospel' usually refers to an account of the life of Jesus that was written to encourage people to believe in him and to follow his way of life. The original Greek word for gospel is evangelion, which means 'good news' (gospel comes from 'godspel', an Old English word for that phrase).

There are four gospels in the Bible: Matthew, Mark, Luke and John. The first three are called the synoptic gospels because they include many of the same stories about Jesus, often in a similar sequence and with similar words. The term *synoptic* comes from the Greek meaning 'seeing all together'. They are different from John whose content is distinct – he misses out details about Jesus' life that are present in the other three gospels and includes information that is not in the other gospels.

The Gospels According to Matthew, Mark, Luke and John

Like each book of the Bible, **the four gospels are divided into chapters, and each chapter is divided into verses**. These verses and chapters aren't found in the original manuscripts, but Christians have found it helpful to use this system so that they don't get lost in all the words.

As there are four gospels it is easier to start by reading smaller chunks rather than by trying to read all four in one stretch. If it helps you, start with Mark first unless you like dipping in and out of all four. If you would like to read a whole gospel in one go you will find it has a power and intensity of its own. Don't forget that because they were written 2,000 years ago some of the language might sound strange or not very clear. If you have questions, try asking your priest, family or friends. Questions can make the gospels come alive; talking about the texts will help you deepen your understanding and faith as well as challenge you to explore your ideas and share them with others.

Some people like to say a short prayer before they read the gospels, asking the Holy Spirit to guide them.

> *Lord,*
> *We ask you to prepare us as we read the gospels.*
> *Open our hearts and minds to your great mysteries and truths.*
> *May your Holy Spirit guide us as we seek to know and love you more deeply.*
> *Amen.*

Others like to read a chosen passage out loud (as we hear things differently when spoken, while others like to take notes, or underline different words or passages. Do whatever works for you. There's no right or wrong way.

Four Gospels, One Christ

Why are there four gospels rather than just the one?

Imagine you are talking about someone who isn't here, you may be thinking of a friend or someone in your family. You will have an idea of what they're like and how you see them. Other people may have a different idea of the same person from a different perspective. All of you will be talking about the same person but bringing a range of memories about who they are, what they have said to you and the kind of life they lead. The four gospels are a bit like this. They are each describing the same person – Jesus Christ, but from a different angle. Although there is much overlap in the synoptic gospels, they have their differences and together with John, form a rich and dynamic picture of Jesus, the Son of God – of his life, death and resurrection.

Here are some of the interesting differences and symbols found in the gospels.

Traditionally there have been four symbols attributed to the four gospel writers and which you can see in many paintings, manuscripts, architecture and stained glass windows in churches.

Matthew – a man, Mark – a lion, Luke – an ox, John – an eagle.

These four symbols are taken from references in two places of the Bible:

The Old Testament book, Ezekiel 1:10-11a *'As for the appearance of their faces: the four had the face of a human being, the face of a lion on the right side, the face of an ox on the left side, and the face of an eagle; such were their faces. Their wings were spread out above.'*

The New Testament book, Revelation 4:7-8a *'the first living creature like a lion, the second living creature like an ox, the third living creature with a face like a human face, and the fourth living creature like a flying eagle. And the four living creatures, each of them with six wings.'*

The Gospels According to Matthew, Mark, Luke and John

Matthew – a man

Matthew's symbol is a man because his gospel represents humanity and is focused on the humanity of Jesus. He begins his gospel with a list all of Jesus' ancestors and Jesus' humility is mentioned throughout the book.

Mark – a lion

Mark's symbol is a lion because his gospel represents leadership and royalty (these qualities are traditionally associated with the lion). Jesus Christ perfectly models real leadership and royalty.

Luke – an ox

Luke's symbol is an ox because the ox was used in sacrifices in the Temple and there is a sacrifice being offered at the beginning of his gospel. The ox is seen as a reminder of the priestly character of Jesus and of his sacrificial death for the sins of all the world.

John – an eagle

John's symbol is an eagle because unlike the three synoptic gospels it begins with a deep meditation upon the meaning of the fact of Christ, as if looking at Christ from above rather than from the ground while he is with his followers. John also includes a description of the disciples receiving the Holy Spirit making the symbol of a winged or flying eagle even more powerful.

These symbols of the gospel writers show their connection to the divine. They are messengers of God so are all portrayed with wings and are bringers of the 'good news'.

Christian Initiation and the Scriptures

The sacraments of *Baptism, Confirmation* and *Eucharist* are gifts from God but they also show us how to live.

❯ *They strengthen us to be followers of Jesus and each have their roots in the Bible.*

Baptism is a beginning. In Mark's Gospel Jesus first appears when he is baptised by John the Baptist (Mark 1:9). Jesus is in the waters of the river Jordan, a sign of cleansing and purification. This is the start of Jesus's public ministry and that's where Mark wants to start. By the end of Mark's first chapter, Jesus has done a lot. Mark's Gospel is fast-paced — he wants you to know about the good news of Jesus.

We associate Confirmation with the idea of being 'sent'. At the end of Luke's Gospel Jesus explains to the disciples that the Scriptures have prepared them for his death and resurrection; and for them to be sent out to preach the good news in his name (Luke 24:44-53). To help them the Holy Spirit will be given to the disciples once Jesus has ascended into heaven and this will take place at Pentecost. Pentecost isn't mentioned in the gospels but in the sequel to Luke's Gospel, the Acts of the Apostles. In Confirmation the Holy Spirit likewise strengthens us to give witness to Jesus in what we say and do.

The story of Jesus' crucifixion and resurrection is the climax of the gospel story. It starts with the account of his Last Supper with his disciples. In Matthew's Gospel the passage is short (Matthew 26:26-29) but familiar. Jesus' invitation to 'Take, eat' and 'Drink' on an evening in the first century has been repeated across the

The Gospels According to Matthew, Mark, Luke and John

centuries and continues today in all of our Eucharists. We, who respond to Jesus' invitation with our 'Amen', stand in a long line of Christians throughout the world.

'Amen' from the biblical text means 'So be it'. When we say Amen at Communion we are not just saying 'Yes' to receiving the body and blood of Jesus but 'Yes' to everything that Jesus says when he proclaims: 'Do this in memory of me'. In John's Gospel Jesus also washes the feet of his disciples (John 13:2–20). He does this to show the disciples that to be a follower of Jesus, to be in communion with him, is to be one who serves others.

The sacraments of Baptism, Confirmation and Eucharist strengthen us to be followers of Jesus and this way of life is built on four pillars of: prayer, understanding, community and outreach. In Luke's Gospel we see this early on when Jesus returns to his home town, Nazareth, and preaches in the synagogue (Luke 4:16–30). This is about public prayer which we call liturgy. It is the Sabbath, Jesus is in the synagogue reading from scripture, the prophet Isaiah. He will then explain the scriptures, relate them to his listeners' lives and deepen their understanding and faith. We believe that scripture is meant to be heard and shared among a community of believers. This is not only true of scripture but for all aspects of our faith which nurtures and grows with the help and influence of others.

Finally, what passage does Jesus choose? Here in Luke 4:16-30, Jesus (referring back to Isaiah 61.1-2) sets out his ministry which will not just be about teaching. It will be about transforming people's lives: bringing good news, giving new sight and setting people free. To be a disciple we not only need a community but we need to look beyond ourselves and offer good news to those in need. Jesus shows us that the scriptures guide us along the way.

Going Deeper into Scripture

To appreciate the gospels, it can really help to discover where they fall within the whole story of the Bible. One way to understand this bigger story is:

1 God created human beings and the wider creation, and loved us completely.

Genesis, Psalms and the beginning of John's Gospel describe this.

2 Humanity chose to turn away from God, trying to make ourselves like mini-gods and creating all sorts of damage (sin) along the way.

Genesis, Psalms and the letter to the Romans describe this, although much of the Old Testament is about humanity choosing to turn away from God.

3 God initiated a rescue plan for humanity, making a series of promises or agreements with his people.

Genesis, Exodus, Joshua, Isaiah, Jeremiah, and much of the Old Testament is about these 'Covenant' promises.

4 Humanity for their part, asked questions about purpose, integrity, wisdom, love and beauty to try to understand God and the world around them.

Proverbs, Ecclesiastes and Song of Songs.

The Gospels According to Matthew, Mark, Luke and John

5 To fulfil his rescue plan, God himself came to be with humanity, in the mystery of Jesus – fully human and fully divine.

The gospels.

6 By coming to be with us, God invited humanity to be with him – to live a new, Spirit-filled life as a child of God.

The Acts of the Apostles.

7 We live this life as a child of God as part of a wider family – the Church – which helps us to live wisely and to receive moments of special grace (sacraments) pointed to by the Scriptures.

The New Testament Letters.

8 We look forward to the day when we will meet Jesus face to face; a vision of a world where the pain and suffering caused by humanity's wrongdoing will be ultimately banished.

Revelation.

Next steps

So once you've read one or all of the gospels, why not try another part of the Bible as suggested above?

If you've got questions about the Bible, why not visit our online FAQs at **biblesociety.org.uk/explore-the-bible**

Reading the Scriptures alongside others can really help. Why not arrange an opportunity to discuss the Bible with friends, or others at church? One really easy way to do this is to use *lyfe* materials from Bible Society at **biblesociety.org.uk/explore-the-bible/lyfe**

As Catholics, we listen to the Bible every single week at Sunday Mass. Why not spend 15 minutes reading through the gospel and considering what it might mean for you before Mass? You can find out what the gospel reading will be at **universalis.com**

There are thousands of tools, apps and websites to help you explore the Scriptures on a regular basis. You can find a directory of some of the best of these on the Bible Society website – **biblesociety.org.uk** and **cbcew.org.uk/bible-studies**

THE GOSPELS

ACCORDING TO MATTHEW, MARK, LUKE AND JOHN

The Gospel According to

Matthew

The Genealogy of Jesus the Messiah

1 An account of the genealogy*a* of Jesus the Messiah,*b* the son of David, the son of Abraham.

²Abraham was the father of Isaac, and Isaac the father of Jacob, and Jacob the father of Judah and his brothers, ³and Judah the father of Perez and Zerah by Tamar, and Perez the father of Hezron, and Hezron the father of Aram, ⁴and Aram the father of Aminadab, and Aminadab the father of Nahshon, and Nahshon the father of Salmon, ⁵and Salmon the father of Boaz by Rahab, and Boaz the father of Obed by Ruth, and Obed the father of Jesse, ⁶and Jesse the father of King David.

And David was the father of Solomon by the wife of Uriah, ⁷and Solomon the father of Rehoboam, and Rehoboam the father of Abijah, and Abijah the father of Asaph,*c* ⁸and Asaph*c* the father of Jehoshaphat, and Jehoshaphat the father of Joram, and Joram the father of Uzziah, ⁹and Uzziah the father of Jotham, and Jotham the father of Ahaz, and Ahaz the father of Hezekiah, ¹⁰and Hezekiah the father of Manasseh, and Manasseh the father of Amos,*d* and Amos*d* the father of Josiah, ¹¹and Josiah the father of Jechoniah and his brothers, at the time of the deportation to Babylon.

¹²And after the deportation to Babylon: Jechoniah was the father of Salathiel, and Salathiel the father of Zerubbabel, ¹³and Zerubbabel the father of Abiud, and Abiud the father of Eliakim, and Eliakim the father of Azor, ¹⁴and Azor the father of Zadok, and

---

a Or *birth*   b Or *Jesus Christ*   c Other ancient authorities read *Asa*   d Other ancient authorities read *Amon*

Zadok the father of Achim, and Achim the father of Eliud, ¹⁵and Eliud the father of Eleazar, and Eleazar the father of Matthan, and Matthan the father of Jacob, ¹⁶and Jacob the father of Joseph the husband of Mary, of whom Jesus was born, who is called the Messiah.ᵉ

¹⁷So all the generations from Abraham to David are fourteen generations; and from David to the deportation to Babylon, fourteen generations; and from the deportation to Babylon to the Messiah,ᵉ fourteen generations.

The Birth of Jesus the Messiah

¹⁸Now the birth of Jesus the Messiahᶠ took place in this way. When his mother Mary had been engaged to Joseph, but before they lived together, she was found to be with child from the Holy Spirit. ¹⁹Her husband Joseph, being a righteous man and unwilling to expose her to public disgrace, planned to dismiss her quietly. ²⁰But just when he had resolved to do this, an angel of the Lord appeared to him in a dream and said, 'Joseph, son of David, do not be afraid to take Mary as your wife, for the child conceived in her is from the Holy Spirit. ²¹She will bear a son, and you are to name him Jesus, for he will save his people from their sins.' ²²All this took place to fulfil what had been spoken by the Lord through the prophet:

²³ 'Look, the virgin shall conceive and bear a son,
    and they shall name him Emmanuel',

which means, 'God is with us.' ²⁴When Joseph awoke from sleep, he did as the angel of the Lord commanded him; he took her as his wife, ²⁵but had no marital relations with her until she had borne a son;ᵍ and he named him Jesus.

The Visit of the Wise Men

2 In the time of King Herod, after Jesus was born in Bethlehem of Judea, wise menʰ from the East came to Jerusalem, ²asking, 'Where is the child who has been born king of the Jews? For we observed his star at its rising,ⁱ and have come to pay him homage.' ³When King Herod heard this, he was frightened, and

---

e Or *the Christ*   f Or *Jesus Christ*   g Other ancient authorities read *her firstborn son*
h Or *astrologers*; Gk *magi*   i Or *in the East*

all Jerusalem with him; [4] and calling together all the chief priests and scribes of the people, he inquired of them where the Messiah[j] was to be born. [5] They told him, 'In Bethlehem of Judea; for so it has been written by the prophet:

[6] "And you, Bethlehem, in the land of Judah,
     are by no means least among the rulers of Judah;
   for from you shall come a ruler
     who is to shepherd[k] my people Israel." '

[7] Then Herod secretly called for the wise men[l] and learned from them the exact time when the star had appeared. [8] Then he sent them to Bethlehem, saying, 'Go and search diligently for the child; and when you have found him, bring me word so that I may also go and pay him homage.' [9] When they had heard the king, they set out; and there, ahead of them, went the star that they had seen at its rising,[m] until it stopped over the place where the child was. [10] When they saw that the star had stopped,[n] they were overwhelmed with joy. [11] On entering the house, they saw the child with Mary his mother; and they knelt down and paid him homage. Then, opening their treasure-chests, they offered him gifts of gold, frankincense, and myrrh. [12] And having been warned in a dream not to return to Herod, they left for their own country by another road.

The Escape to Egypt

[13] Now after they had left, an angel of the Lord appeared to Joseph in a dream and said, 'Get up, take the child and his mother, and flee to Egypt, and remain there until I tell you; for Herod is about to search for the child, to destroy him.' [14] Then Joseph[o] got up, took the child and his mother by night, and went to Egypt, [15] and remained there until the death of Herod. This was to fulfil what had been spoken by the Lord through the prophet, 'Out of Egypt I have called my son.'

The Massacre of the Infants

[16] When Herod saw that he had been tricked by the wise men,[p] he was infuriated, and he sent and killed all the children in and

---

j Or the Christ   k Or rule   l Or astrologers; Gk magi   m Or in the East   n Gk saw the star   o Gk he   p Or astrologers; Gk magi

around Bethlehem who were two years old or under, according to the time that he had learned from the wise men.*p* ¹⁷Then was fulfilled what had been spoken through the prophet Jeremiah:

¹⁸ 'A voice was heard in Ramah,
    wailing and loud lamentation,
  Rachel weeping for her children;
    she refused to be consoled, because they are no
      more.'

The Return from Egypt

¹⁹When Herod died, an angel of the Lord suddenly appeared in a dream to Joseph in Egypt and said, ²⁰'Get up, take the child and his mother, and go to the land of Israel, for those who were seeking the child's life are dead.' ²¹Then Joseph*q* got up, took the child and his mother, and went to the land of Israel. ²²But when he heard that Archelaus was ruling over Judea in place of his father Herod, he was afraid to go there. And after being warned in a dream, he went away to the district of Galilee. ²³There he made his home in a town called Nazareth, so that what had been spoken through the prophets might be fulfilled, 'He will be called a Nazorean.'

The Proclamation of John the Baptist

3 In those days John the Baptist appeared in the wilderness of Judea, proclaiming, ²'Repent, for the kingdom of heaven has come near.'*r* ³This is the one of whom the prophet Isaiah spoke when he said,

  'The voice of one crying out in the wilderness:
  "Prepare the way of the Lord,
    make his paths straight." '

⁴Now John wore clothing of camel's hair with a leather belt around his waist, and his food was locusts and wild honey. ⁵Then the people of Jerusalem and all Judea were going out to him, and all the region along the Jordan, ⁶and they were baptized by him in the river Jordan, confessing their sins.

⁷But when he saw many Pharisees and Sadducees coming for baptism, he said to them, 'You brood of vipers! Who warned you

---

p Or *astrologers*; Gk *magi*   q Gk *he*   r Or *is at hand* to flee from the wrath to come? ⁸Bear fruit worthy of repentance. ⁹Do not presume to say to yourselves, "We have Abraham as our ancestor"; for I tell you, God is able from these stones to raise up children to Abraham. ¹⁰Even now the axe is lying at the root of the trees; every tree therefore that does not bear good fruit is cut down and thrown into the fire.

¹¹'I baptize you with⁵ water for repentance, but one who is more powerful than I is coming after me; I am not worthy to carry his sandals. He will baptize you with⁵ the Holy Spirit and fire. ¹²His winnowing-fork is in his hand, and he will clear his threshing-floor and will gather his wheat into the granary; but the chaff he will burn with unquenchable fire.'

The Baptism of Jesus

¹³Then Jesus came from Galilee to John at the Jordan, to be baptized by him. ¹⁴John would have prevented him, saying, 'I need to be baptized by you, and do you come to me?' ¹⁵But Jesus answered him, 'Let it be so now; for it is proper for us in this way to fulfil all righteousness.' Then he consented. ¹⁶And when Jesus had been baptized, just as he came up from the water, suddenly the heavens were opened to him and he saw the Spirit of God descending like a dove and alighting on him. ¹⁷And a voice from heaven said, 'This is my Son, the Beloved,ᵗ with whom I am well pleased.'

The Temptation of Jesus

4 Then Jesus was led up by the Spirit into the wilderness to be tempted by the devil. ²He fasted for forty days and forty nights, and afterwards he was famished. ³The tempter came and said to him, 'If you are the Son of God, command these stones to become loaves of bread.' ⁴But he answered, 'It is written,

"One does not live by bread alone,
    but by every word that comes from the mouth of
        God." '

⁵Then the devil took him to the holy city and placed him on the pinnacle of the temple, ⁶saying to him, 'If you are the Son of God, throw yourself down; for it is written,

---

s Or *in*   t Or *my beloved Son*

"He will command his angels concerning you",
and "On their hands they will bear you up,
so that you will not dash your foot against a stone." '
⁷Jesus said to him, 'Again it is written, "Do not put the Lord your God to the test." '

⁸Again, the devil took him to a very high mountain and showed him all the kingdoms of the world and their splendour; ⁹and he said to him, 'All these I will give you, if you will fall down and worship me.' ¹⁰Jesus said to him, 'Away with you, Satan! for it is written,

"Worship the Lord your God,
and serve only him." '
¹¹Then the devil left him, and suddenly angels came and waited on him.

Jesus Begins His Ministry in Galilee

¹²Now when Jesus[u] heard that John had been arrested, he withdrew to Galilee. ¹³He left Nazareth and made his home in Capernaum by the lake, in the territory of Zebulun and Naphtali, ¹⁴so that what had been spoken through the prophet Isaiah might be fulfilled:

¹⁵ 'Land of Zebulun, land of Naphtali,
on the road by the sea, across the Jordan, Galilee of the Gentiles—
¹⁶ the people who sat in darkness
have seen a great light,
and for those who sat in the region and shadow of death
light has dawned.'
¹⁷From that time Jesus began to proclaim, 'Repent, for the kingdom of heaven has come near.'[v]

Jesus Calls the First Disciples

¹⁸As he walked by the Sea of Galilee, he saw two brothers, Simon, who is called Peter, and Andrew his brother, casting a net into the lake—for they were fishermen. ¹⁹And he said to them, 'Follow me, and I will make you fish for people.' ²⁰Immediately

---

u Gk *he*   v Or *is at hand*

they left their nets and followed him. ²¹As he went from there, he saw two other brothers, James son of Zebedee and his brother John, in the boat with their father Zebedee, mending their nets, and he called them. ²²Immediately they left the boat and their father, and followed him.

Jesus Ministers to Crowds of People
²³Jesus^w went throughout Galilee, teaching in their synagogues and proclaiming the good news^x of the kingdom and curing every disease and every sickness among the people. ²⁴So his fame spread throughout all Syria, and they brought to him all the sick, those who were afflicted with various diseases and pains, demoniacs, epileptics, and paralytics, and he cured them. ²⁵And great crowds followed him from Galilee, the Decapolis, Jerusalem, Judea, and from beyond the Jordan.

The Beatitudes
5 When Jesus^y saw the crowds, he went up the mountain; and after he sat down, his disciples came to him. ²Then he began to speak, and taught them, saying:

³'Blessed are the poor in spirit, for theirs is the kingdom of heaven.

⁴'Blessed are those who mourn, for they will be comforted.

⁵'Blessed are the meek, for they will inherit the earth.

⁶'Blessed are those who hunger and thirst for righteousness, for they will be filled.

⁷'Blessed are the merciful, for they will receive mercy.

⁸'Blessed are the pure in heart, for they will see God.

⁹'Blessed are the peacemakers, for they will be called children of God.

¹⁰'Blessed are those who are persecuted for righteousness' sake, for theirs is the kingdom of heaven.

¹¹'Blessed are you when people revile you and persecute you and utter all kinds of evil against you falsely^z on my account. ¹²Rejoice and be glad, for your reward is great in heaven, for in the same way they persecuted the prophets who were before you.

_____

w Gk He   x Gk gospel   y Gk he   z Other ancient authorities lack falsely

Salt and Light

¹³'You are the salt of the earth; but if salt has lost its taste, how can its saltiness be restored? It is no longer good for anything, but is thrown out and trampled under foot.

¹⁴'You are the light of the world. A city built on a hill cannot be hidden. ¹⁵No one after lighting a lamp puts it under the bushel basket, but on the lampstand, and it gives light to all in the house. ¹⁶In the same way, let your light shine before others, so that they may see your good works and give glory to your Father in heaven.

The Law and the Prophets

¹⁷'Do not think that I have come to abolish the law or the prophets; I have come not to abolish but to fulfil. ¹⁸For truly I tell you, until heaven and earth pass away, not one letter,ᵃ not one stroke of a letter, will pass from the law until all is accomplished. ¹⁹Therefore, whoever breaksᵇ one of the least of these commandments, and teaches others to do the same, will be called least in the kingdom of heaven; but whoever does them and teaches them will be called great in the kingdom of heaven. ²⁰For I tell you, unless your righteousness exceeds that of the scribes and Pharisees, you will never enter the kingdom of heaven.

Concerning Anger

²¹'You have heard that it was said to those of ancient times, "You shall not murder"; and "whoever murders shall be liable to judgement." ²²But I say to you that if you are angry with a brother or sister,ᶜ you will be liable to judgement; and if you insultᵈ a brother or sister,ᵉ you will be liable to the council; and if you say, "You fool", you will be liable to the hellᶠ of fire. ²³So when you are offering your gift at the altar, if you remember that your brother or sisterᵍ has something against you, ²⁴leave your gift there before the altar and go; first be reconciled to your brother or sister,ᵍ and then come and offer your gift. ²⁵Come

---

a Gk *one iota* b Or *annuls* c Gk *a brother*; other ancient authorities add *without cause*
d Gk *say Raca to* (an obscure term of abuse) e Gk *a brother* f Gk *Gehenna* g Gk *your brother*

to terms quickly with your accuser while you are on the way to court[h] with him, or your accuser may hand you over to the judge, and the judge to the guard, and you will be thrown into prison. ²⁶Truly I tell you, you will never get out until you have paid the last penny.

Concerning Adultery

²⁷'You have heard that it was said, "You shall not commit adultery." ²⁸But I say to you that everyone who looks at a woman with lust has already committed adultery with her in his heart. ²⁹If your right eye causes you to sin, tear it out and throw it away; it is better for you to lose one of your members than for your whole body to be thrown into hell.[i] ³⁰And if your right hand causes you to sin, cut it off and throw it away; it is better for you to lose one of your members than for your whole body to go into hell.[i]

Concerning Divorce

³¹'It was also said, "Whoever divorces his wife, let him give her a certificate of divorce." ³²But I say to you that anyone who divorces his wife, except on the ground of unchastity, causes her to commit adultery; and whoever marries a divorced woman commits adultery.

Concerning Oaths

³³'Again, you have heard that it was said to those of ancient times, "You shall not swear falsely, but carry out the vows you have made to the Lord." ³⁴But I say to you, Do not swear at all, either by heaven, for it is the throne of God, ³⁵or by the earth, for it is his footstool, or by Jerusalem, for it is the city of the great King. ³⁶And do not swear by your head, for you cannot make one hair white or black. ³⁷Let your word be "Yes, Yes" or "No, No"; anything more than this comes from the evil one.[j]

Concerning Retaliation

³⁸'You have heard that it was said, "An eye for an eye and a tooth for a tooth." ³⁹But I say to you, Do not resist an evildoer.

---

h Gk lacks *to court*   i Gk *Gehenna*   j Or *evil*

But if anyone strikes you on the right cheek, turn the other also;
⁴⁰and if anyone wants to sue you and take your coat, give your
cloak as well; ⁴¹and if anyone forces you to go one mile, go also
the second mile. ⁴²Give to everyone who begs from you, and do
not refuse anyone who wants to borrow from you.

Love for Enemies

⁴³'You have heard that it was said, "You shall love your
neighbour and hate your enemy." ⁴⁴But I say to you, Love your
enemies and pray for those who persecute you, ⁴⁵so that you
may be children of your Father in heaven; for he makes his sun
rise on the evil and on the good, and sends rain on the righteous
and on the unrighteous. ⁴⁶For if you love those who love you,
what reward do you have? Do not even the tax-collectors do the
same? ⁴⁷And if you greet only your brothers and sisters,ᵏ what
more are you doing than others? Do not even the Gentiles do the
same? ⁴⁸Be perfect, therefore, as your heavenly Father is perfect.

Concerning Almsgiving

6 'Beware of practising your piety before others in order to
be seen by them; for then you have no reward from your
Father in heaven.

²'So whenever you give alms, do not sound a trumpet before
you, as the hypocrites do in the synagogues and in the streets,
so that they may be praised by others. Truly I tell you, they have
received their reward. ³But when you give alms, do not let your
left hand know what your right hand is doing, ⁴so that your
alms may be done in secret; and your Father who sees in secret
will reward you.ˡ

Concerning Prayer

⁵'And whenever you pray, do not be like the hypocrites; for
they love to stand and pray in the synagogues and at the street
corners, so that they may be seen by others. Truly I tell you, they
have received their reward. ⁶But whenever you pray, go into your
room and shut the door and pray to your Father who is in secret;
and your Father who sees in secret will reward you.ˡ

---

k Gk *your brothers*   l Other ancient authorities add *openly*

7'When you are praying, do not heap up empty phrases as the Gentiles do; for they think that they will be heard because of their many words. 8Do not be like them, for your Father knows what you need before you ask him.

9'Pray then in this way:

Our Father in heaven,
    hallowed be your name.
10   Your kingdom come.
    Your will be done,
        on earth as it is in heaven.
11   Give us this day our daily bread.*m*
12   And forgive us our debts,
        as we also have forgiven our debtors.
13   And do not bring us to the time of trial,*n*
        but rescue us from the evil one.*o*

14For if you forgive others their trespasses, your heavenly Father will also forgive you; 15but if you do not forgive others, neither will your Father forgive your trespasses.

Concerning Fasting

16'And whenever you fast, do not look dismal, like the hypocrites, for they disfigure their faces so as to show others that they are fasting. Truly I tell you, they have received their reward. 17But when you fast, put oil on your head and wash your face, 18so that your fasting may be seen not by others but by your Father who is in secret; and your Father who sees in secret will reward you.*p*

Concerning Treasures

19'Do not store up for yourselves treasures on earth, where moth and rust*q* consume and where thieves break in and steal; 20but store up for yourselves treasures in heaven, where neither moth nor rust*q* consumes and where thieves do not break in and steal. 21For where your treasure is, there your heart will be also.

---

m Or *our bread for tomorrow*   n Or *us into temptation*   o Or *from evil.* Other ancient authorities add, in some form, *For the kingdom and the power and the glory are yours for ever. Amen.*   p Other ancient authorities add *openly*   q Gk *eating*

The Sound Eye

²²'The eye is the lamp of the body. So, if your eye is healthy, your whole body will be full of light; ²³but if your eye is unhealthy, your whole body will be full of darkness. If then the light in you is darkness, how great is the darkness!

Serving Two Masters

²⁴'No one can serve two masters; for a slave will either hate the one and love the other, or be devoted to the one and despise the other. You cannot serve God and wealth.ʳ

Do Not Worry

²⁵'Therefore I tell you, do not worry about your life, what you will eat or what you will drink,ˢ or about your body, what you will wear. Is not life more than food, and the body more than clothing? ²⁶Look at the birds of the air; they neither sow nor reap nor gather into barns, and yet your heavenly Father feeds them. Are you not of more value than they? ²⁷And can any of you by worrying add a single hour to your span of life?ᵗ ²⁸And why do you worry about clothing? Consider the lilies of the field, how they grow; they neither toil nor spin, ²⁹yet I tell you, even Solomon in all his glory was not clothed like one of these. ³⁰But if God so clothes the grass of the field, which is alive today and tomorrow is thrown into the oven, will he not much more clothe you—you of little faith? ³¹Therefore do not worry, saying, "What will we eat?" or "What will we drink?" or "What will we wear?" ³²For it is the Gentiles who strive for all these things; and indeed your heavenly Father knows that you need all these things. ³³But strive first for the kingdom of Godᵘ and hisᵛ righteousness, and all these things will be given to you as well.

³⁴'So do not worry about tomorrow, for tomorrow will bring worries of its own. Today's trouble is enough for today.

Judging Others

7 'Do not judge, so that you may not be judged. ²For with the judgement you make you will be judged, and the measure

---

r Gk *mammon*   s Other ancient authorities lack *or what you will drink*   t Or *add one cubit to your height*   u Other ancient authorities lack *of God*   v Or *its*

you give will be the measure you get. ³Why do you see the speck in your neighbour's^w eye, but do not notice the log in your own eye? ⁴Or how can you say to your neighbour,^x "Let me take the speck out of your eye", while the log is in your own eye? ⁵You hypocrite, first take the log out of your own eye, and then you will see clearly to take the speck out of your neighbour's^y eye.

Profaning the Holy

⁶'Do not give what is holy to dogs; and do not throw your pearls before swine, or they will trample them under foot and turn and maul you.

Ask, Search, Knock

⁷'Ask, and it will be given to you; search, and you will find; knock, and the door will be opened for you. ⁸For everyone who asks receives, and everyone who searches finds, and for everyone who knocks, the door will be opened. ⁹Is there anyone among you who, if your child asks for bread, will give a stone? ¹⁰Or if the child asks for a fish, will give a snake? ¹¹If you then, who are evil, know how to give good gifts to your children, how much more will your Father in heaven give good things to those who ask him!

The Golden Rule

¹²'In everything do to others as you would have them do to you; for this is the law and the prophets.

The Narrow Gate

¹³'Enter through the narrow gate; for the gate is wide and the road is easy^z that leads to destruction, and there are many who take it. ¹⁴For the gate is narrow and the road is hard that leads to life, and there are few who find it.

A Tree and Its Fruit

¹⁵'Beware of false prophets, who come to you in sheep's clothing but inwardly are ravenous wolves. ¹⁶You will know them by their fruits. Are grapes gathered from thorns, or figs from thistles?

---

w Gk *brother's*   x Gk *brother*   y Gk *brother's*   z Other ancient authorities read *for the road is wide and easy*

¹⁷In the same way, every good tree bears good fruit, but the bad tree bears bad fruit. ¹⁸A good tree cannot bear bad fruit, nor can a bad tree bear good fruit. ¹⁹Every tree that does not bear good fruit is cut down and thrown into the fire. ²⁰Thus you will know them by their fruits.

Concerning Self-Deception

²¹'Not everyone who says to me, "Lord, Lord", will enter the kingdom of heaven, but only one who does the will of my Father in heaven. ²²On that day many will say to me, "Lord, Lord, did we not prophesy in your name, and cast out demons in your name, and do many deeds of power in your name?" ²³Then I will declare to them, "I never knew you; go away from me, you evildoers."

Hearers and Doers

²⁴'Everyone then who hears these words of mine and acts on them will be like a wise man who built his house on rock. ²⁵The rain fell, the floods came, and the winds blew and beat on that house, but it did not fall, because it had been founded on rock. ²⁶And everyone who hears these words of mine and does not act on them will be like a foolish man who built his house on sand. ²⁷The rain fell, and the floods came, and the winds blew and beat against that house, and it fell—and great was its fall!'

²⁸Now when Jesus had finished saying these things, the crowds were astounded at his teaching, ²⁹for he taught them as one having authority, and not as their scribes.

Jesus Cleanses a Leper

8 When Jesus*a* had come down from the mountain, great crowds followed him; ²and there was a leper*b* who came to him and knelt before him, saying, 'Lord, if you choose, you can make me clean.' ³He stretched out his hand and touched him, saying, 'I do choose. Be made clean!' Immediately his leprosy*b* was cleansed. ⁴Then Jesus said to him, 'See that you say nothing to anyone; but go, show yourself to the priest, and offer the gift that Moses commanded, as a testimony to them.'

---

a Gk *he*   b The terms *leper* and *leprosy* can refer to several diseases

Jesus Heals a Centurion's Servant

⁵When he entered Capernaum, a centurion came to him, appealing to him ⁶and saying, 'Lord, my servant is lying at home paralysed, in terrible distress.' ⁷And he said to him, 'I will come and cure him.' ⁸The centurion answered, 'Lord, I am not worthy to have you come under my roof; but only speak the word, and my servant will be healed. ⁹For I also am a man under authority, with soldiers under me; and I say to one, "Go", and he goes, and to another, "Come", and he comes, and to my slave, "Do this", and the slave does it.' ¹⁰When Jesus heard him, he was amazed and said to those who followed him, 'Truly I tell you, in no one*c* in Israel have I found such faith. ¹¹I tell you, many will come from east and west and will eat with Abraham and Isaac and Jacob in the kingdom of heaven, ¹²while the heirs of the kingdom will be thrown into the outer darkness, where there will be weeping and gnashing of teeth.' ¹³And to the centurion Jesus said, 'Go; let it be done for you according to your faith.' And the servant was healed in that hour.

Jesus Heals Many at Peter's House

¹⁴When Jesus entered Peter's house, he saw his mother-in-law lying in bed with a fever; ¹⁵he touched her hand, and the fever left her, and she got up and began to serve him. ¹⁶That evening they brought to him many who were possessed by demons; and he cast out the spirits with a word, and cured all who were sick. ¹⁷This was to fulfil what had been spoken through the prophet Isaiah, 'He took our infirmities and bore our diseases.'

Would-Be Followers of Jesus

¹⁸Now when Jesus saw great crowds around him, he gave orders to go over to the other side. ¹⁹A scribe then approached and said, 'Teacher, I will follow you wherever you go.' ²⁰And Jesus said to him, 'Foxes have holes, and birds of the air have nests; but the Son of Man has nowhere to lay his head.' ²¹Another of his disciples said to him, 'Lord, first let me go and bury my father.' ²²But Jesus said to him, 'Follow me, and let the dead bury their own dead.'

---

c Other ancient authorities read *Truly I tell you, not even*

Jesus Stills the Storm

²³And when he got into the boat, his disciples followed him. ²⁴A gale arose on the lake, so great that the boat was being swamped by the waves; but he was asleep. ²⁵And they went and woke him up, saying, 'Lord, save us! We are perishing!' ²⁶And he said to them, 'Why are you afraid, you of little faith?' Then he got up and rebuked the winds and the sea; and there was a dead calm. ²⁷They were amazed, saying, 'What sort of man is this, that even the winds and the sea obey him?'

Jesus Heals the Gadarene Demoniacs

²⁸When he came to the other side, to the country of the Gadarenes,ᵈ two demoniacs coming out of the tombs met him. They were so fierce that no one could pass that way. ²⁹Suddenly they shouted, 'What have you to do with us, Son of God? Have you come here to torment us before the time?' ³⁰Now a large herd of swine was feeding at some distance from them. ³¹The demons begged him, 'If you cast us out, send us into the herd of swine.' ³²And he said to them, 'Go!' So they came out and entered the swine; and suddenly, the whole herd rushed down the steep bank into the lake and perished in the water. ³³The swineherds ran off, and on going into the town, they told the whole story about what had happened to the demoniacs. ³⁴Then the whole town came out to meet Jesus; and when they saw him, they begged him to leave their neighbourhood.

9 And after getting into a boat he crossed the water and came to his own town.

Jesus Heals a Paralytic

²And just then some people were carrying a paralysed man lying on a bed. When Jesus saw their faith, he said to the paralytic, 'Take heart, son; your sins are forgiven.' ³Then some of the scribes said to themselves, 'This man is blaspheming.' ⁴But Jesus, perceiving their thoughts, said, 'Why do you think evil in your hearts? ⁵For which is easier, to say, "Your sins are forgiven", or to say, "Stand up and walk"? ⁶But so that you may know that the Son of Man has authority on earth to forgive sins'–he

---

d Other ancient authorities read *Gergesenes*; others, *Gerasenes*

then said to the paralytic—'Stand up, take your bed and go to your home.' ⁷And he stood up and went to his home. ⁸When the crowds saw it, they were filled with awe, and they glorified God, who had given such authority to human beings.

The Calling of Matthew

⁹As Jesus was walking along, he saw a man called Matthew sitting at the tax booth; and he said to him, 'Follow me.' And he got up and followed him.

¹⁰And as he sat at dinner*e* in the house, many tax-collectors and sinners came and were sitting*f* with him and his disciples. ¹¹When the Pharisees saw this, they said to his disciples, 'Why does your teacher eat with tax-collectors and sinners?' ¹²But when he heard this, he said, 'Those who are well have no need of a physician, but those who are sick. ¹³Go and learn what this means, "I desire mercy, not sacrifice." For I have come to call not the righteous but sinners.'

The Question about Fasting

¹⁴Then the disciples of John came to him, saying, 'Why do we and the Pharisees fast often,*g* but your disciples do not fast?' ¹⁵And Jesus said to them, 'The wedding-guests cannot mourn as long as the bridegroom is with them, can they? The days will come when the bridegroom is taken away from them, and then they will fast. ¹⁶No one sews a piece of unshrunk cloth on an old cloak, for the patch pulls away from the cloak, and a worse tear is made. ¹⁷Neither is new wine put into old wineskins; otherwise, the skins burst, and the wine is spilled, and the skins are destroyed; but new wine is put into fresh wineskins, and so both are preserved.'

A Girl Restored to Life and a Woman Healed

¹⁸While he was saying these things to them, suddenly a leader of the synagogue*h* came in and knelt before him, saying, 'My daughter has just died; but come and lay your hand on her, and she will live.' ¹⁹And Jesus got up and followed him, with his

---

e Gk *reclined*   f Gk *were reclining*   g Other ancient authorities lack *often*   h Gk lacks *of the synagogue*

disciples. ²⁰Then suddenly a woman who had been suffering from haemorrhages for twelve years came up behind him and touched the fringe of his cloak, ²¹for she said to herself, 'If I only touch his cloak, I will be made well.' ²²Jesus turned, and seeing her he said, 'Take heart, daughter; your faith has made you well.' And instantly the woman was made well. ²³When Jesus came to the leader's house and saw the flute-players and the crowd making a commotion, ²⁴he said, 'Go away; for the girl is not dead but sleeping.' And they laughed at him. ²⁵But when the crowd had been put outside, he went in and took her by the hand, and the girl got up. ²⁶And the report of this spread throughout that district.

Jesus Heals Two Blind Men

²⁷As Jesus went on from there, two blind men followed him, crying loudly, 'Have mercy on us, Son of David!' ²⁸When he entered the house, the blind men came to him; and Jesus said to them, 'Do you believe that I am able to do this?' They said to him, 'Yes, Lord.' ²⁹Then he touched their eyes and said, 'According to your faith let it be done to you.' ³⁰And their eyes were opened. Then Jesus sternly ordered them, 'See that no one knows of this.' ³¹But they went away and spread the news about him throughout that district.

Jesus Heals One Who Was Mute

³²After they had gone away, a demoniac who was mute was brought to him. ³³And when the demon had been cast out, the one who had been mute spoke; and the crowds were amazed and said, 'Never has anything like this been seen in Israel.' ³⁴But the Pharisees said, 'By the ruler of the demons he casts out the demons.'[i]

The Harvest Is Great, the Labourers Few

³⁵Then Jesus went about all the cities and villages, teaching in their synagogues, and proclaiming the good news of the kingdom, and curing every disease and every sickness. ³⁶When he saw the crowds, he had compassion for them, because they were harassed

---

i Other ancient authorities lack this verse

and helpless, like sheep without a shepherd. ³⁷Then he said to his disciples, 'The harvest is plentiful, but the labourers are few; ³⁸therefore ask the Lord of the harvest to send out labourers into his harvest.'

The Twelve Apostles

10 Then Jesus^j summoned his twelve disciples and gave them authority over unclean spirits, to cast them out, and to cure every disease and every sickness. ²These are the names of the twelve apostles: first, Simon, also known as Peter, and his brother Andrew; James son of Zebedee, and his brother John; ³Philip and Bartholomew; Thomas and Matthew the tax-collector; James son of Alphaeus, and Thaddaeus;^k ⁴Simon the Cananaean, and Judas Iscariot, the one who betrayed him.

The Mission of the Twelve

⁵These twelve Jesus sent out with the following instructions: 'Go nowhere among the Gentiles, and enter no town of the Samaritans, ⁶but go rather to the lost sheep of the house of Israel. ⁷As you go, proclaim the good news, "The kingdom of heaven has come near."^l ⁸Cure the sick, raise the dead, cleanse the lepers,^m cast out demons. You received without payment; give without payment. ⁹Take no gold, or silver, or copper in your belts, ¹⁰no bag for your journey, or two tunics, or sandals, or a staff; for labourers deserve their food. ¹¹Whatever town or village you enter, find out who in it is worthy, and stay there until you leave. ¹²As you enter the house, greet it. ¹³If the house is worthy, let your peace come upon it; but if it is not worthy, let your peace return to you. ¹⁴If anyone will not welcome you or listen to your words, shake off the dust from your feet as you leave that house or town. ¹⁵Truly I tell you, it will be more tolerable for the land of Sodom and Gomorrah on the day of judgement than for that town.

Coming Persecutions

¹⁶'See, I am sending you out like sheep into the midst of wolves; so be wise as serpents and innocent as doves. ¹⁷Beware of them,

---

j Gk *he*   k Other ancient authorities read *Lebbaeus*, or *Lebbaeus called Thaddaeus*   l Or *is at hand*   m The terms *leper* and *leprosy* can refer to several diseases

for they will hand you over to councils and flog you in their synagogues; [18]and you will be dragged before governors and kings because of me, as a testimony to them and the Gentiles. [19]When they hand you over, do not worry about how you are to speak or what you are to say; for what you are to say will be given to you at that time; [20]for it is not you who speak, but the Spirit of your Father speaking through you. [21]Brother will betray brother to death, and a father his child, and children will rise against parents and have them put to death; [22]and you will be hated by all because of my name. But the one who endures to the end will be saved. [23]When they persecute you in one town, flee to the next; for truly I tell you, you will not have gone through all the towns of Israel before the Son of Man comes.

[24]'A disciple is not above the teacher, nor a slave above the master; [25]it is enough for the disciple to be like the teacher, and the slave like the master. If they have called the master of the house Beelzebul, how much more will they malign those of his household!

Whom to Fear

[26]'So have no fear of them; for nothing is covered up that will not be uncovered, and nothing secret that will not become known. [27]What I say to you in the dark, tell in the light; and what you hear whispered, proclaim from the housetops. [28]Do not fear those who kill the body but cannot kill the soul; rather fear him who can destroy both soul and body in hell.[n] [29]Are not two sparrows sold for a penny? Yet not one of them will fall to the ground unperceived by your Father. [30]And even the hairs of your head are all counted. [31]So do not be afraid; you are of more value than many sparrows.

[32]'Everyone therefore who acknowledges me before others, I also will acknowledge before my Father in heaven; [33]but whoever denies me before others, I also will deny before my Father in heaven.

Not Peace, but a Sword

[34]'Do not think that I have come to bring peace to the earth; I have not come to bring peace, but a sword.

---

n Gk *Gehenna*

35 For I have come to set a man against his father,
   and a daughter against her mother,
   and a daughter-in-law against her mother-in-law;
36 and one's foes will be members of one's own household.
37 Whoever loves father or mother more than me is not worthy of me; and whoever loves son or daughter more than me is not worthy of me; 38 and whoever does not take up the cross and follow me is not worthy of me. 39 Those who find their life will lose it, and those who lose their life for my sake will find it.

Rewards

40 'Whoever welcomes you welcomes me, and whoever welcomes me welcomes the one who sent me. 41 Whoever welcomes a prophet in the name of a prophet will receive a prophet's reward; and whoever welcomes a righteous person in the name of a righteous person will receive the reward of the righteous; 42 and whoever gives even a cup of cold water to one of these little ones in the name of a disciple—truly I tell you, none of these will lose their reward.'

11 Now when Jesus had finished instructing his twelve disciples, he went on from there to teach and proclaim his message in their cities.

Messengers from John the Baptist

2 When John heard in prison what the Messiah*o* was doing, he sent word by his*p* disciples 3 and said to him, 'Are you the one who is to come, or are we to wait for another?' 4 Jesus answered them, 'Go and tell John what you hear and see: 5 the blind receive their sight, the lame walk, the lepers*q* are cleansed, the deaf hear, the dead are raised, and the poor have good news brought to them. 6 And blessed is anyone who takes no offence at me.'

Jesus Praises John the Baptist

7 As they went away, Jesus began to speak to the crowds about John: 'What did you go out into the wilderness to look at? A reed shaken by the wind? 8 What then did you go out to see? Someone*r*

---

o Or *the Christ*   p Other ancient authorities read *two of his*   q The terms *leper* and *leprosy* can refer to several diseases   r Or *Why then did you go out? To see someone* dressed in soft robes? Look, those who wear soft robes are in royal palaces. ⁹What then did you go out to see? A prophet?ˢ Yes, I tell you, and more than a prophet. ¹⁰This is the one about whom it is written,

> "See, I am sending my messenger ahead of you,
>   who will prepare your way before you."

¹¹Truly I tell you, among those born of women no one has arisen greater than John the Baptist; yet the least in the kingdom of heaven is greater than he. ¹²From the days of John the Baptist until now the kingdom of heaven has suffered violence,ᵗ and the violent take it by force. ¹³For all the prophets and the law prophesied until John came; ¹⁴and if you are willing to accept it, he is Elijah who is to come. ¹⁵Let anyone with earsᵘ listen!

¹⁶'But to what will I compare this generation? It is like children sitting in the market-places and calling to one another,

> ¹⁷ "We played the flute for you, and you did not dance;
>   we wailed, and you did not mourn."

¹⁸For John came neither eating nor drinking, and they say, "He has a demon"; ¹⁹the Son of Man came eating and drinking, and they say, "Look, a glutton and a drunkard, a friend of tax-collectors and sinners!" Yet wisdom is vindicated by her deeds.'ᵛ

Woes to Unrepentant Cities

²⁰Then he began to reproach the cities in which most of his deeds of power had been done, because they did not repent. ²¹'Woe to you, Chorazin! Woe to you, Bethsaida! For if the deeds of power done in you had been done in Tyre and Sidon, they would have repented long ago in sackcloth and ashes. ²²But I tell you, on the day of judgement it will be more tolerable for Tyre and Sidon than for you.

> ²³ And you, Capernaum,
>   will you be exalted to heaven?
>   No, you will be brought down to Hades.

For if the deeds of power done in you had been done in Sodom, it would have remained until this day. ²⁴But I tell you that on

---

s Other ancient authorities read *Why then did you go out? To see a prophet?*   t Or *has been coming violently*   u Other ancient authorities add *to hear*   v Other ancient authorities read *children*

the day of judgement it will be more tolerable for the land of Sodom than for you.'

Jesus Thanks His Father

²⁵At that time Jesus said, 'I thank^w you, Father, Lord of heaven and earth, because you have hidden these things from the wise and the intelligent and have revealed them to infants; ²⁶yes, Father, for such was your gracious will.^{x} ²⁷All things have been handed over to me by my Father; and no one knows the Son except the Father, and no one knows the Father except the Son and anyone to whom the Son chooses to reveal him.

²⁸'Come to me, all you that are weary and are carrying heavy burdens, and I will give you rest. ²⁹Take my yoke upon you, and learn from me; for I am gentle and humble in heart, and you will find rest for your souls. ³⁰For my yoke is easy, and my burden is light.'

Plucking Grain on the Sabbath

12 At that time Jesus went through the cornfields on the sabbath; his disciples were hungry, and they began to pluck heads of grain and to eat. ²When the Pharisees saw it, they said to him, 'Look, your disciples are doing what is not lawful to do on the sabbath.' ³He said to them, 'Have you not read what David did when he and his companions were hungry? ⁴He entered the house of God and ate the bread of the Presence, which it was not lawful for him or his companions to eat, but only for the priests. ⁵Or have you not read in the law that on the sabbath the priests in the temple break the sabbath and yet are guiltless? ⁶I tell you, something greater than the temple is here. ⁷But if you had known what this means, "I desire mercy and not sacrifice", you would not have condemned the guiltless. ⁸For the Son of Man is lord of the sabbath.'

The Man with a Withered Hand

⁹He left that place and entered their synagogue; ¹⁰a man was there with a withered hand, and they asked him, 'Is it lawful to cure on the sabbath?' so that they might accuse him. ¹¹He said

---

w Or praise   **x** Or for so it was well-pleasing in your sight

to them, 'Suppose one of you has only one sheep and it falls into a pit on the sabbath; will you not lay hold of it and lift it out? [12] How much more valuable is a human being than a sheep! So it is lawful to do good on the sabbath.' [13] Then he said to the man, 'Stretch out your hand.' He stretched it out, and it was restored, as sound as the other. [14] But the Pharisees went out and conspired against him, how to destroy him.

God's Chosen Servant

[15] When Jesus became aware of this, he departed. Many crowds[y] followed him, and he cured all of them, [16] and he ordered them not to make him known. [17] This was to fulfil what had been spoken through the prophet Isaiah:

[18] 'Here is my servant, whom I have chosen,
    my beloved, with whom my soul is well pleased.
I will put my Spirit upon him,
    and he will proclaim justice to the Gentiles.
[19] He will not wrangle or cry aloud,
    nor will anyone hear his voice in the streets.
[20] He will not break a bruised reed
    or quench a smouldering wick
until he brings justice to victory.
[21]   And in his name the Gentiles will hope.'

Jesus and Beelzebul

[22] Then they brought to him a demoniac who was blind and mute; and he cured him, so that the one who had been mute could speak and see. [23] All the crowds were amazed and said, 'Can this be the Son of David?' [24] But when the Pharisees heard it, they said, 'It is only by Beelzebul, the ruler of the demons, that this fellow casts out the demons.' [25] He knew what they were thinking and said to them, 'Every kingdom divided against itself is laid waste, and no city or house divided against itself will stand. [26] If Satan casts out Satan, he is divided against himself; how then will his kingdom stand? [27] If I cast out demons by Beelzebul, by whom do your own exorcists[z] cast them out? Therefore they will be your judges. [28] But if it is by the Spirit of God that I cast out demons,

---

y Other ancient authorities lack *crowds*   z Gk *sons*

then the kingdom of God has come to you. ²⁹Or how can one enter a strong man's house and plunder his property, without first tying up the strong man? Then indeed the house can be plundered. ³⁰Whoever is not with me is against me, and whoever does not gather with me scatters. ³¹Therefore I tell you, people will be forgiven for every sin and blasphemy, but blasphemy against the Spirit will not be forgiven. ³²Whoever speaks a word against the Son of Man will be forgiven, but whoever speaks against the Holy Spirit will not be forgiven, either in this age or in the age to come.

A Tree and Its Fruit

³³'Either make the tree good, and its fruit good; or make the tree bad, and its fruit bad; for the tree is known by its fruit. ³⁴You brood of vipers! How can you speak good things, when you are evil? For out of the abundance of the heart the mouth speaks. ³⁵The good person brings good things out of a good treasure, and the evil person brings evil things out of an evil treasure. ³⁶I tell you, on the day of judgement you will have to give an account for every careless word you utter; ³⁷for by your words you will be justified, and by your words you will be condemned.'

The Sign of Jonah

³⁸Then some of the scribes and Pharisees said to him, 'Teacher, we wish to see a sign from you.' ³⁹But he answered them, 'An evil and adulterous generation asks for a sign, but no sign will be given to it except the sign of the prophet Jonah. ⁴⁰For just as Jonah was for three days and three nights in the belly of the sea monster, so for three days and three nights the Son of Man will be in the heart of the earth. ⁴¹The people of Nineveh will rise up at the judgement with this generation and condemn it, because they repented at the proclamation of Jonah, and see, something greater than Jonah is here! ⁴²The queen of the South will rise up at the judgement with this generation and condemn it, because she came from the ends of the earth to listen to the wisdom of Solomon, and see, something greater than Solomon is here!

The Return of the Unclean Spirit

⁴³'When the unclean spirit has gone out of a person, it wanders through waterless regions looking for a resting-place, but it finds

none. ⁴⁴Then it says, "I will return to my house from which I came." When it comes, it finds it empty, swept, and put in order. ⁴⁵Then it goes and brings along seven other spirits more evil than itself, and they enter and live there; and the last state of that person is worse than the first. So will it be also with this evil generation.'

The True Kindred of Jesus

⁴⁶While he was still speaking to the crowds, his mother and his brothers were standing outside, wanting to speak to him. ⁴⁷Someone told him, 'Look, your mother and your brothers are standing outside, wanting to speak to you.'ᵃ ⁴⁸But to the one who had told him this, Jesusᵇ replied, 'Who is my mother, and who are my brothers?' ⁴⁹And pointing to his disciples, he said, 'Here are my mother and my brothers! ⁵⁰For whoever does the will of my Father in heaven is my brother and sister and mother.'

The Parable of the Sower

13 That same day Jesus went out of the house and sat beside the lake. ²Such great crowds gathered around him that he got into a boat and sat there, while the whole crowd stood on the beach. ³And he told them many things in parables, saying: 'Listen! A sower went out to sow. ⁴And as he sowed, some seeds fell on the path, and the birds came and ate them up. ⁵Other seeds fell on rocky ground, where they did not have much soil, and they sprang up quickly, since they had no depth of soil. ⁶But when the sun rose, they were scorched; and since they had no root, they withered away. ⁷Other seeds fell among thorns, and the thorns grew up and choked them. ⁸Other seeds fell on good soil and brought forth grain, some a hundredfold, some sixty, some thirty. ⁹Let anyone with earsᶜ listen!'

The Purpose of the Parables

¹⁰Then the disciples came and asked him, 'Why do you speak to them in parables?' ¹¹He answered, 'To you it has been given

---

a Other ancient authorities lack verse 47   b Gk *he*   c Other ancient authorities add *to hear*   d Or *mysteries* to know the secrets*d* of the kingdom of heaven, but to them it has not been given. ¹²For to those who have, more will be given, and they will have an abundance; but from those who have nothing, even what they have will be taken away. ¹³The reason I speak to them in parables is that "seeing they do not perceive, and hearing they do not listen, nor do they understand." ¹⁴With them indeed is fulfilled the prophecy of Isaiah that says:

> "You will indeed listen, but never understand,
>   and you will indeed look, but never perceive.
> ¹⁵ For this people's heart has grown dull,
>   and their ears are hard of hearing,
>   and they have shut their eyes;
>   so that they might not look with their eyes,
>   and listen with their ears,
> and understand with their heart and turn—
>   and I would heal them."

¹⁶But blessed are your eyes, for they see, and your ears, for they hear. ¹⁷Truly I tell you, many prophets and righteous people longed to see what you see, but did not see it, and to hear what you hear, but did not hear it.

The Parable of the Sower Explained

¹⁸'Hear then the parable of the sower. ¹⁹When anyone hears the word of the kingdom and does not understand it, the evil one comes and snatches away what is sown in the heart; this is what was sown on the path. ²⁰As for what was sown on rocky ground, this is the one who hears the word and immediately receives it with joy; ²¹yet such a person has no root, but endures only for a while, and when trouble or persecution arises on account of the word, that person immediately falls away.*e* ²²As for what was sown among thorns, this is the one who hears the word, but the cares of the world and the lure of wealth choke the word, and it yields nothing. ²³But as for what was sown on good soil, this is the one who hears the word and understands it, who indeed bears fruit and yields, in one case a hundredfold, in another sixty, and in another thirty.'

---

e Gk *stumbles*

The Parable of Weeds among the Wheat

²⁴He put before them another parable: 'The kingdom of heaven may be compared to someone who sowed good seed in his field; ²⁵but while everybody was asleep, an enemy came and sowed weeds among the wheat, and then went away. ²⁶So when the plants came up and bore grain, then the weeds appeared as well. ²⁷And the slaves of the householder came and said to him, "Master, did you not sow good seed in your field? Where, then, did these weeds come from?" ²⁸He answered, "An enemy has done this." The slaves said to him, "Then do you want us to go and gather them?" ²⁹But he replied, "No; for in gathering the weeds you would uproot the wheat along with them. ³⁰Let both of them grow together until the harvest; and at harvest time I will tell the reapers, Collect the weeds first and bind them in bundles to be burned, but gather the wheat into my barn." '

The Parable of the Mustard Seed

³¹He put before them another parable: 'The kingdom of heaven is like a mustard seed that someone took and sowed in his field; ³²it is the smallest of all the seeds, but when it has grown it is the greatest of shrubs and becomes a tree, so that the birds of the air come and make nests in its branches.'

The Parable of the Yeast

³³He told them another parable: 'The kingdom of heaven is like yeast that a woman took and mixed in with*f* three measures of flour until all of it was leavened.'

The Use of Parables

³⁴Jesus told the crowds all these things in parables; without a parable he told them nothing. ³⁵This was to fulfil what had been spoken through the prophet:*g*

'I will open my mouth to speak in parables;
    I will proclaim what has been hidden from the
        foundation of the world.'*h*

---

f Gk *hid in*   g Other ancient authorities read *the prophet Isaiah*   h Other ancient authorities lack *of the world*

Jesus Explains the Parable of the Weeds

³⁶Then he left the crowds and went into the house. And his disciples approached him, saying, 'Explain to us the parable of the weeds of the field.' ³⁷He answered, 'The one who sows the good seed is the Son of Man; ³⁸the field is the world, and the good seed are the children of the kingdom; the weeds are the children of the evil one, ³⁹and the enemy who sowed them is the devil; the harvest is the end of the age, and the reapers are angels. ⁴⁰Just as the weeds are collected and burned up with fire, so will it be at the end of the age. ⁴¹The Son of Man will send his angels, and they will collect out of his kingdom all causes of sin and all evildoers, ⁴²and they will throw them into the furnace of fire, where there will be weeping and gnashing of teeth. ⁴³Then the righteous will shine like the sun in the kingdom of their Father. Let anyone with earsⁱ listen!

Three Parables

⁴⁴'The kingdom of heaven is like treasure hidden in a field, which someone found and hid; then in his joy he goes and sells all that he has and buys that field.

⁴⁵'Again, the kingdom of heaven is like a merchant in search of fine pearls; ⁴⁶on finding one pearl of great value, he went and sold all that he had and bought it.

⁴⁷'Again, the kingdom of heaven is like a net that was thrown into the sea and caught fish of every kind; ⁴⁸when it was full, they drew it ashore, sat down, and put the good into baskets but threw out the bad. ⁴⁹So it will be at the end of the age. The angels will come out and separate the evil from the righteous ⁵⁰and throw them into the furnace of fire, where there will be weeping and gnashing of teeth.

Treasures New and Old

⁵¹'Have you understood all this?' They answered, 'Yes.' ⁵²And he said to them, 'Therefore every scribe who has been trained for the kingdom of heaven is like the master of a household who brings out of his treasure what is new and what is old.' ⁵³When Jesus had finished these parables, he left that place.

---

i Other ancient authorities add *to hear*

The Rejection of Jesus at Nazareth

54 He came to his home town and began to teach the people[j] in their synagogue, so that they were astounded and said, 'Where did this man get this wisdom and these deeds of power? 55 Is not this the carpenter's son? Is not his mother called Mary? And are not his brothers James and Joseph and Simon and Judas? 56 And are not all his sisters with us? Where then did this man get all this?' 57 And they took offence at him. But Jesus said to them, 'Prophets are not without honour except in their own country and in their own house.' 58 And he did not do many deeds of power there, because of their unbelief.

The Death of John the Baptist

14 At that time Herod the ruler[k] heard reports about Jesus; 2 and he said to his servants, 'This is John the Baptist; he has been raised from the dead, and for this reason these powers are at work in him.' 3 For Herod had arrested John, bound him, and put him in prison on account of Herodias, his brother Philip's wife,[l] 4 because John had been telling him, 'It is not lawful for you to have her.' 5 Though Herod[m] wanted to put him to death, he feared the crowd, because they regarded him as a prophet. 6 But when Herod's birthday came, the daughter of Herodias danced before the company, and she pleased Herod 7 so much that he promised on oath to grant her whatever she might ask. 8 Prompted by her mother, she said, 'Give me the head of John the Baptist here on a platter.' 9 The king was grieved, yet out of regard for his oaths and for the guests, he commanded it to be given; 10 he sent and had John beheaded in the prison. 11 The head was brought on a platter and given to the girl, who brought it to her mother. 12 His disciples came and took the body and buried it; then they went and told Jesus.

Feeding the Five Thousand

13 Now when Jesus heard this, he withdrew from there in a boat to a deserted place by himself. But when the crowds heard it, they followed him on foot from the towns. 14 When he went ashore, he saw a great crowd; and he had compassion for them

---

j Gk *them*   k Gk *tetrarch*   l Other ancient authorities read *his brother's wife*   m Gk *he*

and cured their sick. ¹⁵When it was evening, the disciples came to him and said, 'This is a deserted place, and the hour is now late; send the crowds away so that they may go into the villages and buy food for themselves.' ¹⁶Jesus said to them, 'They need not go away; you give them something to eat.' ¹⁷They replied, 'We have nothing here but five loaves and two fish.' ¹⁸And he said, 'Bring them here to me.' ¹⁹Then he ordered the crowds to sit down on the grass. Taking the five loaves and the two fish, he looked up to heaven, and blessed and broke the loaves, and gave them to the disciples, and the disciples gave them to the crowds. ²⁰And all ate and were filled; and they took up what was left over of the broken pieces, twelve baskets full. ²¹And those who ate were about five thousand men, besides women and children.

Jesus Walks on the Water

²²Immediately he made the disciples get into the boat and go on ahead to the other side, while he dismissed the crowds. ²³And after he had dismissed the crowds, he went up the mountain by himself to pray. When evening came, he was there alone, ²⁴but by this time the boat, battered by the waves, was far from the land,ⁿ for the wind was against them. ²⁵And early in the morning he came walking towards them on the lake. ²⁶But when the disciples saw him walking on the lake, they were terrified, saying, 'It is a ghost!' And they cried out in fear. ²⁷But immediately Jesus spoke to them and said, 'Take heart, it is I; do not be afraid.'

²⁸Peter answered him, 'Lord, if it is you, command me to come to you on the water.' ²⁹He said, 'Come.' So Peter got out of the boat, started walking on the water, and came towards Jesus. ³⁰But when he noticed the strong wind,ᵒ he became frightened, and beginning to sink, he cried out, 'Lord, save me!' ³¹Jesus immediately reached out his hand and caught him, saying to him, 'You of little faith, why did you doubt?' ³²When they got into the boat, the wind ceased. ³³And those in the boat worshipped him, saying, 'Truly you are the Son of God.'

---

n Other ancient authorities read *was out on the lake*   o Other ancient authorities read *the wind*

Jesus Heals the Sick in Gennesaret

34 When they had crossed over, they came to land at Gennesaret.
35 After the people of that place recognized him, they sent word
throughout the region and brought all who were sick to him,
36 and begged him that they might touch even the fringe of his
cloak; and all who touched it were healed.

The Tradition of the Elders

15 Then Pharisees and scribes came to Jesus from Jerusalem
and said, 2 'Why do your disciples break the tradition of the
elders? For they do not wash their hands before they eat.' 3 He
answered them, 'And why do you break the commandment of
God for the sake of your tradition? 4 For God said,[p] "Honour your
father and your mother," and, "Whoever speaks evil of father or
mother must surely die." 5 But you say that whoever tells father or
mother, "Whatever support you might have had from me is given
to God",[q] then that person need not honour the father.[r] 6 So, for
the sake of your tradition, you make void the word[s] of God. 7 You
hypocrites! Isaiah prophesied rightly about you when he said:

8 "This people honours me with their lips,
but their hearts are far from me;
9 in vain do they worship me,
teaching human precepts as doctrines." '

Things That Defile

10 Then he called the crowd to him and said to them, 'Listen
and understand: 11 it is not what goes into the mouth that defiles
a person, but it is what comes out of the mouth that defiles.'
12 Then the disciples approached and said to him, 'Do you know
that the Pharisees took offence when they heard what you said?'
13 He answered, 'Every plant that my heavenly Father has not
planted will be uprooted. 14 Let them alone; they are blind guides
of the blind.[t] And if one blind person guides another, both will
fall into a pit.' 15 But Peter said to him, 'Explain this parable to us.'
16 Then he said, 'Are you also still without understanding? 17 Do you

---

p Other ancient authorities read *commanded, saying* q Or *is an offering* r Other ancient authorities add *or the mother* s Other ancient authorities read *law*; others, *commandment* t Other ancient authorities lack *of the blind*

not see that whatever goes into the mouth enters the stomach, and goes out into the sewer? [18] But what comes out of the mouth proceeds from the heart, and this is what defiles. [19] For out of the heart come evil intentions, murder, adultery, fornication, theft, false witness, slander. [20] These are what defile a person, but to eat with unwashed hands does not defile.'

The Canaanite Woman's Faith

[21] Jesus left that place and went away to the district of Tyre and Sidon. [22] Just then a Canaanite woman from that region came out and started shouting, 'Have mercy on me, Lord, Son of David; my daughter is tormented by a demon.' [23] But he did not answer her at all. And his disciples came and urged him, saying, 'Send her away, for she keeps shouting after us.' [24] He answered, 'I was sent only to the lost sheep of the house of Israel.' [25] But she came and knelt before him, saying, 'Lord, help me.' [26] He answered, 'It is not fair to take the children's food and throw it to the dogs.' [27] She said, 'Yes, Lord, yet even the dogs eat the crumbs that fall from their masters' table.' [28] Then Jesus answered her, 'Woman, great is your faith! Let it be done for you as you wish.' And her daughter was healed instantly.

Jesus Cures Many People

[29] After Jesus had left that place, he passed along the Sea of Galilee, and he went up the mountain, where he sat down. [30] Great crowds came to him, bringing with them the lame, the maimed, the blind, the mute, and many others. They put them at his feet, and he cured them, [31] so that the crowd was amazed when they saw the mute speaking, the maimed whole, the lame walking, and the blind seeing. And they praised the God of Israel.

Feeding the Four Thousand

[32] Then Jesus called his disciples to him and said, 'I have compassion for the crowd, because they have been with me now for three days and have nothing to eat; and I do not want to send them away hungry, for they might faint on the way.' [33] The disciples said to him, 'Where are we to get enough bread in the desert to feed so great a crowd?' [34] Jesus asked

them, 'How many loaves have you?' They said, 'Seven, and a few small fish.' [35]Then ordering the crowd to sit down on the ground, [36]he took the seven loaves and the fish; and after giving thanks he broke them and gave them to the disciples, and the disciples gave them to the crowds. [37]And all of them ate and were filled; and they took up the broken pieces left over, seven baskets full. [38]Those who had eaten were four thousand men, besides women and children. [39]After sending away the crowds, he got into the boat and went to the region of Magadan.[u]

The Demand for a Sign

16 The Pharisees and Sadducees came, and to test Jesus[v] they asked him to show them a sign from heaven. [2]He answered them, 'When it is evening, you say, "It will be fair weather, for the sky is red." [3]And in the morning, "It will be stormy today, for the sky is red and threatening." You know how to interpret the appearance of the sky, but you cannot interpret the signs of the times.[w] [4]An evil and adulterous generation asks for a sign, but no sign will be given to it except the sign of Jonah.' Then he left them and went away.

The Yeast of the Pharisees and Sadducees

[5]When the disciples reached the other side, they had forgotten to bring any bread. [6]Jesus said to them, 'Watch out, and beware of the yeast of the Pharisees and Sadducees.' [7]They said to one another, 'It is because we have brought no bread.' [8]And becoming aware of it, Jesus said, 'You of little faith, why are you talking about having no bread? [9]Do you still not perceive? Do you not remember the five loaves for the five thousand, and how many baskets you gathered? [10]Or the seven loaves for the four thousand, and how many baskets you gathered? [11]How could you fail to perceive that I was not speaking about bread? Beware of the yeast of the Pharisees and Sadducees!' [12]Then they understood that he had not told them to beware of the yeast of bread, but of the teaching of the Pharisees and Sadducees.

---

u Other ancient authorities read *Magdala* or *Magdalan*   v Gk *him*   w Other ancient authorities lack [2] *When it is…of the times*

Peter's Declaration about Jesus

¹³Now when Jesus came into the district of Caesarea Philippi, he asked his disciples, 'Who do people say that the Son of Man is?' ¹⁴And they said, 'Some say John the Baptist, but others Elijah, and still others Jeremiah or one of the prophets.' ¹⁵He said to them, 'But who do you say that I am?' ¹⁶Simon Peter answered, 'You are the Messiah,ˣ the Son of the living God.' ¹⁷And Jesus answered him, 'Blessed are you, Simon son of Jonah! For flesh and blood has not revealed this to you, but my Father in heaven. ¹⁸And I tell you, you are Peter,ʸ and on this rockᶻ I will build my church, and the gates of Hades will not prevail against it. ¹⁹I will give you the keys of the kingdom of heaven, and whatever you bind on earth will be bound in heaven, and whatever you loose on earth will be loosed in heaven.' ²⁰Then he sternly ordered the disciples not to tell anyone that he wasᵃ the Messiah.ᵇ

Jesus Foretells His Death and Resurrection

²¹From that time on, Jesus began to show his disciples that he must go to Jerusalem and undergo great suffering at the hands of the elders and chief priests and scribes, and be killed, and on the third day be raised. ²²And Peter took him aside and began to rebuke him, saying, 'God forbid it, Lord! This must never happen to you.' ²³But he turned and said to Peter, 'Get behind me, Satan! You are a stumbling-block to me; for you are setting your mind not on divine things but on human things.'

The Cross and Self-Denial

²⁴Then Jesus told his disciples, 'If any want to become my followers, let them deny themselves and take up their cross and follow me. ²⁵For those who want to save their life will lose it, and those who lose their life for my sake will find it. ²⁶For what will it profit them if they gain the whole world but forfeit their life? Or what will they give in return for their life?

²⁷'For the Son of Man is to come with his angels in the glory of his Father, and then he will repay everyone for what has been done. ²⁸Truly I tell you, there are some standing here who will

---

x Or *the Christ*   y Gk *Petros*   z Gk *petra*   a Other ancient authorities add *Jesus*
b Or *the Christ*

not taste death before they see the Son of Man coming in his kingdom.'

The Transfiguration

17 Six days later, Jesus took with him Peter and James and his brother John and led them up a high mountain, by themselves. ²And he was transfigured before them, and his face shone like the sun, and his clothes became dazzling white. ³Suddenly there appeared to them Moses and Elijah, talking with him. ⁴Then Peter said to Jesus, 'Lord, it is good for us to be here; if you wish, I*c* will make three dwellings*d* here, one for you, one for Moses, and one for Elijah.' ⁵While he was still speaking, suddenly a bright cloud overshadowed them, and from the cloud a voice said, 'This is my Son, the Beloved;*e* with him I am well pleased; listen to him!' ⁶When the disciples heard this, they fell to the ground and were overcome by fear. ⁷But Jesus came and touched them, saying, 'Get up and do not be afraid.' ⁸And when they looked up, they saw no one except Jesus himself alone.

⁹As they were coming down the mountain, Jesus ordered them, 'Tell no one about the vision until after the Son of Man has been raised from the dead.' ¹⁰And the disciples asked him, 'Why, then, do the scribes say that Elijah must come first?' ¹¹He replied, 'Elijah is indeed coming and will restore all things; ¹²but I tell you that Elijah has already come, and they did not recognize him, but they did to him whatever they pleased. So also the Son of Man is about to suffer at their hands.' ¹³Then the disciples understood that he was speaking to them about John the Baptist.

Jesus Cures a Boy with a Demon

¹⁴When they came to the crowd, a man came to him, knelt before him, ¹⁵and said, 'Lord, have mercy on my son, for he is an epileptic and he suffers terribly; he often falls into the fire and often into the water. ¹⁶And I brought him to your disciples, but they could not cure him.' ¹⁷Jesus answered, 'You faithless and perverse generation, how much longer must I be with you? How much longer must I put up with you? Bring him here to me.'

---

c Other ancient authorities read *we*   d Or *tents*   e Or *my beloved Son*

¹⁸ And Jesus rebuked the demon,[f] and it[g] came out of him, and the boy was cured instantly. ¹⁹ Then the disciples came to Jesus privately and said, 'Why could we not cast it out?' ²⁰ He said to them, 'Because of your little faith. For truly I tell you, if you have faith the size of a[h] mustard seed, you will say to this mountain, "Move from here to there", and it will move; and nothing will be impossible for you.'[i]

Jesus Again Foretells His Death and Resurrection

²² As they were gathering[j] in Galilee, Jesus said to them, 'The Son of Man is going to be betrayed into human hands, ²³ and they will kill him, and on the third day he will be raised.' And they were greatly distressed.

Jesus and the Temple Tax

²⁴ When they reached Capernaum, the collectors of the temple tax[k] came to Peter and said, 'Does your teacher not pay the temple tax?'[k] ²⁵ He said, 'Yes, he does.' And when he came home, Jesus spoke of it first, asking, 'What do you think, Simon? From whom do kings of the earth take toll or tribute? From their children or from others?' ²⁶ When Peter[l] said, 'From others', Jesus said to him, 'Then the children are free. ²⁷ However, so that we do not give offence to them, go to the lake and cast a hook; take the first fish that comes up; and when you open its mouth, you will find a coin;[m] take that and give it to them for you and me.'

True Greatness

18 At that time the disciples came to Jesus and asked, 'Who is the greatest in the kingdom of heaven?' ² He called a child, whom he put among them, ³ and said, 'Truly I tell you, unless you change and become like children, you will never enter the kingdom of heaven. ⁴ Whoever becomes humble like this child is the greatest in the kingdom of heaven. ⁵ Whoever welcomes one such child in my name welcomes me.

---

f Gk *it* or *him*   g Gk *the demon*   h Gk *faith as a grain of*   i Other ancient authorities add verse 21, *But this kind does not come out except by prayer and fasting*   j Other ancient authorities read *living*   k Gk *didrachma*   l Gk *he*   m Gk *stater*; the stater was worth two didrachmas

Temptations to Sin

6 'If any of you put a stumbling-block before one of these little ones who believe in me, it would be better for you if a great millstone were fastened around your neck and you were drowned in the depth of the sea. 7 Woe to the world because of stumbling-blocks! Occasions for stumbling are bound to come, but woe to the one by whom the stumbling-block comes!

8 'If your hand or your foot causes you to stumble, cut it off and throw it away; it is better for you to enter life maimed or lame than to have two hands or two feet and to be thrown into the eternal fire. 9 And if your eye causes you to stumble, tear it out and throw it away; it is better for you to enter life with one eye than to have two eyes and to be thrown into the hell[n] of fire.

The Parable of the Lost Sheep

10 'Take care that you do not despise one of these little ones; for, I tell you, in heaven their angels continually see the face of my Father in heaven.[o] 12 What do you think? If a shepherd has a hundred sheep, and one of them has gone astray, does he not leave the ninety-nine on the mountains and go in search of the one that went astray? 13 And if he finds it, truly I tell you, he rejoices over it more than over the ninety-nine that never went astray. 14 So it is not the will of your[p] Father in heaven that one of these little ones should be lost.

Reproving Another Who Sins

15 'If another member of the church[q] sins against you,[r] go and point out the fault when the two of you are alone. If the member listens to you, you have regained that one.[s] 16 But if you are not listened to, take one or two others along with you, so that every word may be confirmed by the evidence of two or three witnesses. 17 If the member refuses to listen to them, tell it to the church; and if the offender refuses to listen even to the church, let such a one be to you as a Gentile and a tax-

---

n Gk *Gehenna*   o Other ancient authorities add verse 11, *For the Son of Man came to save the lost*   p Other ancient authorities read *my*   q Gk *If your brother*   r Other ancient authorities lack *against you*   s Gk *the brother*

collector. ¹⁸Truly I tell you, whatever you bind on earth will be bound in heaven, and whatever you loose on earth will be loosed in heaven. ¹⁹Again, truly I tell you, if two of you agree on earth about anything you ask, it will be done for you by my Father in heaven. ²⁰For where two or three are gathered in my name, I am there among them.'

Forgiveness

²¹Then Peter came and said to him, 'Lord, if another member of the church^t sins against me, how often should I forgive? As many as seven times?' ²²Jesus said to him, 'Not seven times, but, I tell you, seventy-seven^u times.

The Parable of the Unforgiving Servant

²³'For this reason the kingdom of heaven may be compared to a king who wished to settle accounts with his slaves. ²⁴When he began the reckoning, one who owed him ten thousand talents^v was brought to him; ²⁵and, as he could not pay, his lord ordered him to be sold, together with his wife and children and all his possessions, and payment to be made. ²⁶So the slave fell on his knees before him, saying, "Have patience with me, and I will pay you everything." ²⁷And out of pity for him, the lord of that slave released him and forgave him the debt. ²⁸But that same slave, as he went out, came upon one of his fellow-slaves who owed him a hundred denarii;^w and seizing him by the throat, he said, "Pay what you owe." ²⁹Then his fellow-slave fell down and pleaded with him, "Have patience with me, and I will pay you." ³⁰But he refused; then he went and threw him into prison until he should pay the debt. ³¹When his fellow-slaves saw what had happened, they were greatly distressed, and they went and reported to their lord all that had taken place. ³²Then his lord summoned him and said to him, "You wicked slave! I forgave you all that debt because you pleaded with me. ³³Should you not have had mercy on your fellow-slave, as I had mercy on you?" ³⁴And in anger his lord handed him over to be tortured until he should pay his entire debt. ³⁵So my heavenly Father will also do

---

t Gk *if my brother*   u Or *seventy times seven*   v A talent was worth more than fifteen years' wages of a labourer   w The denarius was the usual day's wage for a labourer

to every one of you, if you do not forgive your brother or sister[x] from your heart.'

Teaching about Divorce

19 When Jesus had finished saying these things, he left Galilee and went to the region of Judea beyond the Jordan. ²Large crowds followed him, and he cured them there.

³Some Pharisees came to him, and to test him they asked, 'Is it lawful for a man to divorce his wife for any cause?' ⁴He answered, 'Have you not read that the one who made them at the beginning "made them male and female", ⁵and said, "For this reason a man shall leave his father and mother and be joined to his wife, and the two shall become one flesh"? ⁶So they are no longer two, but one flesh. Therefore what God has joined together, let no one separate.' ⁷They said to him, 'Why then did Moses command us to give a certificate of dismissal and to divorce her?' ⁸He said to them, 'It was because you were so hard-hearted that Moses allowed you to divorce your wives, but at the beginning it was not so. ⁹And I say to you, whoever divorces his wife, except for unchastity, and marries another commits adultery.'[y]

¹⁰His disciples said to him, 'If such is the case of a man with his wife, it is better not to marry.' ¹¹But he said to them, 'Not everyone can accept this teaching, but only those to whom it is given. ¹²For there are eunuchs who have been so from birth, and there are eunuchs who have been made eunuchs by others, and there are eunuchs who have made themselves eunuchs for the sake of the kingdom of heaven. Let anyone accept this who can.'

Jesus Blesses Little Children

¹³Then little children were being brought to him in order that he might lay his hands on them and pray. The disciples spoke sternly to those who brought them; ¹⁴but Jesus said, 'Let the little children come to me, and do not stop them; for it is to such as these that the kingdom of heaven belongs.' ¹⁵And he laid his hands on them and went on his way.

---

x Gk *brother*   y Other ancient authorities read *except on the ground of unchastity, causes her to commit adultery*; others add at the end of the verse *and he who marries a divorced woman commits adultery*

The Rich Young Man

¹⁶Then someone came to him and said, 'Teacher, what good deed must I do to have eternal life?' ¹⁷And he said to him, 'Why do you ask me about what is good? There is only one who is good. If you wish to enter into life, keep the commandments.' ¹⁸He said to him, 'Which ones?' And Jesus said, 'You shall not murder; You shall not commit adultery; You shall not steal; You shall not bear false witness; ¹⁹Honour your father and mother; also, You shall love your neighbour as yourself.' ²⁰The young man said to him, 'I have kept all these;ᶻ what do I still lack?' ²¹Jesus said to him, 'If you wish to be perfect, go, sell your possessions, and give the moneyᵃ to the poor, and you will have treasure in heaven; then come, follow me.' ²²When the young man heard this word, he went away grieving, for he had many possessions.

²³Then Jesus said to his disciples, 'Truly I tell you, it will be hard for a rich person to enter the kingdom of heaven. ²⁴Again I tell you, it is easier for a camel to go through the eye of a needle than for someone who is rich to enter the kingdom of God.' ²⁵When the disciples heard this, they were greatly astounded and said, 'Then who can be saved?' ²⁶But Jesus looked at them and said, 'For mortals it is impossible, but for God all things are possible.'

²⁷Then Peter said in reply, 'Look, we have left everything and followed you. What then will we have?' ²⁸Jesus said to them, 'Truly I tell you, at the renewal of all things, when the Son of Man is seated on the throne of his glory, you who have followed me will also sit on twelve thrones, judging the twelve tribes of Israel. ²⁹And everyone who has left houses or brothers or sisters or father or mother or children or fields, for my name's sake, will receive a hundredfold,ᵇ and will inherit eternal life. ³⁰But many who are first will be last, and the last will be first.

The Labourers in the Vineyard

20 'For the kingdom of heaven is like a landowner who went out early in the morning to hire labourers for his vineyard. ²After agreeing with the labourers for the usual daily wage,ᶜ he sent them into his vineyard. ³When he went out about

---

z Other ancient authorities add *from my youth*   a Gk lacks *the money*   b Other ancient authorities read *manifold*   c Gk *a denarius*

nine o'clock, he saw others standing idle in the market-place; [4]and he said to them, "You also go into the vineyard, and I will pay you whatever is right." So they went. [5]When he went out again about noon and about three o'clock, he did the same. [6]And about five o'clock he went out and found others standing around; and he said to them, "Why are you standing here idle all day?" [7]They said to him, "Because no one has hired us." He said to them, "You also go into the vineyard." [8]When evening came, the owner of the vineyard said to his manager, "Call the labourers and give them their pay, beginning with the last and then going to the first." [9]When those hired about five o'clock came, each of them received the usual daily wage.[c] [10]Now when the first came, they thought they would receive more; but each of them also received the usual daily wage.[c] [11]And when they received it, they grumbled against the landowner, [12]saying, "These last worked only one hour, and you have made them equal to us who have borne the burden of the day and the scorching heat." [13]But he replied to one of them, "Friend, I am doing you no wrong; did you not agree with me for the usual daily wage?[c] [14]Take what belongs to you and go; I choose to give to this last the same as I give to you. [15]Am I not allowed to do what I choose with what belongs to me? Or are you envious because I am generous?"[d] [16]So the last will be first, and the first will be last.'[e]

A Third Time Jesus Foretells His Death and Resurrection

[17]While Jesus was going up to Jerusalem, he took the twelve disciples aside by themselves, and said to them on the way, [18]'See, we are going up to Jerusalem, and the Son of Man will be handed over to the chief priests and scribes, and they will condemn him to death; [19]then they will hand him over to the Gentiles to be mocked and flogged and crucified; and on the third day he will be raised.'

The Request of the Mother of James and John

[20]Then the mother of the sons of Zebedee came to him with her sons, and kneeling before him, she asked a favour of him. [21]And

---

c Gk *a denarius*   d Gk *is your eye evil because I am good?*   e Other ancient authorities add *for many are called but few are chosen*

he said to her, 'What do you want?' She said to him, 'Declare that these two sons of mine will sit, one at your right hand and one at your left, in your kingdom.' ²²But Jesus answered, 'You do not know what you are asking. Are you able to drink the cup that I am about to drink?'ᶠ They said to him, 'We are able.' ²³He said to them, 'You will indeed drink my cup, but to sit at my right hand and at my left, this is not mine to grant, but it is for those for whom it has been prepared by my Father.'

²⁴When the ten heard it, they were angry with the two brothers. ²⁵But Jesus called them to him and said, 'You know that the rulers of the Gentiles lord it over them, and their great ones are tyrants over them. ²⁶It will not be so among you; but whoever wishes to be great among you must be your servant, ²⁷and whoever wishes to be first among you must be your slave; ²⁸just as the Son of Man came not to be served but to serve, and to give his life a ransom for many.'

Jesus Heals Two Blind Men

²⁹As they were leaving Jericho, a large crowd followed him. ³⁰There were two blind men sitting by the roadside. When they heard that Jesus was passing by, they shouted, 'Lord,ᵍ have mercy on us, Son of David!' ³¹The crowd sternly ordered them to be quiet; but they shouted even more loudly, 'Have mercy on us, Lord, Son of David!' ³²Jesus stood still and called them, saying, 'What do you want me to do for you?' ³³They said to him, 'Lord, let our eyes be opened.' ³⁴Moved with compassion, Jesus touched their eyes. Immediately they regained their sight and followed him.

Jesus' Triumphal Entry into Jerusalem

21 When they had come near Jerusalem and had reached Bethphage, at the Mount of Olives, Jesus sent two disciples, ²saying to them, 'Go into the village ahead of you, and immediately you will find a donkey tied, and a colt with her; untie them and bring them to me. ³If anyone says anything to you, just say this, "The Lord needs them." And he will send them

---

f Other ancient authorities add *or to be baptized with the baptism that I am baptized with?*
g Other ancient authorities lack *Lord*

immediately.'[h] 4 This took place to fulfil what had been spoken through the prophet, saying,

> 5 'Tell the daughter of Zion,
>> Look, your king is coming to you,
>>> humble, and mounted on a donkey,
>>> and on a colt, the foal of a donkey.'

6 The disciples went and did as Jesus had directed them; 7 they brought the donkey and the colt, and put their cloaks on them, and he sat on them. 8 A very large crowd[i] spread their cloaks on the road, and others cut branches from the trees and spread them on the road. 9 The crowds that went ahead of him and that followed were shouting,

> 'Hosanna to the Son of David!
>> Blessed is the one who comes in the name of the Lord!
> Hosanna in the highest heaven!'

10 When he entered Jerusalem, the whole city was in turmoil, asking, 'Who is this?' 11 The crowds were saying, 'This is the prophet Jesus from Nazareth in Galilee.'

Jesus Cleanses the Temple

12 Then Jesus entered the temple[j] and drove out all who were selling and buying in the temple, and he overturned the tables of the money-changers and the seats of those who sold doves. 13 He said to them, 'It is written,

> "My house shall be called a house of prayer";
>> but you are making it a den of robbers.'

14 The blind and the lame came to him in the temple, and he cured them. 15 But when the chief priests and the scribes saw the amazing things that he did, and heard[k] the children crying out in the temple, 'Hosanna to the Son of David', they became angry 16 and said to him, 'Do you hear what these are saying?' Jesus said to them, 'Yes; have you never read,

> "Out of the mouths of infants and nursing babies
>> you have prepared praise for yourself"?'

17 He left them, went out of the city to Bethany, and spent the night there.

---

h Or *"The Lord needs them and will send them back immediately."*   i Or *Most of the crowd*
j Other ancient authorities add *of God*   k Gk lacks *heard*

Jesus Curses the Fig Tree

¹⁸ In the morning, when he returned to the city, he was hungry. ¹⁹ And seeing a fig tree by the side of the road, he went to it and found nothing at all on it but leaves. Then he said to it, 'May no fruit ever come from you again!' And the fig tree withered at once. ²⁰ When the disciples saw it, they were amazed, saying, 'How did the fig tree wither at once?' ²¹ Jesus answered them, 'Truly I tell you, if you have faith and do not doubt, not only will you do what has been done to the fig tree, but even if you say to this mountain, "Be lifted up and thrown into the sea", it will be done. ²² Whatever you ask for in prayer with faith, you will receive.'

The Authority of Jesus Questioned

²³ When he entered the temple, the chief priests and the elders of the people came to him as he was teaching, and said, 'By what authority are you doing these things, and who gave you this authority?' ²⁴ Jesus said to them, 'I will also ask you one question; if you tell me the answer, then I will also tell you by what authority I do these things. ²⁵ Did the baptism of John come from heaven, or was it of human origin?' And they argued with one another, 'If we say, "From heaven", he will say to us, "Why then did you not believe him?" ²⁶ But if we say, "Of human origin", we are afraid of the crowd; for all regard John as a prophet.' ²⁷ So they answered Jesus, 'We do not know.' And he said to them, 'Neither will I tell you by what authority I am doing these things.

The Parable of the Two Sons

²⁸ 'What do you think? A man had two sons; he went to the first and said, "Son, go and work in the vineyard today." ²⁹ He answered, "I will not"; but later he changed his mind and went. ³⁰ The father*¹* went to the second and said the same; and he answered, "I go, sir"; but he did not go. ³¹ Which of the two did the will of his father?' They said, 'The first.' Jesus said to them, 'Truly I tell you, the tax-collectors and the prostitutes are going into the kingdom of God ahead of you. ³² For John came to you in the way of righteousness and you did not believe him, but

---

1 Gk *He*

the tax-collectors and the prostitutes believed him; and even
after you saw it, you did not change your minds and believe him.

The Parable of the Wicked Tenants

33 'Listen to another parable. There was a landowner who
planted a vineyard, put a fence around it, dug a wine press in it,
and built a watch-tower. Then he leased it to tenants and went
to another country. 34 When the harvest time had come, he sent
his slaves to the tenants to collect his produce. 35 But the tenants
seized his slaves and beat one, killed another, and stoned another.
36 Again he sent other slaves, more than the first; and they treated
them in the same way. 37 Finally he sent his son to them, saying,
"They will respect my son." 38 But when the tenants saw the son,
they said to themselves, "This is the heir; come, let us kill him
and get his inheritance." 39 So they seized him, threw him out
of the vineyard, and killed him. 40 Now when the owner of the
vineyard comes, what will he do to those tenants?' 41 They said to
him, 'He will put those wretches to a miserable death, and lease
the vineyard to other tenants who will give him the produce at
the harvest time.'

42 Jesus said to them, 'Have you never read in the scriptures:
   "The stone that the builders rejected
      has become the cornerstone; *m*
   this was the Lord's doing,
      and it is amazing in our eyes"?
43 Therefore I tell you, the kingdom of God will be taken away
from you and given to a people that produces the fruits of the
kingdom. *n* 44 The one who falls on this stone will be broken to
pieces; and it will crush anyone on whom it falls.' *o*

45 When the chief priests and the Pharisees heard his parables,
they realized that he was speaking about them. 46 They wanted
to arrest him, but they feared the crowds, because they regarded
him as a prophet.

The Parable of the Wedding Banquet

22 Once more Jesus spoke to them in parables, saying: 2 'The
kingdom of heaven may be compared to a king who gave

---

m Or *keystone*   n Gk *the fruits of it*   o Other ancient authorities lack verse 44

a wedding banquet for his son. ³He sent his slaves to call those who had been invited to the wedding banquet, but they would not come. ⁴Again he sent other slaves, saying, "Tell those who have been invited: Look, I have prepared my dinner, my oxen and my fat calves have been slaughtered, and everything is ready; come to the wedding banquet." ⁵But they made light of it and went away, one to his farm, another to his business, ⁶while the rest seized his slaves, maltreated them, and killed them. ⁷The king was enraged. He sent his troops, destroyed those murderers, and burned their city. ⁸Then he said to his slaves, "The wedding is ready, but those invited were not worthy. ⁹Go therefore into the main streets, and invite everyone you find to the wedding banquet." ¹⁰Those slaves went out into the streets and gathered all whom they found, both good and bad; so the wedding hall was filled with guests.

¹¹'But when the king came in to see the guests, he noticed a man there who was not wearing a wedding robe, ¹²and he said to him, "Friend, how did you get in here without a wedding robe?" And he was speechless. ¹³Then the king said to the attendants, "Bind him hand and foot, and throw him into the outer darkness, where there will be weeping and gnashing of teeth." ¹⁴For many are called, but few are chosen.'

The Question about Paying Taxes

¹⁵Then the Pharisees went and plotted to entrap him in what he said. ¹⁶So they sent their disciples to him, along with the Herodians, saying, 'Teacher, we know that you are sincere, and teach the way of God in accordance with truth, and show deference to no one; for you do not regard people with partiality. ¹⁷Tell us, then, what you think. Is it lawful to pay taxes to the emperor, or not?' ¹⁸But Jesus, aware of their malice, said, 'Why are you putting me to the test, you hypocrites? ¹⁹Show me the coin used for the tax.' And they brought him a denarius. ²⁰Then he said to them, 'Whose head is this, and whose title?' ²¹They answered, 'The emperor's.' Then he said to them, 'Give therefore to the emperor the things that are the emperor's, and to God the things that are God's.' ²²When they heard this, they were amazed; and they left him and went away.

The Question about the Resurrection

23The same day some Sadducees came to him, saying there is no
resurrection;[p] and they asked him a question, saying, 24'Teacher,
Moses said, "If a man dies childless, his brother shall marry the
widow, and raise up children for his brother." 25Now there were
seven brothers among us; the first married, and died childless,
leaving the widow to his brother. 26The second did the same,
so also the third, down to the seventh. 27Last of all, the woman
herself died. 28In the resurrection, then, whose wife of the seven
will she be? For all of them had married her.'
29Jesus answered them, 'You are wrong, because you know
neither the scriptures nor the power of God. 30For in the
resurrection they neither marry nor are given in marriage, but
are like angels[q] in heaven. 31And as for the resurrection of the
dead, have you not read what was said to you by God, 32"I am
the God of Abraham, the God of Isaac, and the God of Jacob"? He
is God not of the dead, but of the living.' 33And when the crowd
heard it, they were astounded at his teaching.

The Greatest Commandment

34When the Pharisees heard that he had silenced the Sadducees,
they gathered together, 35and one of them, a lawyer, asked him
a question to test him. 36'Teacher, which commandment in the
law is the greatest?' 37He said to him, ' "You shall love the Lord
your God with all your heart, and with all your soul, and with
all your mind." 38This is the greatest and first commandment.
39And a second is like it: "You shall love your neighbour as
yourself." 40On these two commandments hang all the law and
the prophets.'

The Question about David's Son

41Now while the Pharisees were gathered together, Jesus asked
them this question: 42'What do you think of the Messiah?[r] Whose
son is he?' They said to him, 'The son of David.' 43He said to them,
'How is it then that David by the Spirit[s] calls him Lord, saying,
44 "The Lord said to my Lord,

---

p Other ancient authorities read *who say that there is no resurrection* q Other ancient authorities add *of God* r Or *Christ* s Gk *in spirit*

'Sit at my right hand,
     until I put your enemies under your feet' "?
⁴⁵If David thus calls him Lord, how can he be his son?' ⁴⁶No one was able to give him an answer, nor from that day did anyone dare to ask him any more questions.

Jesus Denounces Scribes and Pharisees

23 Then Jesus said to the crowds and to his disciples, ²'The scribes and the Pharisees sit on Moses' seat; ³therefore, do whatever they teach you and follow it; but do not do as they do, for they do not practise what they teach. ⁴They tie up heavy burdens, hard to bear,ᵗ and lay them on the shoulders of others; but they themselves are unwilling to lift a finger to move them. ⁵They do all their deeds to be seen by others; for they make their phylacteries broad and their fringes long. ⁶They love to have the place of honour at banquets and the best seats in the synagogues, ⁷and to be greeted with respect in the market-places, and to have people call them rabbi. ⁸But you are not to be called rabbi, for you have one teacher, and you are all students.ᵘ ⁹And call no one your father on earth, for you have one Father—the one in heaven. ¹⁰Nor are you to be called instructors, for you have one instructor, the Messiah.ᵛ ¹¹The greatest among you will be your servant. ¹²All who exalt themselves will be humbled, and all who humble themselves will be exalted.

¹³'But woe to you, scribes and Pharisees, hypocrites! For you lock people out of the kingdom of heaven. For you do not go in yourselves, and when others are going in, you stop them.ʷ ¹⁵Woe to you, scribes and Pharisees, hypocrites! For you cross sea and land to make a single convert, and you make the new convert twice as much a child of hellˣ as yourselves.

¹⁶'Woe to you, blind guides, who say, "Whoever swears by the sanctuary is bound by nothing, but whoever swears by the gold of the sanctuary is bound by the oath." ¹⁷You blind fools! For which is greater, the gold or the sanctuary that has made the gold sacred? ¹⁸And you say, "Whoever swears by the altar

---

t Other ancient authorities lack *hard to bear*   u Gk *brothers*   v Or *the Christ*   w Other authorities add here (or after verse 12) verse 14, *Woe to you, scribes and Pharisees, hypocrites! For you devour widows' houses and for the sake of appearance you make long prayers; therefore you will receive the greater condemnation*   x Gk *Gehenna*

is bound by nothing, but whoever swears by the gift that is on the altar is bound by the oath." ¹⁹ How blind you are! For which is greater, the gift or the altar that makes the gift sacred? ²⁰ So whoever swears by the altar, swears by it and by everything on it; ²¹ and whoever swears by the sanctuary, swears by it and by the one who dwells in it; ²² and whoever swears by heaven, swears by the throne of God and by the one who is seated upon it.

²³ 'Woe to you, scribes and Pharisees, hypocrites! For you tithe mint, dill, and cummin, and have neglected the weightier matters of the law: justice and mercy and faith. It is these you ought to have practised without neglecting the others. ²⁴ You blind guides! You strain out a gnat but swallow a camel!

²⁵ 'Woe to you, scribes and Pharisees, hypocrites! For you clean the outside of the cup and of the plate, but inside they are full of greed and self-indulgence. ²⁶ You blind Pharisee! First clean the inside of the cup,^{y} so that the outside also may become clean.

²⁷ 'Woe to you, scribes and Pharisees, hypocrites! For you are like whitewashed tombs, which on the outside look beautiful, but inside they are full of the bones of the dead and of all kinds of filth. ²⁸ So you also on the outside look righteous to others, but inside you are full of hypocrisy and lawlessness.

²⁹ 'Woe to you, scribes and Pharisees, hypocrites! For you build the tombs of the prophets and decorate the graves of the righteous, ³⁰ and you say, "If we had lived in the days of our ancestors, we would not have taken part with them in shedding the blood of the prophets." ³¹ Thus you testify against yourselves that you are descendants of those who murdered the prophets. ³² Fill up, then, the measure of your ancestors. ³³ You snakes, you brood of vipers! How can you escape being sentenced to hell?^{z} ³⁴ Therefore I send you prophets, sages, and scribes, some of whom you will kill and crucify, and some you will flog in your synagogues and pursue from town to town, ³⁵ so that upon you may come all the righteous blood shed on earth, from the blood of righteous Abel to the blood of Zechariah son of Barachiah, whom you murdered between the sanctuary and the altar. ³⁶ Truly I tell you, all this will come upon this generation.

---

y Other ancient authorities add *and of the plate*   z Gk *Gehenna*

The Lament over Jerusalem

[37]'Jerusalem, Jerusalem, the city that kills the prophets and stones those who are sent to it! How often have I desired to gather your children together as a hen gathers her brood under her wings, and you were not willing! [38]See, your house is left to you, desolate.[a] [39]For I tell you, you will not see me again until you say, "Blessed is the one who comes in the name of the Lord." '

The Destruction of the Temple Foretold

24 As Jesus came out of the temple and was going away, his disciples came to point out to him the buildings of the temple. [2]Then he asked them, 'You see all these, do you not? Truly I tell you, not one stone will be left here upon another; all will be thrown down.'

Signs of the End of the Age

[3]When he was sitting on the Mount of Olives, the disciples came to him privately, saying, 'Tell us, when will this be, and what will be the sign of your coming and of the end of the age?' [4]Jesus answered them, 'Beware that no one leads you astray. [5]For many will come in my name, saying, "I am the Messiah!"[b] and they will lead many astray. [6]And you will hear of wars and rumours of wars; see that you are not alarmed; for this must take place, but the end is not yet. [7]For nation will rise against nation, and kingdom against kingdom, and there will be famines[c] and earthquakes in various places: [8]all this is but the beginning of the birth pangs.

Persecutions Foretold

[9]'Then they will hand you over to be tortured and will put you to death, and you will be hated by all nations because of my name. [10]Then many will fall away,[d] and they will betray one another and hate one another. [11]And many false prophets will arise and lead many astray. [12]And because of the increase of lawlessness, the love of many will grow cold. [13]But anyone who endures to the end will be saved. [14]And this good news[e] of the

---

a Other ancient authorities lack *desolate*   b Or *the Christ*   c Other ancient authorities add *and pestilences*   d Or *stumble*   e Or *gospel*

kingdom will be proclaimed throughout the world, as a testimony to all the nations; and then the end will come.

The Desolating Sacrilege

¹⁵'So when you see the desolating sacrilege standing in the holy place, as was spoken of by the prophet Daniel (let the reader understand), ¹⁶then those in Judea must flee to the mountains; ¹⁷someone on the housetop must not go down to take what is in the house; ¹⁸someone in the field must not turn back to get a coat. ¹⁹Woe to those who are pregnant and to those who are nursing infants in those days! ²⁰Pray that your flight may not be in winter or on a sabbath. ²¹For at that time there will be great suffering, such as has not been from the beginning of the world until now, no, and never will be. ²²And if those days had not been cut short, no one would be saved; but for the sake of the elect those days will be cut short. ²³Then if anyone says to you, "Look! Here is the Messiah!"ᶠ or "There he is!"—do not believe it. ²⁴For false messiahsᵍ and false prophets will appear and produce great signs and omens, to lead astray, if possible, even the elect. ²⁵Take note, I have told you beforehand. ²⁶So, if they say to you, "Look! He is in the wilderness", do not go out. If they say, "Look! He is in the inner rooms", do not believe it. ²⁷For as the lightning comes from the east and flashes as far as the west, so will be the coming of the Son of Man. ²⁸Wherever the corpse is, there the vultures will gather.

The Coming of the Son of Man

²⁹ 'Immediately after the suffering of those days
    the sun will be darkened,
        and the moon will not give its light;
    the stars will fall from heaven,
        and the powers of heaven will be shaken.
³⁰Then the sign of the Son of Man will appear in heaven, and then all the tribes of the earth will mourn, and they will see "the Son of Man coming on the clouds of heaven" with power and great glory. ³¹And he will send out his angels with a loud trumpet call, and they will gather his elect from the four winds, from one end of heaven to the other.

---

f Or *the Christ*   g Or *christs*

The Lesson of the Fig Tree

³²'From the fig tree learn its lesson: as soon as its branch becomes tender and puts forth its leaves, you know that summer is near. ³³So also, when you see all these things, you know that he*h* is near, at the very gates. ³⁴Truly I tell you, this generation will not pass away until all these things have taken place. ³⁵Heaven and earth will pass away, but my words will not pass away.

The Necessity for Watchfulness

³⁶'But about that day and hour no one knows, neither the angels of heaven, nor the Son,*i* but only the Father. ³⁷For as the days of Noah were, so will be the coming of the Son of Man. ³⁸For as in those days before the flood they were eating and drinking, marrying and giving in marriage, until the day Noah entered the ark, ³⁹and they knew nothing until the flood came and swept them all away, so too will be the coming of the Son of Man. ⁴⁰Then two will be in the field; one will be taken and one will be left. ⁴¹Two women will be grinding meal together; one will be taken and one will be left. ⁴²Keep awake therefore, for you do not know on what day*j* your Lord is coming. ⁴³But understand this: if the owner of the house had known in what part of the night the thief was coming, he would have stayed awake and would not have let his house be broken into. ⁴⁴Therefore you also must be ready, for the Son of Man is coming at an unexpected hour.

The Faithful or the Unfaithful Slave

⁴⁵'Who then is the faithful and wise slave, whom his master has put in charge of his household, to give the other slaves*k* their allowance of food at the proper time? ⁴⁶Blessed is that slave whom his master will find at work when he arrives. ⁴⁷Truly I tell you, he will put that one in charge of all his possessions. ⁴⁸But if that wicked slave says to himself, "My master is delayed", ⁴⁹and he begins to beat his fellow-slaves, and eats and drinks with drunkards, ⁵⁰the master of that slave will come on a day when he does not expect him and at an hour that he does not know.

---

h Or *it*   i Other ancient authorities lack *nor the Son*   j Other ancient authorities read *at what hour*   k Gk *to give them*

⁵¹He will cut him in pieces*l* and put him with the hypocrites, where there will be weeping and gnashing of teeth.

The Parable of the Ten Bridesmaids

25 ¹'Then the kingdom of heaven will be like this. Ten bridesmaids*m* took their lamps and went to meet the bridegroom.*n* ²Five of them were foolish, and five were wise. ³When the foolish took their lamps, they took no oil with them; ⁴but the wise took flasks of oil with their lamps. ⁵As the bridegroom was delayed, all of them became drowsy and slept. ⁶But at midnight there was a shout, "Look! Here is the bridegroom! Come out to meet him." ⁷Then all those bridesmaids*o* got up and trimmed their lamps. ⁸The foolish said to the wise, "Give us some of your oil, for our lamps are going out." ⁹But the wise replied, "No! there will not be enough for you and for us; you had better go to the dealers and buy some for yourselves." ¹⁰And while they went to buy it, the bridegroom came, and those who were ready went with him into the wedding banquet; and the door was shut. ¹¹Later the other bridesmaids*o* came also, saying, "Lord, lord, open to us." ¹²But he replied, "Truly I tell you, I do not know you." ¹³Keep awake therefore, for you know neither the day nor the hour.*p*

The Parable of the Talents

¹⁴'For it is as if a man, going on a journey, summoned his slaves and entrusted his property to them; ¹⁵to one he gave five talents,*q* to another two, to another one, to each according to his ability. Then he went away. ¹⁶The one who had received the five talents went off at once and traded with them, and made five more talents. ¹⁷In the same way, the one who had the two talents made two more talents. ¹⁸But the one who had received the one talent went off and dug a hole in the ground and hid his master's money. ¹⁹After a long time the master of those slaves came and settled accounts with them. ²⁰Then the one who had received the five talents came forward, bringing five more talents, saying,

---

l Or *cut him off*   m Gk *virgins*   n Other ancient authorities add *and the bride*
o Gk *virgins*   p Other ancient authorities add *in which the Son of Man is coming*
q A talent was worth more than fifteen years' wages of a labourer

"Master, you handed over to me five talents; see, I have made five more talents." [21]His master said to him, "Well done, good and trustworthy slave; you have been trustworthy in a few things, I will put you in charge of many things; enter into the joy of your master." [22]And the one with the two talents also came forward, saying, "Master, you handed over to me two talents; see, I have made two more talents." [23]His master said to him, "Well done, good and trustworthy slave; you have been trustworthy in a few things, I will put you in charge of many things; enter into the joy of your master." [24]Then the one who had received the one talent also came forward, saying, "Master, I knew that you were a harsh man, reaping where you did not sow, and gathering where you did not scatter seed; [25]so I was afraid, and I went and hid your talent in the ground. Here you have what is yours." [26]But his master replied, "You wicked and lazy slave! You knew, did you, that I reap where I did not sow, and gather where I did not scatter? [27]Then you ought to have invested my money with the bankers, and on my return I would have received what was my own with interest. [28]So take the talent from him, and give it to the one with the ten talents. [29]For to all those who have, more will be given, and they will have an abundance; but from those who have nothing, even what they have will be taken away. [30]As for this worthless slave, throw him into the outer darkness, where there will be weeping and gnashing of teeth."

The Judgement of the Nations

[31]'When the Son of Man comes in his glory, and all the angels with him, then he will sit on the throne of his glory. [32]All the nations will be gathered before him, and he will separate people one from another as a shepherd separates the sheep from the goats, [33]and he will put the sheep at his right hand and the goats at the left. [34]Then the king will say to those at his right hand, "Come, you that are blessed by my Father, inherit the kingdom prepared for you from the foundation of the world; [35]for I was hungry and you gave me food, I was thirsty and you gave me something to drink, I was a stranger and you welcomed me, [36]I was naked and you gave me clothing, I was sick and you took care of me, I was in prison and you visited me." [37]Then the righteous will answer him, "Lord, when was it that we saw you

hungry and gave you food, or thirsty and gave you something to drink? ³⁸And when was it that we saw you a stranger and welcomed you, or naked and gave you clothing? ³⁹And when was it that we saw you sick or in prison and visited you?" ⁴⁰And the king will answer them, "Truly I tell you, just as you did it to one of the least of these who are members of my family,ʳ you did it to me." ⁴¹Then he will say to those at his left hand, "You that are accursed, depart from me into the eternal fire prepared for the devil and his angels; ⁴²for I was hungry and you gave me no food, I was thirsty and you gave me nothing to drink, ⁴³I was a stranger and you did not welcome me, naked and you did not give me clothing, sick and in prison and you did not visit me." ⁴⁴Then they also will answer, "Lord, when was it that we saw you hungry or thirsty or a stranger or naked or sick or in prison, and did not take care of you?" ⁴⁵Then he will answer them, "Truly I tell you, just as you did not do it to one of the least of these, you did not do it to me." ⁴⁶And these will go away into eternal punishment, but the righteous into eternal life.'

The Plot to Kill Jesus

26 When Jesus had finished saying all these things, he said to his disciples, ²'You know that after two days the Passover is coming, and the Son of Man will be handed over to be crucified.'

³Then the chief priests and the elders of the people gathered in the palace of the high priest, who was called Caiaphas, ⁴and they conspired to arrest Jesus by stealth and kill him. ⁵But they said, 'Not during the festival, or there may be a riot among the people.'

The Anointing at Bethany

⁶Now while Jesus was at Bethany in the house of Simon the leper,ˢ ⁷a woman came to him with an alabaster jar of very costly ointment, and she poured it on his head as he sat at the table. ⁸But when the disciples saw it, they were angry and said, 'Why this waste? ⁹For this ointment could have been sold for a large sum, and the money given to the poor.' ¹⁰But Jesus, aware of this, said to them, 'Why do you trouble the woman? She has

---

r Gk *these my brothers*   s The terms *leper* and *leprosy* can refer to several diseases

performed a good service for me. ¹¹For you always have the poor with you, but you will not always have me. ¹²By pouring this ointment on my body she has prepared me for burial. ¹³Truly I tell you, wherever this good news[t] is proclaimed in the whole world, what she has done will be told in remembrance of her.'

Judas Agrees to Betray Jesus

¹⁴Then one of the twelve, who was called Judas Iscariot, went to the chief priests ¹⁵and said, 'What will you give me if I betray him to you?' They paid him thirty pieces of silver. ¹⁶And from that moment he began to look for an opportunity to betray him.

The Passover with the Disciples

¹⁷On the first day of Unleavened Bread the disciples came to Jesus, saying, 'Where do you want us to make the preparations for you to eat the Passover?' ¹⁸He said, 'Go into the city to a certain man, and say to him, "The Teacher says, My time is near; I will keep the Passover at your house with my disciples." ' ¹⁹So the disciples did as Jesus had directed them, and they prepared the Passover meal.

²⁰When it was evening, he took his place with the twelve;[u] ²¹and while they were eating, he said, 'Truly I tell you, one of you will betray me.' ²²And they became greatly distressed and began to say to him one after another, 'Surely not I, Lord?' ²³He answered, 'The one who has dipped his hand into the bowl with me will betray me. ²⁴The Son of Man goes as it is written of him, but woe to that one by whom the Son of Man is betrayed! It would have been better for that one not to have been born.' ²⁵Judas, who betrayed him, said, 'Surely not I, Rabbi?' He replied, 'You have said so.'

The Institution of the Lord's Supper

²⁶While they were eating, Jesus took a loaf of bread, and after blessing it he broke it, gave it to the disciples, and said, 'Take, eat; this is my body.' ²⁷Then he took a cup, and after giving thanks he gave it to them, saying, 'Drink from it, all of you; ²⁸for this is my blood of the[v] covenant, which is poured out for many for the

---

t Or *gospel*   u Other ancient authorities add *disciples*   v Other ancient authorities add *new*

forgiveness of sins. ²⁹I tell you, I will never again drink of this fruit of the vine until that day when I drink it new with you in my Father's kingdom.'

³⁰When they had sung the hymn, they went out to the Mount of Olives.

Peter's Denial Foretold

³¹Then Jesus said to them, 'You will all become deserters because of me this night; for it is written,

"I will strike the shepherd,
and the sheep of the flock will be scattered."

³²But after I am raised up, I will go ahead of you to Galilee.' ³³Peter said to him, 'Though all become deserters because of you, I will never desert you.' ³⁴Jesus said to him, 'Truly I tell you, this very night, before the cock crows, you will deny me three times.' ³⁵Peter said to him, 'Even though I must die with you, I will not deny you.' And so said all the disciples.

Jesus Prays in Gethsemane

³⁶Then Jesus went with them to a place called Gethsemane; and he said to his disciples, 'Sit here while I go over there and pray.' ³⁷He took with him Peter and the two sons of Zebedee, and began to be grieved and agitated. ³⁸Then he said to them, 'I am deeply grieved, even to death; remain here, and stay awake with me.' ³⁹And going a little farther, he threw himself on the ground and prayed, 'My Father, if it is possible, let this cup pass from me; yet not what I want but what you want.' ⁴⁰Then he came to the disciples and found them sleeping; and he said to Peter, 'So, could you not stay awake with me one hour? ⁴¹Stay awake and pray that you may not come into the time of trial;ʷ the spirit indeed is willing, but the flesh is weak.' ⁴²Again he went away for the second time and prayed, 'My Father, if this cannot pass unless I drink it, your will be done.' ⁴³Again he came and found them sleeping, for their eyes were heavy. ⁴⁴So leaving them again, he went away and prayed for the third time, saying the same words. ⁴⁵Then he came to the disciples and said to them, 'Are you still sleeping and taking your rest? See, the hour is at hand, and the

---

ʷ Or into temptation

Son of Man is betrayed into the hands of sinners. ⁴⁶Get up, let us be going. See, my betrayer is at hand.'

The Betrayal and Arrest of Jesus

⁴⁷While he was still speaking, Judas, one of the twelve, arrived; with him was a large crowd with swords and clubs, from the chief priests and the elders of the people. ⁴⁸Now the betrayer had given them a sign, saying, 'The one I will kiss is the man; arrest him.' ⁴⁹At once he came up to Jesus and said, 'Greetings, Rabbi!' and kissed him. ⁵⁰Jesus said to him, 'Friend, do what you are here to do.' Then they came and laid hands on Jesus and arrested him. ⁵¹Suddenly, one of those with Jesus put his hand on his sword, drew it, and struck the slave of the high priest, cutting off his ear. ⁵²Then Jesus said to him, 'Put your sword back into its place; for all who take the sword will perish by the sword. ⁵³Do you think that I cannot appeal to my Father, and he will at once send me more than twelve legions of angels? ⁵⁴But how then would the scriptures be fulfilled, which say it must happen in this way?' ⁵⁵At that hour Jesus said to the crowds, 'Have you come out with swords and clubs to arrest me as though I were a bandit? Day after day I sat in the temple teaching, and you did not arrest me. ⁵⁶But all this has taken place, so that the scriptures of the prophets may be fulfilled.' Then all the disciples deserted him and fled.

Jesus before the High Priest

⁵⁷Those who had arrested Jesus took him to Caiaphas the high priest, in whose house the scribes and the elders had gathered. ⁵⁸But Peter was following him at a distance, as far as the courtyard of the high priest; and going inside, he sat with the guards in order to see how this would end. ⁵⁹Now the chief priests and the whole council were looking for false testimony against Jesus so that they might put him to death, ⁶⁰but they found none, though many false witnesses came forward. At last two came forward ⁶¹and said, 'This fellow said, "I am able to destroy the temple of God and to build it in three days." ' ⁶²The high priest stood up and said, 'Have you no answer? What is it that they testify against you?' ⁶³But Jesus was silent. Then the high priest said to him, 'I put you under oath before the living

God, tell us if you are the Messiah,ˣ the Son of God.' ⁶⁴Jesus said to him,

> 'You have said so. But I tell you,
> From now on you will see the Son of Man
>   seated at the right hand of Power
>   and coming on the clouds of heaven.'

⁶⁵Then the high priest tore his clothes and said, 'He has blasphemed! Why do we still need witnesses? You have now heard his blasphemy. ⁶⁶What is your verdict?' They answered, 'He deserves death.' ⁶⁷Then they spat in his face and struck him; and some slapped him, ⁶⁸saying, 'Prophesy to us, you Messiah!ˣ Who is it that struck you?'

Peter's Denial of Jesus

⁶⁹Now Peter was sitting outside in the courtyard. A servant-girl came to him and said, 'You also were with Jesus the Galilean.' ⁷⁰But he denied it before all of them, saying, 'I do not know what you are talking about.' ⁷¹When he went out to the porch, another servant-girl saw him, and she said to the bystanders, 'This man was with Jesus of Nazareth.'ʸ ⁷²Again he denied it with an oath, 'I do not know the man.' ⁷³After a little while the bystanders came up and said to Peter, 'Certainly you are also one of them, for your accent betrays you.' ⁷⁴Then he began to curse, and he swore an oath, 'I do not know the man!' At that moment the cock crowed. ⁷⁵Then Peter remembered what Jesus had said: 'Before the cock crows, you will deny me three times.' And he went out and wept bitterly.

Jesus Brought before Pilate

27 When morning came, all the chief priests and the elders of the people conferred together against Jesus in order to bring about his death. ²They bound him, led him away, and handed him over to Pilate the governor.

The Suicide of Judas

³When Judas, his betrayer, saw that Jesusᶻ was condemned, he repented and brought back the thirty pieces of silver to the

---

x Or *Christ*   y Gk *the Nazorean*   z Gk *he*

chief priests and the elders. ⁴He said, 'I have sinned by betraying innocent*ᵃ* blood.' But they said, 'What is that to us? See to it yourself.' ⁵Throwing down the pieces of silver in the temple, he departed; and he went and hanged himself. ⁶But the chief priests, taking the pieces of silver, said, 'It is not lawful to put them into the treasury, since they are blood money.' ⁷After conferring together, they used them to buy the potter's field as a place to bury foreigners. ⁸For this reason that field has been called the Field of Blood to this day. ⁹Then was fulfilled what had been spoken through the prophet Jeremiah,*ᵇ* 'And they took*ᶜ* the thirty pieces of silver, the price of the one on whom a price had been set,*ᵈ* on whom some of the people of Israel had set a price, ¹⁰and they gave*ᵉ* them for the potter's field, as the Lord commanded me.'

Pilate Questions Jesus

¹¹Now Jesus stood before the governor; and the governor asked him, 'Are you the King of the Jews?' Jesus said, 'You say so.' ¹²But when he was accused by the chief priests and elders, he did not answer. ¹³Then Pilate said to him, 'Do you not hear how many accusations they make against you?' ¹⁴But he gave him no answer, not even to a single charge, so that the governor was greatly amazed.

Barabbas or Jesus?

¹⁵Now at the festival the governor was accustomed to release a prisoner for the crowd, anyone whom they wanted. ¹⁶At that time they had a notorious prisoner, called Jesus*ᶠ* Barabbas. ¹⁷So after they had gathered, Pilate said to them, 'Whom do you want me to release for you, Jesus*ᶠ* Barabbas or Jesus who is called the Messiah?'*ᵍ* ¹⁸For he realized that it was out of jealousy that they had handed him over. ¹⁹While he was sitting on the judgement seat, his wife sent word to him, 'Have nothing to do with that innocent man, for today I have suffered a great deal because of a dream about him.' ²⁰Now the chief priests and the elders

---

a Other ancient authorities read *righteous*   b Other ancient authorities read *Zechariah* or *Isaiah*   c Or *I took*   d Or *the price of the precious One*   e Other ancient authorities read *I gave*   f Other ancient authorities lack *Jesus*   g Or *the Christ*

persuaded the crowds to ask for Barabbas and to have Jesus killed. ²¹The governor again said to them, 'Which of the two do you want me to release for you?' And they said, 'Barabbas.' ²²Pilate said to them, 'Then what should I do with Jesus who is called the Messiah?'ᵍ All of them said, 'Let him be crucified!' ²³Then he asked, 'Why, what evil has he done?' But they shouted all the more, 'Let him be crucified!'

Pilate Hands Jesus over to Be Crucified

²⁴So when Pilate saw that he could do nothing, but rather that a riot was beginning, he took some water and washed his hands before the crowd, saying, 'I am innocent of this man's blood;ʰ see to it yourselves.' ²⁵Then the people as a whole answered, 'His blood be on us and on our children!' ²⁶So he released Barabbas for them; and after flogging Jesus, he handed him over to be crucified.

The Soldiers Mock Jesus

²⁷Then the soldiers of the governor took Jesus into the governor's headquarters,ⁱ and they gathered the whole cohort around him. ²⁸They stripped him and put a scarlet robe on him, ²⁹and after twisting some thorns into a crown, they put it on his head. They put a reed in his right hand and knelt before him and mocked him, saying, 'Hail, King of the Jews!' ³⁰They spat on him, and took the reed and struck him on the head. ³¹After mocking him, they stripped him of the robe and put his own clothes on him. Then they led him away to crucify him.

The Crucifixion of Jesus

³²As they went out, they came upon a man from Cyrene named Simon; they compelled this man to carry his cross. ³³And when they came to a place called Golgotha (which means Place of a Skull), ³⁴they offered him wine to drink, mixed with gall; but when he tasted it, he would not drink it. ³⁵And when they had crucified him, they divided his clothes among themselves by casting lots;ʲ ³⁶then they sat down there and kept watch over

---

g Or *the Christ*   h Other ancient authorities read *this righteous blood*, or *this righteous man's blood*   i Gk *the praetorium*   j Other ancient authorities add *in order that what had been spoken through the prophet might be fulfilled, 'They divided my clothes among themselves, and for my clothing they cast lots.*

him. ³⁷Over his head they put the charge against him, which read, 'This is Jesus, the King of the Jews.'

³⁸Then two bandits were crucified with him, one on his right and one on his left. ³⁹Those who passed by derided*ᵏ* him, shaking their heads ⁴⁰and saying, 'You who would destroy the temple and build it in three days, save yourself! If you are the Son of God, come down from the cross.' ⁴¹In the same way the chief priests also, along with the scribes and elders, were mocking him, saying, ⁴²'He saved others; he cannot save himself.*ˡ* He is the King of Israel; let him come down from the cross now, and we will believe in him. ⁴³He trusts in God; let God deliver him now, if he wants to; for he said, "I am God's Son." ' ⁴⁴The bandits who were crucified with him also taunted him in the same way.

The Death of Jesus

⁴⁵From noon on, darkness came over the whole land*ᵐ* until three in the afternoon. ⁴⁶And about three o'clock Jesus cried with a loud voice, 'Eli, Eli, lema sabachthani?' that is, 'My God, my God, why have you forsaken me?' ⁴⁷When some of the bystanders heard it, they said, 'This man is calling for Elijah.' ⁴⁸At once one of them ran and got a sponge, filled it with sour wine, put it on a stick, and gave it to him to drink. ⁴⁹But the others said, 'Wait, let us see whether Elijah will come to save him.'*ⁿ* ⁵⁰Then Jesus cried again with a loud voice and breathed his last.*ᵒ* ⁵¹At that moment the curtain of the temple was torn in two, from top to bottom. The earth shook, and the rocks were split. ⁵²The tombs also were opened, and many bodies of the saints who had fallen asleep were raised. ⁵³After his resurrection they came out of the tombs and entered the holy city and appeared to many. ⁵⁴Now when the centurion and those with him, who were keeping watch over Jesus, saw the earthquake and what took place, they were terrified and said, 'Truly this man was God's Son!'*ᵖ*

⁵⁵Many women were also there, looking on from a distance; they had followed Jesus from Galilee and had provided for him. ⁵⁶Among them were Mary Magdalene, and Mary the mother of James and Joseph, and the mother of the sons of Zebedee.

---

k Or *blasphemed*   l Or *is he unable to save himself?*   m Or *earth*   n Other ancient authorities add *And another took a spear and pierced his side, and out came water and blood*   o Or *gave up his spirit*   p Or *a son of God*

The Burial of Jesus

⁵⁷When it was evening, there came a rich man from Arimathea, named Joseph, who was also a disciple of Jesus. ⁵⁸He went to Pilate and asked for the body of Jesus; then Pilate ordered it to be given to him. ⁵⁹So Joseph took the body and wrapped it in a clean linen cloth ⁶⁰and laid it in his own new tomb, which he had hewn in the rock. He then rolled a great stone to the door of the tomb and went away. ⁶¹Mary Magdalene and the other Mary were there, sitting opposite the tomb.

The Guard at the Tomb

⁶²The next day, that is, after the day of Preparation, the chief priests and the Pharisees gathered before Pilate ⁶³and said, 'Sir, we remember what that impostor said while he was still alive, "After three days I will rise again." ⁶⁴Therefore command that the tomb be made secure until the third day; otherwise his disciples may go and steal him away, and tell the people, "He has been raised from the dead", and the last deception would be worse than the first.' ⁶⁵Pilate said to them, 'You have a guard^q of soldiers; go, make it as secure as you can.'^r ⁶⁶So they went with the guard and made the tomb secure by sealing the stone.

The Resurrection of Jesus

28 After the sabbath, as the first day of the week was dawning, Mary Magdalene and the other Mary went to see the tomb. ²And suddenly there was a great earthquake; for an angel of the Lord, descending from heaven, came and rolled back the stone and sat on it. ³His appearance was like lightning, and his clothing white as snow. ⁴For fear of him the guards shook and became like dead men. ⁵But the angel said to the women, 'Do not be afraid; I know that you are looking for Jesus who was crucified. ⁶He is not here; for he has been raised, as he said. Come, see the place where he^s lay. ⁷Then go quickly and tell his disciples, "He has been raised from the dead,^t and indeed he is going ahead of you to Galilee; there you will see him." This is my message for you.' ⁸So they left the tomb quickly with fear and

---

q Or *Take a guard*   r Gk *you know how*   s Other ancient authorities read *the Lord*
t Other ancient authorities lack *from the dead*

great joy, and ran to tell his disciples. [9]Suddenly Jesus met them and said, 'Greetings!' And they came to him, took hold of his feet, and worshipped him. [10]Then Jesus said to them, 'Do not be afraid; go and tell my brothers to go to Galilee; there they will see me.'

The Report of the Guard

[11]While they were going, some of the guard went into the city and told the chief priests everything that had happened. [12]After the priests[u] had assembled with the elders, they devised a plan to give a large sum of money to the soldiers, [13]telling them, 'You must say, "His disciples came by night and stole him away while we were asleep." [14]If this comes to the governor's ears, we will satisfy him and keep you out of trouble.' [15]So they took the money and did as they were directed. And this story is still told among the Jews to this day.

The Commissioning of the Disciples

[16]Now the eleven disciples went to Galilee, to the mountain to which Jesus had directed them. [17]When they saw him, they worshipped him; but some doubted. [18]And Jesus came and said to them, 'All authority in heaven and on earth has been given to me. [19]Go therefore and make disciples of all nations, baptizing them in the name of the Father and of the Son and of the Holy Spirit, [20]and teaching them to obey everything that I have commanded you. And remember, I am with you always, to the end of the age.'[v]

---

u Gk *they*   v Other ancient authorities add *Amen*

The Gospel According to

Mark

The Proclamation of John the Baptist

1 The beginning of the good news[a] of Jesus Christ, the Son of God.[b]

[2] As it is written in the prophet Isaiah,[c]

'See, I am sending my messenger ahead of you,[d]
who will prepare your way;
[3] the voice of one crying out in the wilderness:
"Prepare the way of the Lord,
make his paths straight" ',

[4] John the baptizer appeared[e] in the wilderness, proclaiming a baptism of repentance for the forgiveness of sins. [5] And people from the whole Judean countryside and all the people of Jerusalem were going out to him, and were baptized by him in the river Jordan, confessing their sins. [6] Now John was clothed with camel's hair, with a leather belt around his waist, and he ate locusts and wild honey. [7] He proclaimed, 'The one who is more powerful than I is coming after me; I am not worthy to stoop down and untie the thong of his sandals. [8] I have baptized you with[f] water; but he will baptize you with[f] the Holy Spirit.'

The Baptism of Jesus

[9] In those days Jesus came from Nazareth of Galilee and was baptized by John in the Jordan. [10] And just as he was coming up

---

a Or *gospel*   b Other ancient authorities lack *the Son of God*   c Other ancient authorities read *in the prophets*   d Gk *before your face*   e Other ancient authorities read *John was baptizing*   f Or *in*

out of the water, he saw the heavens torn apart and the Spirit descending like a dove on him. ¹¹And a voice came from heaven, 'You are my Son, the Beloved;ᵍ with you I am well pleased.'

The Temptation of Jesus

¹²And the Spirit immediately drove him out into the wilderness. ¹³He was in the wilderness for forty days, tempted by Satan; and he was with the wild beasts; and the angels waited on him.

The Beginning of the Galilean Ministry

¹⁴Now after John was arrested, Jesus came to Galilee, proclaiming the good newsʰ of God,ⁱ ¹⁵and saying, 'The time is fulfilled, and the kingdom of God has come near;ʲ repent, and believe in the good news.'ᵏ

Jesus Calls the First Disciples

¹⁶As Jesus passed along the Sea of Galilee, he saw Simon and his brother Andrew casting a net into the lake—for they were fishermen. ¹⁷And Jesus said to them, 'Follow me and I will make you fish for people.' ¹⁸And immediately they left their nets and followed him. ¹⁹As he went a little farther, he saw James son of Zebedee and his brother John, who were in their boat mending the nets. ²⁰Immediately he called them; and they left their father Zebedee in the boat with the hired men, and followed him.

The Man with an Unclean Spirit

²¹They went to Capernaum; and when the sabbath came, he entered the synagogue and taught. ²²They were astounded at his teaching, for he taught them as one having authority, and not as the scribes. ²³Just then there was in their synagogue a man with an unclean spirit, ²⁴and he cried out, 'What have you to do with us, Jesus of Nazareth? Have you come to destroy us? I know who you are, the Holy One of God.' ²⁵But Jesus rebuked him, saying, 'Be silent, and come out of him!' ²⁶And the unclean spirit, throwing him into convulsions and crying with a loud voice, came out of him. ²⁷They were all amazed, and they kept on asking one another,

---

g Or *my beloved Son*   h Or *gospel*   i Other ancient authorities read *of the kingdom*
j Or *is at hand*   k Or *gospel*

'What is this? A new teaching—with authority! He^l commands even the unclean spirits, and they obey him.' ^{28}At once his fame began to spread throughout the surrounding region of Galilee.

Jesus Heals Many at Simon's House

^{29}As soon as they^m left the synagogue, they entered the house of Simon and Andrew, with James and John. ^{30}Now Simon's mother-in-law was in bed with a fever, and they told him about her at once. ^{31}He came and took her by the hand and lifted her up. Then the fever left her, and she began to serve them.

^{32}That evening, at sunset, they brought to him all who were sick or possessed with demons. ^{33}And the whole city was gathered around the door. ^{34}And he cured many who were sick with various diseases, and cast out many demons; and he would not permit the demons to speak, because they knew him.

A Preaching Tour in Galilee

^{35}In the morning, while it was still very dark, he got up and went out to a deserted place, and there he prayed. ^{36}And Simon and his companions hunted for him. ^{37}When they found him, they said to him, 'Everyone is searching for you.' ^{38}He answered, 'Let us go on to the neighbouring towns, so that I may proclaim the message there also; for that is what I came out to do.' ^{39}And he went throughout Galilee, proclaiming the message in their synagogues and casting out demons.

Jesus Cleanses a Leper

^{40}A leper^n came to him begging him, and kneeling^o he said to him, 'If you choose, you can make me clean.' ^{41}Moved with pity,^{p} Jesus^q stretched out his hand and touched him, and said to him, 'I do choose. Be made clean!' ^{42}Immediately the leprosy^r left him, and he was made clean. ^{43}After sternly warning him he sent him away at once, ^{44}saying to him, 'See that you say nothing to anyone; but go, show yourself to the priest, and offer for your cleansing what Moses commanded, as a testimony to

---

l Or *A new teaching! With authority he*   m Other ancient authorities read *he*   n The terms *leper* and *leprosy* can refer to several diseases   o Other ancient authorities lack *kneeling*
p Other ancient authorities read *anger*   q Gk *he*   r The terms *leper* and *leprosy* can refer to several diseases

them.' ⁴⁵But he went out and began to proclaim it freely, and to spread the word, so that Jesus^s could no longer go into a town openly, but stayed out in the country; and people came to him from every quarter.

Jesus Heals a Paralytic

2 When he returned to Capernaum after some days, it was reported that he was at home. ²So many gathered around that there was no longer room for them, not even in front of the door; and he was speaking the word to them. ³Then some people^t came, bringing to him a paralysed man, carried by four of them. ⁴And when they could not bring him to Jesus because of the crowd, they removed the roof above him; and after having dug through it, they let down the mat on which the paralytic lay. ⁵When Jesus saw their faith, he said to the paralytic, 'Son, your sins are forgiven.' ⁶Now some of the scribes were sitting there, questioning in their hearts, ⁷'Why does this fellow speak in this way? It is blasphemy! Who can forgive sins but God alone?' ⁸At once Jesus perceived in his spirit that they were discussing these questions among themselves; and he said to them, 'Why do you raise such questions in your hearts? ⁹Which is easier, to say to the paralytic, "Your sins are forgiven", or to say, "Stand up and take your mat and walk"? ¹⁰But so that you may know that the Son of Man has authority on earth to forgive sins'–he said to the paralytic– ¹¹'I say to you, stand up, take your mat and go to your home.' ¹²And he stood up, and immediately took the mat and went out before all of them; so that they were all amazed and glorified God, saying, 'We have never seen anything like this!'

Jesus Calls Levi

¹³Jesus^u went out again beside the lake; the whole crowd gathered around him, and he taught them. ¹⁴As he was walking along, he saw Levi son of Alphaeus sitting at the tax booth, and he said to him, 'Follow me.' And he got up and followed him.

¹⁵And as he sat at dinner^v in Levi's^w house, many tax-collectors and sinners were also sitting^x with Jesus and his disciples–for there were many who followed him. ¹⁶When the scribes of^y

---

s Gk *he*   t Gk *they*   u Gk *He*   v Gk *reclined*   w Gk *his*   x Gk *reclining*   y Other ancient authorities read *and*

the Pharisees saw that he was eating with sinners and tax-collectors, they said to his disciples, 'Why does he eat ^{z} with tax-collectors and sinners?' ^{17}When Jesus heard this, he said to them, 'Those who are well have no need of a physician, but those who are sick; I have come to call not the righteous but sinners.'

The Question about Fasting

^{18}Now John's disciples and the Pharisees were fasting; and people^a came and said to him, 'Why do John's disciples and the disciples of the Pharisees fast, but your disciples do not fast?' ^{19}Jesus said to them, 'The wedding-guests cannot fast while the bridegroom is with them, can they? As long as they have the bridegroom with them, they cannot fast. ^{20}The days will come when the bridegroom is taken away from them, and then they will fast on that day.

^{21}'No one sews a piece of unshrunk cloth on an old cloak; otherwise, the patch pulls away from it, the new from the old, and a worse tear is made. ^{22}And no one puts new wine into old wineskins; otherwise, the wine will burst the skins, and the wine is lost, and so are the skins; but one puts new wine into fresh wineskins.'^{b}

Pronouncement about the Sabbath

^{23}One sabbath he was going through the cornfields; and as they made their way his disciples began to pluck heads of grain. ^{24}The Pharisees said to him, 'Look, why are they doing what is not lawful on the sabbath?' ^{25}And he said to them, 'Have you never read what David did when he and his companions were hungry and in need of food? ^{26}He entered the house of God, when Abiathar was high priest, and ate the bread of the Presence, which it is not lawful for any but the priests to eat, and he gave some to his companions.' ^{27}Then he said to them, 'The sabbath was made for humankind, and not humankind for the sabbath; ^{28}so the Son of Man is lord even of the sabbath.'

---

z Other ancient authorities add *and drink*   a Gk *they*   b Other ancient authorities lack *but one puts new wine into fresh wineskins*

The Man with a Withered Hand

3 Again he entered the synagogue, and a man was there who had a withered hand. ²They watched him to see whether he would cure him on the sabbath, so that they might accuse him. ³And he said to the man who had the withered hand, 'Come forward.' ⁴Then he said to them, 'Is it lawful to do good or to do harm on the sabbath, to save life or to kill?' But they were silent. ⁵He looked around at them with anger; he was grieved at their hardness of heart and said to the man, 'Stretch out your hand.' He stretched it out, and his hand was restored. ⁶The Pharisees went out and immediately conspired with the Herodians against him, how to destroy him.

A Multitude at the Lakeside

⁷Jesus departed with his disciples to the lake, and a great multitude from Galilee followed him; ⁸hearing all that he was doing, they came to him in great numbers from Judea, Jerusalem, Idumea, beyond the Jordan, and the region around Tyre and Sidon. ⁹He told his disciples to have a boat ready for him because of the crowd, so that they would not crush him; ¹⁰for he had cured many, so that all who had diseases pressed upon him to touch him. ¹¹Whenever the unclean spirits saw him, they fell down before him and shouted, 'You are the Son of God!' ¹²But he sternly ordered them not to make him known.

Jesus Appoints the Twelve

¹³He went up the mountain and called to him those whom he wanted, and they came to him. ¹⁴And he appointed twelve, whom he also named apostles,ᶜ to be with him, and to be sent out to proclaim the message, ¹⁵and to have authority to cast out demons. ¹⁶So he appointed the twelve:ᵈ Simon (to whom he gave the name Peter); ¹⁷James son of Zebedee and John the brother of James (to whom he gave the name Boanerges, that is, Sons of Thunder); ¹⁸and Andrew, and Philip, and Bartholomew, and Matthew, and Thomas, and James son of Alphaeus, and Thaddaeus, and Simon the Cananaean, ¹⁹and Judas Iscariot, who betrayed him.

---

c Other ancient authorities lack *whom he also named apostles*   d Other ancient authorities lack *So he appointed the twelve*

Jesus and Beelzebul

Then he went home; 20 and the crowd came together again, so that they could not even eat. 21 When his family heard it, they went out to restrain him, for people were saying, 'He has gone out of his mind.' 22 And the scribes who came down from Jerusalem said; 'He has Beelzebul, and by the ruler of the demons he casts out demons.' 23 And he called them to him, and spoke to them in parables, 'How can Satan cast out Satan? 24 If a kingdom is divided against itself, that kingdom cannot stand. 25 And if a house is divided against itself, that house will not be able to stand. 26 And if Satan has risen up against himself and is divided, he cannot stand, but his end has come. 27 But no one can enter a strong man's house and plunder his property without first tying up the strong man; then indeed the house can be plundered.

28 'Truly I tell you, people will be forgiven for their sins and whatever blasphemies they utter; 29 but whoever blasphemes against the Holy Spirit can never have forgiveness, but is guilty of an eternal sin'— 30 for they had said, 'He has an unclean spirit.'

The True Kindred of Jesus

31 Then his mother and his brothers came; and standing outside, they sent to him and called him. 32 A crowd was sitting around him; and they said to him, 'Your mother and your brothers and sisters[e] are outside, asking for you.' 33 And he replied, 'Who are my mother and my brothers?' 34 And looking at those who sat around him, he said, 'Here are my mother and my brothers! 35 Whoever does the will of God is my brother and sister and mother.'

The Parable of the Sower

4 Again he began to teach beside the lake. Such a very large crowd gathered around him that he got into a boat on the lake and sat there, while the whole crowd was beside the lake on the land. 2 He began to teach them many things in parables, and in his teaching he said to them: 3 'Listen! A sower went out to sow. 4 And as he sowed, some seed fell on the path, and the birds came and ate it up. 5 Other seed fell on rocky ground, where it did not have much soil, and it sprang up quickly, since it had

---

e Other ancient authorities lack *and sisters*

no depth of soil. ⁶And when the sun rose, it was scorched; and since it had no root, it withered away. ⁷Other seed fell among thorns, and the thorns grew up and choked it, and it yielded no grain. ⁸Other seed fell into good soil and brought forth grain, growing up and increasing and yielding thirty and sixty and a hundredfold.' ⁹And he said, 'Let anyone with ears to hear listen!'

The Purpose of the Parables

¹⁰When he was alone, those who were around him along with the twelve asked him about the parables. ¹¹And he said to them, 'To you has been given the secretᶠ of the kingdom of God, but for those outside, everything comes in parables; ¹²in order that

"they may indeed look, but not perceive,
    and may indeed listen, but not understand;
  so that they may not turn again and be forgiven." '

¹³And he said to them, 'Do you not understand this parable? Then how will you understand all the parables? ¹⁴The sower sows the word. ¹⁵These are the ones on the path where the word is sown: when they hear, Satan immediately comes and takes away the word that is sown in them. ¹⁶And these are the ones sown on rocky ground: when they hear the word, they immediately receive it with joy. ¹⁷But they have no root, and endure only for a while; then, when trouble or persecution arises on account of the word, immediately they fall away.ᵍ ¹⁸And others are those sown among the thorns: these are the ones who hear the word, ¹⁹but the cares of the world, and the lure of wealth, and the desire for other things come in and choke the word, and it yields nothing. ²⁰And these are the ones sown on the good soil: they hear the word and accept it and bear fruit, thirty and sixty and a hundredfold.'

A Lamp under a Bushel Basket

²¹He said to them, 'Is a lamp brought in to be put under the bushel basket, or under the bed, and not on the lampstand? ²²For there is nothing hidden, except to be disclosed; nor is anything secret, except to come to light. ²³Let anyone with ears to hear listen!' ²⁴And he said to them, 'Pay attention to what you hear;

---

f Or *mystery*   g Or *stumble*

the measure you give will be the measure you get, and still more will be given you. ²⁵For to those who have, more will be given; and from those who have nothing, even what they have will be taken away.'

The Parable of the Growing Seed

²⁶He also said, 'The kingdom of God is as if someone would scatter seed on the ground, ²⁷and would sleep and rise night and day, and the seed would sprout and grow, he does not know how. ²⁸The earth produces of itself, first the stalk, then the head, then the full grain in the head. ²⁹But when the grain is ripe, at once he goes in with his sickle, because the harvest has come.'

The Parable of the Mustard Seed

³⁰He also said, 'With what can we compare the kingdom of God, or what parable will we use for it? ³¹It is like a mustard seed, which, when sown upon the ground, is the smallest of all the seeds on earth; ³²yet when it is sown it grows up and becomes the greatest of all shrubs, and puts forth large branches, so that the birds of the air can make nests in its shade.'

The Use of Parables

³³With many such parables he spoke the word to them, as they were able to hear it; ³⁴he did not speak to them except in parables, but he explained everything in private to his disciples.

Jesus Stills a Storm

³⁵On that day, when evening had come, he said to them, 'Let us go across to the other side.' ³⁶And leaving the crowd behind, they took him with them in the boat, just as he was. Other boats were with him. ³⁷A great gale arose, and the waves beat into the boat, so that the boat was already being swamped. ³⁸But he was in the stern, asleep on the cushion; and they woke him up and said to him, 'Teacher, do you not care that we are perishing?' ³⁹He woke up and rebuked the wind, and said to the sea, 'Peace! Be still!' Then the wind ceased, and there was a dead calm. ⁴⁰He said to them, 'Why are you afraid? Have you still no faith?' ⁴¹And they were filled with great awe and said to one another, 'Who then is this, that even the wind and the sea obey him?'

Jesus Heals the Gerasene Demoniac

5 They came to the other side of the lake, to the country of the Gerasenes.[h] [2]And when he had stepped out of the boat, immediately a man out of the tombs with an unclean spirit met him. [3]He lived among the tombs; and no one could restrain him any more, even with a chain; [4]for he had often been restrained with shackles and chains, but the chains he wrenched apart, and the shackles he broke in pieces; and no one had the strength to subdue him. [5]Night and day among the tombs and on the mountains he was always howling and bruising himself with stones. [6]When he saw Jesus from a distance, he ran and bowed down before him; [7]and he shouted at the top of his voice, 'What have you to do with me, Jesus, Son of the Most High God? I adjure you by God, do not torment me.' [8]For he had said to him, 'Come out of the man, you unclean spirit!' [9]Then Jesus[i] asked him, 'What is your name?' He replied, 'My name is Legion; for we are many.' [10]He begged him earnestly not to send them out of the country. [11]Now there on the hillside a great herd of swine was feeding; [12]and the unclean spirits[j] begged him, 'Send us into the swine; let us enter them.' [13]So he gave them permission. And the unclean spirits came out and entered the swine; and the herd, numbering about two thousand, rushed down the steep bank into the lake, and were drowned in the lake.

[14]The swineherds ran off and told it in the city and in the country. Then people came to see what it was that had happened. [15]They came to Jesus and saw the demoniac sitting there, clothed and in his right mind, the very man who had had the legion; and they were afraid. [16]Those who had seen what had happened to the demoniac and to the swine reported it. [17]Then they began to beg Jesus[k] to leave their neighbourhood. [18]As he was getting into the boat, the man who had been possessed by demons begged him that he might be with him. [19]But Jesus[l] refused, and said to him, 'Go home to your friends, and tell them how much the Lord has done for you, and what mercy he has shown you.' [20]And he went away and began to proclaim in the Decapolis how much Jesus had done for him; and everyone was amazed.

---

h Other ancient authorities read *Gergesenes*; others, *Gadarenes*   i Gk *he*   j Gk *they*
k Gk *him*   l Gk *he*

A Girl Restored to Life and a Woman Healed

²¹When Jesus had crossed again in the boat *m* to the other side, a great crowd gathered round him; and he was by the lake. ²²Then one of the leaders of the synagogue named Jairus came and, when he saw him, fell at his feet ²³and begged him repeatedly, 'My little daughter is at the point of death. Come and lay your hands on her, so that she may be made well, and live.' ²⁴So he went with him.

And a large crowd followed him and pressed in on him. ²⁵Now there was a woman who had been suffering from haemorrhages for twelve years. ²⁶She had endured much under many physicians, and had spent all that she had; and she was no better, but rather grew worse. ²⁷She had heard about Jesus, and came up behind him in the crowd and touched his cloak, ²⁸for she said, 'If I but touch his clothes, I will be made well.' ²⁹Immediately her haemorrhage stopped; and she felt in her body that she was healed of her disease. ³⁰Immediately aware that power had gone forth from him, Jesus turned about in the crowd and said, 'Who touched my clothes?' ³¹And his disciples said to him, 'You see the crowd pressing in on you; how can you say, "Who touched me?" ' ³²He looked all round to see who had done it. ³³But the woman, knowing what had happened to her, came in fear and trembling, fell down before him, and told him the whole truth. ³⁴He said to her, 'Daughter, your faith has made you well; go in peace, and be healed of your disease.'

³⁵While he was still speaking, some people came from the leader's house to say, 'Your daughter is dead. Why trouble the teacher any further?' ³⁶But overhearing *n* what they said, Jesus said to the leader of the synagogue, 'Do not fear, only believe.' ³⁷He allowed no one to follow him except Peter, James, and John, the brother of James. ³⁸When they came to the house of the leader of the synagogue, he saw a commotion, people weeping and wailing loudly. ³⁹When he had entered, he said to them, 'Why do you make a commotion and weep? The child is not dead but sleeping.' ⁴⁰And they laughed at him. Then he put

---

m Other ancient authorities lack *in the boat*   n Or *ignoring*; other ancient authorities read *hearing*

them all outside, and took the child's father and mother and those who were with him, and went in where the child was. ⁴¹He took her by the hand and said to her, 'Talitha cum', which means, 'Little girl, get up!' ⁴²And immediately the girl got up and began to walk about (she was twelve years of age). At this they were overcome with amazement. ⁴³He strictly ordered them that no one should know this, and told them to give her something to eat.

The Rejection of Jesus at Nazareth

6 He left that place and came to his home town, and his disciples followed him. ²On the sabbath he began to teach in the synagogue, and many who heard him were astounded. They said, 'Where did this man get all this? What is this wisdom that has been given to him? What deeds of power are being done by his hands! ³Is not this the carpenter, the son of Maryᵒ and brother of James and Joses and Judas and Simon, and are not his sisters here with us?' And they took offenceᵖ at him. ⁴Then Jesus said to them, 'Prophets are not without honour, except in their home town, and among their own kin, and in their own house.' ⁵And he could do no deed of power there, except that he laid his hands on a few sick people and cured them. ⁶And he was amazed at their unbelief.

The Mission of the Twelve

Then he went about among the villages teaching. ⁷He called the twelve and began to send them out two by two, and gave them authority over the unclean spirits. ⁸He ordered them to take nothing for their journey except a staff; no bread, no bag, no money in their belts; ⁹but to wear sandals and not to put on two tunics. ¹⁰He said to them, 'Wherever you enter a house, stay there until you leave the place. ¹¹If any place will not welcome you and they refuse to hear you, as you leave, shake off the dust that is on your feet as a testimony against them.' ¹²So they went out and proclaimed that all should repent. ¹³They cast out many demons, and anointed with oil many who were sick and cured them.

---

o Other ancient authorities read *son of the carpenter and of Mary*   p Or *stumbled*

The Death of John the Baptist

¹⁴King Herod heard of it, for Jesus'*q* name had become known. Some were*r* saying, 'John the baptizer has been raised from the dead; and for this reason these powers are at work in him.' ¹⁵But others said, 'It is Elijah.' And others said, 'It is a prophet, like one of the prophets of old.' ¹⁶But when Herod heard of it, he said, 'John, whom I beheaded, has been raised.'

¹⁷For Herod himself had sent men who arrested John, bound him, and put him in prison on account of Herodias, his brother Philip's wife, because Herod*s* had married her. ¹⁸For John had been telling Herod, 'It is not lawful for you to have your brother's wife.' ¹⁹And Herodias had a grudge against him, and wanted to kill him. But she could not, ²⁰for Herod feared John, knowing that he was a righteous and holy man, and he protected him. When he heard him, he was greatly perplexed;*t* and yet he liked to listen to him. ²¹But an opportunity came when Herod on his birthday gave a banquet for his courtiers and officers and for the leaders of Galilee. ²²When his daughter Herodias*u* came in and danced, she pleased Herod and his guests; and the king said to the girl, 'Ask me for whatever you wish, and I will give it.' ²³And he solemnly swore to her, 'Whatever you ask me, I will give you, even half of my kingdom.' ²⁴She went out and said to her mother, 'What should I ask for?' She replied, 'The head of John the baptizer.' ²⁵Immediately she rushed back to the king and requested, 'I want you to give me at once the head of John the Baptist on a platter.' ²⁶The king was deeply grieved; yet out of regard for his oaths and for the guests, he did not want to refuse her. ²⁷Immediately the king sent a soldier of the guard with orders to bring John's*v* head. He went and beheaded him in the prison, ²⁸brought his head on a platter, and gave it to the girl. Then the girl gave it to her mother. ²⁹When his disciples heard about it, they came and took his body, and laid it in a tomb.

Feeding the Five Thousand

³⁰The apostles gathered around Jesus, and told him all that they had done and taught. ³¹He said to them, 'Come away to a deserted

---

q Gk *his*   *r* Other ancient authorities read *He was*   *s* Gk *he*   *t* Other ancient authorities read *he did many things*   *u* Other ancient authorities read *the daughter of Herodias herself*
v Gk *his*

place all by yourselves and rest a while.' For many were coming and going, and they had no leisure even to eat. ³²And they went away in the boat to a deserted place by themselves. ³³Now many saw them going and recognized them, and they hurried there on foot from all the towns and arrived ahead of them. ³⁴As he went ashore, he saw a great crowd; and he had compassion for them, because they were like sheep without a shepherd; and he began to teach them many things. ³⁵When it grew late, his disciples came to him and said, 'This is a deserted place, and the hour is now very late; ³⁶send them away so that they may go into the surrounding country and villages and buy something for themselves to eat.' ³⁷But he answered them, 'You give them something to eat.' They said to him, 'Are we to go and buy two hundred denarii^w worth of bread, and give it to them to eat?' ³⁸And he said to them, 'How many loaves have you? Go and see.' When they had found out, they said, 'Five, and two fish.' ³⁹Then he ordered them to get all the people to sit down in groups on the green grass. ⁴⁰So they sat down in groups of hundreds and of fifties. ⁴¹Taking the five loaves and the two fish, he looked up to heaven, and blessed and broke the loaves, and gave them to his disciples to set before the people; and he divided the two fish among them all. ⁴²And all ate and were filled; ⁴³and they took up twelve baskets full of broken pieces and of the fish. ⁴⁴Those who had eaten the loaves numbered five thousand men.

Jesus Walks on the Water

⁴⁵Immediately he made his disciples get into the boat and go on ahead to the other side, to Bethsaida, while he dismissed the crowd. ⁴⁶After saying farewell to them, he went up on the mountain to pray.

⁴⁷When evening came, the boat was out on the lake, and he was alone on the land. ⁴⁸When he saw that they were straining at the oars against an adverse wind, he came towards them early in the morning, walking on the lake. He intended to pass them by. ⁴⁹But when they saw him walking on the lake, they thought it was a ghost and cried out; ⁵⁰for they all saw him and were terrified. But immediately he spoke to them and said, 'Take heart, it is I;

---

w The denarius was the usual day's wage for a labourer

do not be afraid.' ⁵¹Then he got into the boat with them and the wind ceased. And they were utterly astounded, ⁵²for they did not understand about the loaves, but their hearts were hardened.

Healing the Sick in Gennesaret

⁵³When they had crossed over, they came to land at Gennesaret and moored the boat. ⁵⁴When they got out of the boat, people at once recognized him, ⁵⁵and rushed about that whole region and began to bring the sick on mats to wherever they heard he was. ⁵⁶And wherever he went, into villages or cities or farms, they laid the sick in the market-places, and begged him that they might touch even the fringe of his cloak; and all who touched it were healed.

The Tradition of the Elders

7 Now when the Pharisees and some of the scribes who had come from Jerusalem gathered around him, ²they noticed that some of his disciples were eating with defiled hands, that is, without washing them. ³(For the Pharisees, and all the Jews, do not eat unless they thoroughly wash their hands,ˣ thus observing the tradition of the elders; ⁴and they do not eat anything from the market unless they wash it;ʸ and there are also many other traditions that they observe, the washing of cups, pots, and bronze kettles.ᶻ) ⁵So the Pharisees and the scribes asked him, 'Why do your disciples not liveᵃ according to the tradition of the elders, but eat with defiled hands?' ⁶He said to them, 'Isaiah prophesied rightly about you hypocrites, as it is written,

"This people honours me with their lips,
    but their hearts are far from me;
⁷ in vain do they worship me,
    teaching human precepts as doctrines."

⁸You abandon the commandment of God and hold to human tradition.'

⁹Then he said to them, 'You have a fine way of rejecting the commandment of God in order to keep your tradition!

---

x Meaning of Gk uncertain   y Other ancient authorities read *and when they come from the market-place, they do not eat unless they purify themselves*   z Other ancient authorities add *and beds*   a Gk *walk*

¹⁰For Moses said, "Honour your father and your mother"; and, "Whoever speaks evil of father or mother must surely die." ¹¹But you say that if anyone tells father or mother, "Whatever support you might have had from me is Corban" (that is, an offering to God^b)— ¹²then you no longer permit doing anything for a father or mother, ¹³thus making void the word of God through your tradition that you have handed on. And you do many things like this.'

¹⁴Then he called the crowd again and said to them, 'Listen to me, all of you, and understand: ¹⁵there is nothing outside a person that by going in can defile, but the things that come out are what defile.'^c

¹⁷When he had left the crowd and entered the house, his disciples asked him about the parable. ¹⁸He said to them, 'Then do you also fail to understand? Do you not see that whatever goes into a person from outside cannot defile, ¹⁹since it enters, not the heart but the stomach, and goes out into the sewer?' (Thus he declared all foods clean.) ²⁰And he said, 'It is what comes out of a person that defiles. ²¹For it is from within, from the human heart, that evil intentions come: fornication, theft, murder, ²²adultery, avarice, wickedness, deceit, licentiousness, envy, slander, pride, folly. ²³All these evil things come from within, and they defile a person.'

The Syrophoenician Woman's Faith

²⁴From there he set out and went away to the region of Tyre.^d He entered a house and did not want anyone to know he was there. Yet he could not escape notice, ²⁵but a woman whose little daughter had an unclean spirit immediately heard about him, and she came and bowed down at his feet. ²⁶Now the woman was a Gentile, of Syrophoenician origin. She begged him to cast the demon out of her daughter. ²⁷He said to her, 'Let the children be fed first, for it is not fair to take the children's food and throw it to the dogs.' ²⁸But she answered him, 'Sir,^e even the dogs under the table eat the children's crumbs.' ²⁹Then he

---

b Gk lacks *to God*   c Other ancient authorities add verse 16, *'Let anyone with ears to hear listen'*   d Other ancient authorities add *and Sidon*   e Or *Lord;* other ancient authorities prefix *Yes*

said to her, 'For saying that, you may go—the demon has left your daughter.' [30] So she went home, found the child lying on the bed, and the demon gone.

Jesus Cures a Deaf Man

[31] Then he returned from the region of Tyre, and went by way of Sidon towards the Sea of Galilee, in the region of the Decapolis. [32] They brought to him a deaf man who had an impediment in his speech; and they begged him to lay his hand on him. [33] He took him aside in private, away from the crowd, and put his fingers into his ears, and he spat and touched his tongue. [34] Then looking up to heaven, he sighed and said to him, 'Ephphatha', that is, 'Be opened.' [35] And immediately his ears were opened, his tongue was released, and he spoke plainly. [36] Then Jesus[f] ordered them to tell no one; but the more he ordered them, the more zealously they proclaimed it. [37] They were astounded beyond measure, saying, 'He has done everything well; he even makes the deaf to hear and the mute to speak.'

Feeding the Four Thousand

8 In those days when there was again a great crowd without anything to eat, he called his disciples and said to them, [2] 'I have compassion for the crowd, because they have been with me now for three days and have nothing to eat. [3] If I send them away hungry to their homes, they will faint on the way—and some of them have come from a great distance.' [4] His disciples replied, 'How can one feed these people with bread here in the desert?' [5] He asked them, 'How many loaves do you have?' They said, 'Seven.' [6] Then he ordered the crowd to sit down on the ground; and he took the seven loaves, and after giving thanks he broke them and gave them to his disciples to distribute; and they distributed them to the crowd. [7] They had also a few small fish; and after blessing them, he ordered that these too should be distributed. [8] They ate and were filled; and they took up the broken pieces left over, seven baskets full. [9] Now there were about four thousand people. And he sent them away. [10] And

---

f Gk *he*

immediately he got into the boat with his disciples and went to the district of Dalmanutha.^{g}

The Demand for a Sign

^{11}The Pharisees came and began to argue with him, asking him for a sign from heaven, to test him. ^{12}And he sighed deeply in his spirit and said, 'Why does this generation ask for a sign? Truly I tell you, no sign will be given to this generation.' ^{13}And he left them, and getting into the boat again, he went across to the other side.

The Yeast of the Pharisees and of Herod

^{14}Now the disciples^h had forgotten to bring any bread; and they had only one loaf with them in the boat. ^{15}And he cautioned them, saying, 'Watch out—beware of the yeast of the Pharisees and the yeast of Herod.'^{i} ^{16}They said to one another, 'It is because we have no bread.' ^{17}And becoming aware of it, Jesus said to them, 'Why are you talking about having no bread? Do you still not perceive or understand? Are your hearts hardened? ^{18}Do you have eyes, and fail to see? Do you have ears, and fail to hear? And do you not remember? ^{19}When I broke the five loaves for the five thousand, how many baskets full of broken pieces did you collect?' They said to him, 'Twelve.' ^{20}'And the seven for the four thousand, how many baskets full of broken pieces did you collect?' And they said to him, 'Seven.' ^{21}Then he said to them, 'Do you not yet understand?'

Jesus Cures a Blind Man at Bethsaida

^{22}They came to Bethsaida. Some people^j brought a blind man to him and begged him to touch him. ^{23}He took the blind man by the hand and led him out of the village; and when he had put saliva on his eyes and laid his hands on him, he asked him, 'Can you see anything?' ^{24}And the man^k looked up and said, 'I can see people, but they look like trees, walking.' ^{25}Then Jesus^k laid his hands on his eyes again; and he looked intently and his sight was restored, and he saw everything

---

g Other ancient authorities read *Mageda* or *Magdala*   h Gk *they*   i Other ancient authorities read *the Herodians*   j Gk *They*   k Gk *he*

clearly. 26Then he sent him away to his home, saying, 'Do not even go into the village.'[l]

Peter's Declaration about Jesus

27Jesus went on with his disciples to the villages of Caesarea Philippi; and on the way he asked his disciples, 'Who do people say that I am?' 28And they answered him, 'John the Baptist; and others, Elijah; and still others, one of the prophets.' 29He asked them, 'But who do you say that I am?' Peter answered him, 'You are the Messiah.'[m] 30And he sternly ordered them not to tell anyone about him.

Jesus Foretells His Death and Resurrection

31Then he began to teach them that the Son of Man must undergo great suffering, and be rejected by the elders, the chief priests, and the scribes, and be killed, and after three days rise again. 32He said all this quite openly. And Peter took him aside and began to rebuke him. 33But turning and looking at his disciples, he rebuked Peter and said, 'Get behind me, Satan! For you are setting your mind not on divine things but on human things.'

34He called the crowd with his disciples, and said to them, 'If any want to become my followers, let them deny themselves and take up their cross and follow me. 35For those who want to save their life will lose it, and those who lose their life for my sake, and for the sake of the gospel,[n] will save it. 36For what will it profit them to gain the whole world and forfeit their life? 37Indeed, what can they give in return for their life? 38Those who are ashamed of me and of my words[o] in this adulterous and sinful generation, of them the Son of Man will also be ashamed when he comes in the glory of his Father with the holy angels.'

9 And he said to them, 'Truly I tell you, there are some standing here who will not taste death until they see that the kingdom of God has come with[p] power.'

---

l Other ancient authorities add *or tell anyone in the village*   m Or *the Christ*   n Other ancient authorities read *lose their life for the sake of the gospel*   o Other ancient authorities read *and of mine*   p Or *in*

The Transfiguration

²Six days later, Jesus took with him Peter and James and John, and led them up a high mountain apart, by themselves. And he was transfigured before them, ³and his clothes became dazzling white, such as no one*q* on earth could bleach them. ⁴And there appeared to them Elijah with Moses, who were talking with Jesus. ⁵Then Peter said to Jesus, 'Rabbi, it is good for us to be here; let us make three dwellings,*r* one for you, one for Moses, and one for Elijah.' ⁶He did not know what to say, for they were terrified. ⁷Then a cloud overshadowed them, and from the cloud there came a voice, 'This is my Son, the Beloved;*s* listen to him!' ⁸Suddenly when they looked around, they saw no one with them any more, but only Jesus.

The Coming of Elijah

⁹As they were coming down the mountain, he ordered them to tell no one about what they had seen, until after the Son of Man had risen from the dead. ¹⁰So they kept the matter to themselves, questioning what this rising from the dead could mean. ¹¹Then they asked him, 'Why do the scribes say that Elijah must come first?' ¹²He said to them, 'Elijah is indeed coming first to restore all things. How then is it written about the Son of Man, that he is to go through many sufferings and be treated with contempt? ¹³But I tell you that Elijah has come, and they did to him whatever they pleased, as it is written about him.'

The Healing of a Boy with a Spirit

¹⁴When they came to the disciples, they saw a great crowd around them, and some scribes arguing with them. ¹⁵When the whole crowd saw him, they were immediately overcome with awe, and they ran forward to greet him. ¹⁶He asked them, 'What are you arguing about with them?' ¹⁷Someone from the crowd answered him, 'Teacher, I brought you my son; he has a spirit that makes him unable to speak; ¹⁸and whenever it seizes him, it dashes him down; and he foams and grinds his teeth and becomes rigid; and I asked your disciples to cast

---

q Gk *no fuller*   r Or *tents*   s Or *my beloved Son*

it out, but they could not do so.' ¹⁹He answered them, 'You faithless generation, how much longer must I be among you? How much longer must I put up with you? Bring him to me.' ²⁰And they brought the boy^t to him. When the spirit saw him, immediately it threw the boy^t into convulsions, and he fell on the ground and rolled about, foaming at the mouth. ²¹Jesus^u asked the father, 'How long has this been happening to him?' And he said, 'From childhood. ²²It has often cast him into the fire and into the water, to destroy him; but if you are able to do anything, have pity on us and help us.' ²³Jesus said to him, 'If you are able!—All things can be done for the one who believes.' ²⁴Immediately the father of the child cried out,^v 'I believe; help my unbelief!' ²⁵When Jesus saw that a crowd came running together, he rebuked the unclean spirit, saying to it, 'You spirit that keep this boy from speaking and hearing, I command you, come out of him, and never enter him again!' ²⁶After crying out and convulsing him terribly, it came out, and the boy was like a corpse, so that most of them said, 'He is dead.' ²⁷But Jesus took him by the hand and lifted him up, and he was able to stand. ²⁸When he had entered the house, his disciples asked him privately, 'Why could we not cast it out?' ²⁹He said to them, 'This kind can come out only through prayer.'^w

Jesus Again Foretells His Death and Resurrection

³⁰They went on from there and passed through Galilee. He did not want anyone to know it; ³¹for he was teaching his disciples, saying to them, 'The Son of Man is to be betrayed into human hands, and they will kill him, and three days after being killed, he will rise again.' ³²But they did not understand what he was saying and were afraid to ask him.

Who Is the Greatest?

³³Then they came to Capernaum; and when he was in the house he asked them, 'What were you arguing about on the way?' ³⁴But they were silent, for on the way they had argued with one another about who was the greatest. ³⁵He sat down,

---

t Gk *him*   u Gk *He*   v Other ancient authorities add *with tears*   w Other ancient authorities add *and fasting*

called the twelve, and said to them, 'Whoever wants to be first must be last of all and servant of all.' ³⁶Then he took a little child and put it among them; and taking it in his arms, he said to them, ³⁷'Whoever welcomes one such child in my name welcomes me, and whoever welcomes me welcomes not me but the one who sent me.'

Another Exorcist

³⁸John said to him, 'Teacher, we saw someoneˣ casting out demons in your name, and we tried to stop him, because he was not following us.' ³⁹But Jesus said, 'Do not stop him; for no one who does a deed of power in my name will be able soon afterwards to speak evil of me. ⁴⁰Whoever is not against us is for us. ⁴¹For truly I tell you, whoever gives you a cup of water to drink because you bear the name of Christ will by no means lose the reward.

Temptations to Sin

⁴²'If any of you put a stumbling-block before one of these little ones who believe in me,ʸ it would be better for you if a great millstone were hung around your neck and you were thrown into the sea. ⁴³If your hand causes you to stumble, cut it off; it is better for you to enter life maimed than to have two hands and to go to hell,ᶻ to the unquenchable fire.ᵃ ⁴⁵And if your foot causes you to stumble, cut it off; it is better for you to enter life lame than to have two feet and to be thrown into hell.ᵇ ᶜ ⁴⁷And if your eye causes you to stumble, tear it out; it is better for you to enter the kingdom of God with one eye than to have two eyes and to be thrown into hell,ᵈ ⁴⁸where their worm never dies, and the fire is never quenched.

⁴⁹'For everyone will be salted with fire.ᵉ ⁵⁰Salt is good; but if salt has lost its saltiness, how can you season it?ᶠ Have salt in yourselves, and be at peace with one another.'

---

x Other ancient authorities add *who does not follow us*   y Other ancient authorities lack *in me*   z Gk *Gehenna*   a Verses 44 and 46 (which are identical with verse 48) are lacking in the best ancient authorities   b Gk *Gehenna*   c Verses 44 and 46 (which are identical with verse 48) are lacking in the best ancient authorities   d Gk *Gehenna*   e Other ancient authorities either add or substitute *and every sacrifice will be salted with salt*   f Or *how can you restore its saltiness?*

Teaching about Divorce

10 He left that place and went to the region of Judea and[g] beyond the Jordan. And crowds again gathered around him; and, as was his custom, he again taught them.

[2] Some Pharisees came, and to test him they asked, 'Is it lawful for a man to divorce his wife?' [3] He answered them, 'What did Moses command you?' [4] They said, 'Moses allowed a man to write a certificate of dismissal and to divorce her.' [5] But Jesus said to them, 'Because of your hardness of heart he wrote this commandment for you. [6] But from the beginning of creation, "God made them male and female." [7] "For this reason a man shall leave his father and mother and be joined to his wife,[h] [8] and the two shall become one flesh." So they are no longer two, but one flesh. [9] Therefore what God has joined together, let no one separate.'

[10] Then in the house the disciples asked him again about this matter. [11] He said to them, 'Whoever divorces his wife and marries another commits adultery against her; [12] and if she divorces her husband and marries another, she commits adultery.'

Jesus Blesses Little Children

[13] People were bringing little children to him in order that he might touch them; and the disciples spoke sternly to them. [14] But when Jesus saw this, he was indignant and said to them, 'Let the little children come to me; do not stop them; for it is to such as these that the kingdom of God belongs. [15] Truly I tell you, whoever does not receive the kingdom of God as a little child will never enter it.' [16] And he took them up in his arms, laid his hands on them, and blessed them.

The Rich Man

[17] As he was setting out on a journey, a man ran up and knelt before him, and asked him, 'Good Teacher, what must I do to inherit eternal life?' [18] Jesus said to him, 'Why do you call me good? No one is good but God alone. [19] You know the commandments: "You shall not murder; You shall not commit adultery; You shall not steal; You shall not bear false witness; You

---

g Other ancient authorities lack *and*   h Other ancient authorities lack *and be joined to his wife*

shall not defraud; Honour your father and mother." ' ²⁰He said to him, 'Teacher, I have kept all these since my youth.' ²¹Jesus, looking at him, loved him and said, 'You lack one thing; go, sell what you own, and give the money^i to the poor, and you will have treasure in heaven; then come, follow me.' ²²When he heard this, he was shocked and went away grieving, for he had many possessions.

²³Then Jesus looked around and said to his disciples, 'How hard it will be for those who have wealth to enter the kingdom of God!' ²⁴And the disciples were perplexed at these words. But Jesus said to them again, 'Children, how hard it is^j to enter the kingdom of God! ²⁵It is easier for a camel to go through the eye of a needle than for someone who is rich to enter the kingdom of God.' ²⁶They were greatly astounded and said to one another,^k 'Then who can be saved?' ²⁷Jesus looked at them and said, 'For mortals it is impossible, but not for God; for God all things are possible.'

²⁸Peter began to say to him, 'Look, we have left everything and followed you.' ²⁹Jesus said, 'Truly I tell you, there is no one who has left house or brothers or sisters or mother or father or children or fields, for my sake and for the sake of the good news,^l ³⁰who will not receive a hundredfold now in this age—houses, brothers and sisters, mothers and children, and fields, with persecutions—and in the age to come eternal life. ³¹But many who are first will be last, and the last will be first.'

A Third Time Jesus Foretells His Death and Resurrection

³²They were on the road, going up to Jerusalem, and Jesus was walking ahead of them; they were amazed, and those who followed were afraid. He took the twelve aside again and began to tell them what was to happen to him, ³³saying, 'See, we are going up to Jerusalem, and the Son of Man will be handed over to the chief priests and the scribes, and they will condemn him to death; then they will hand him over to the Gentiles; ³⁴they will mock him, and spit upon him, and flog him, and kill him; and after three days he will rise again.'

---

i Gk lacks *the money*   j Other ancient authorities add *for those who trust in riches*
k Other ancient authorities read *to him*   l Or *gospel*

The Request of James and John

³⁵James and John, the sons of Zebedee, came forward to him and said to him, 'Teacher, we want you to do for us whatever we ask of you.' ³⁶And he said to them, 'What is it you want me to do for you?' ³⁷And they said to him, 'Grant us to sit, one at your right hand and one at your left, in your glory.' ³⁸But Jesus said to them, 'You do not know what you are asking. Are you able to drink the cup that I drink, or be baptized with the baptism that I am baptized with?' ³⁹They replied, 'We are able.' Then Jesus said to them, 'The cup that I drink you will drink; and with the baptism with which I am baptized, you will be baptized; ⁴⁰but to sit at my right hand or at my left is not mine to grant, but it is for those for whom it has been prepared.'

⁴¹When the ten heard this, they began to be angry with James and John. ⁴²So Jesus called them and said to them, 'You know that among the Gentiles those whom they recognize as their rulers lord it over them, and their great ones are tyrants over them. ⁴³But it is not so among you; but whoever wishes to become great among you must be your servant, ⁴⁴and whoever wishes to be first among you must be slave of all. ⁴⁵For the Son of Man came not to be served but to serve, and to give his life a ransom for many.'

The Healing of Blind Bartimaeus

⁴⁶They came to Jericho. As he and his disciples and a large crowd were leaving Jericho, Bartimaeus son of Timaeus, a blind beggar, was sitting by the roadside. ⁴⁷When he heard that it was Jesus of Nazareth, he began to shout out and say, 'Jesus, Son of David, have mercy on me!' ⁴⁸Many sternly ordered him to be quiet, but he cried out even more loudly, 'Son of David, have mercy on me!' ⁴⁹Jesus stood still and said, 'Call him here.' And they called the blind man, saying to him, 'Take heart; get up, he is calling you.' ⁵⁰So throwing off his cloak, he sprang up and came to Jesus. ⁵¹Then Jesus said to him, 'What do you want me to do for you?' The blind man said to him, 'My teacher,ᵐ let me see again.' ⁵²Jesus said to him, 'Go; your faith has made you well.' Immediately he regained his sight and followed him on the way.

---

m Aramaic *Rabbouni*

Jesus' Triumphal Entry into Jerusalem

11 When they were approaching Jerusalem, at Bethphage and Bethany, near the Mount of Olives, he sent two of his disciples ²and said to them, 'Go into the village ahead of you, and immediately as you enter it, you will find tied there a colt that has never been ridden; untie it and bring it. ³If anyone says to you, "Why are you doing this?" just say this, "The Lord needs it and will send it back here immediately." ' ⁴They went away and found a colt tied near a door, outside in the street. As they were untying it, ⁵some of the bystanders said to them, 'What are you doing, untying the colt?' ⁶They told them what Jesus had said; and they allowed them to take it. ⁷Then they brought the colt to Jesus and threw their cloaks on it; and he sat on it. ⁸Many people spread their cloaks on the road, and others spread leafy branches that they had cut in the fields. ⁹Then those who went ahead and those who followed were shouting,

'Hosanna!

Blessed is the one who comes in the name of the Lord!
¹⁰   Blessed is the coming kingdom of our ancestor David!

Hosanna in the highest heaven!'

¹¹Then he entered Jerusalem and went into the temple; and when he had looked around at everything, as it was already late, he went out to Bethany with the twelve.

Jesus Curses the Fig Tree

¹²On the following day, when they came from Bethany, he was hungry. ¹³Seeing in the distance a fig tree in leaf, he went to see whether perhaps he would find anything on it. When he came to it, he found nothing but leaves, for it was not the season for figs. ¹⁴He said to it, 'May no one ever eat fruit from you again.' And his disciples heard it.

Jesus Cleanses the Temple

¹⁵Then they came to Jerusalem. And he entered the temple and began to drive out those who were selling and those who were buying in the temple, and he overturned the tables of the money-changers and the seats of those who sold doves; ¹⁶and he would not allow anyone to carry anything through the temple. ¹⁷He was teaching and saying, 'Is it not written,

"My house shall be called a house of prayer for all the
        nations"?
    But you have made it a den of robbers.'
[18] And when the chief priests and the scribes heard it, they kept
looking for a way to kill him; for they were afraid of him, because
the whole crowd was spellbound by his teaching. [19] And when
evening came, Jesus and his disciples[n] went out of the city.

The Lesson from the Withered Fig Tree

[20] In the morning as they passed by, they saw the fig tree
withered away to its roots. [21] Then Peter remembered and said
to him, 'Rabbi, look! The fig tree that you cursed has withered.'
[22] Jesus answered them, 'Have[o] faith in God. [23] Truly I tell you, if
you say to this mountain, "Be taken up and thrown into the sea",
and if you do not doubt in your heart, but believe that what
you say will come to pass, it will be done for you. [24] So I tell you,
whatever you ask for in prayer, believe that you have received[p]
it, and it will be yours.
    [25] 'Whenever you stand praying, forgive, if you have anything
against anyone; so that your Father in heaven may also forgive
you your trespasses.'[q]

Jesus' Authority Is Questioned

[27] Again they came to Jerusalem. As he was walking in the temple,
the chief priests, the scribes, and the elders came to him [28] and
said, 'By what authority are you doing these things? Who gave you
this authority to do them?' [29] Jesus said to them, 'I will ask you one
question; answer me, and I will tell you by what authority I do
these things. [30] Did the baptism of John come from heaven, or was
it of human origin? Answer me.' [31] They argued with one another, 'If
we say, "From heaven", he will say, "Why then did you not believe
him?" [32] But shall we say, "Of human origin"?'–they were afraid
of the crowd, for all regarded John as truly a prophet. [33] So they
answered Jesus, 'We do not know.' And Jesus said to them, 'Neither
will I tell you by what authority I am doing these things.'

---

n Gk *they*: other ancient authorities read *he*   o Other ancient authorities read *'If you have*
p Other ancient authorities read *are receiving*   q Other ancient authorities add verse 26,
'But if you do not forgive, neither will your Father in heaven forgive your trespasses.'

The Parable of the Wicked Tenants

12 Then he began to speak to them in parables. 'A man planted a vineyard, put a fence around it, dug a pit for the wine press, and built a watch-tower; then he leased it to tenants and went to another country. ²When the season came, he sent a slave to the tenants to collect from them his share of the produce of the vineyard. ³But they seized him, and beat him, and sent him away empty-handed. ⁴And again he sent another slave to them; this one they beat over the head and insulted. ⁵Then he sent another, and that one they killed. And so it was with many others; some they beat, and others they killed. ⁶He had still one other, a beloved son. Finally he sent him to them, saying, "They will respect my son." ⁷But those tenants said to one another, "This is the heir; come, let us kill him, and the inheritance will be ours." ⁸So they seized him, killed him, and threw him out of the vineyard. ⁹What then will the owner of the vineyard do? He will come and destroy the tenants and give the vineyard to others. ¹⁰Have you not read this scripture:

"The stone that the builders rejected
    has become the cornerstone;ʳ
¹¹ this was the Lord's doing,
    and it is amazing in our eyes"?'

¹²When they realized that he had told this parable against them, they wanted to arrest him, but they feared the crowd. So they left him and went away.

The Question about Paying Taxes

¹³Then they sent to him some Pharisees and some Herodians to trap him in what he said. ¹⁴And they came and said to him, 'Teacher, we know that you are sincere, and show deference to no one; for you do not regard people with partiality, but teach the way of God in accordance with truth. Is it lawful to pay taxes to the emperor, or not? ¹⁵Should we pay them, or should we not?' But knowing their hypocrisy, he said to them, 'Why are you putting me to the test? Bring me a denarius and let me see it.' ¹⁶And they brought one. Then he said to them, 'Whose head is this, and whose title?' They answered, 'The emperor's.'

_____

r Or *keystone*

¹⁷Jesus said to them, 'Give to the emperor the things that are the emperor's, and to God the things that are God's.' And they were utterly amazed at him.

The Question about the Resurrection

¹⁸Some Sadducees, who say there is no resurrection, came to him and asked him a question, saying, ¹⁹'Teacher, Moses wrote for us that if a man's brother dies, leaving a wife but no child, the man⁵ shall marry the widow and raise up children for his brother. ²⁰There were seven brothers; the first married and, when he died, left no children; ²¹and the second married the widowᵗ and died, leaving no children; and the third likewise; ²²none of the seven left children. Last of all the woman herself died. ²³In the resurrectionᵘ whose wife will she be? For the seven had married her.'

²⁴Jesus said to them, 'Is not this the reason you are wrong, that you know neither the scriptures nor the power of God? ²⁵For when they rise from the dead, they neither marry nor are given in marriage, but are like angels in heaven. ²⁶And as for the dead being raised, have you not read in the book of Moses, in the story about the bush, how God said to him, "I am the God of Abraham, the God of Isaac, and the God of Jacob"? ²⁷He is God not of the dead, but of the living; you are quite wrong.'

The First Commandment

²⁸One of the scribes came near and heard them disputing with one another, and seeing that he answered them well, he asked him, 'Which commandment is the first of all?' ²⁹Jesus answered, 'The first is, "Hear, O Israel: the Lord our God, the Lord is one; ³⁰you shall love the Lord your God with all your heart, and with all your soul, and with all your mind, and with all your strength." ³¹The second is this, "You shall love your neighbour as yourself." There is no other commandment greater than these.' ³²Then the scribe said to him, 'You are right, Teacher; you have truly said that "he is one, and besides him there is no other"; ³³and "to love him with all the heart, and with all the understanding, and with all the strength", and "to love one's neighbour as oneself",—

---

s Gk *his brother*   t Gk *her*   u Other ancient authorities add *when they rise*

this is much more important than all whole burnt-offerings and sacrifices.' ³⁴When Jesus saw that he answered wisely, he said to him, 'You are not far from the kingdom of God.' After that no one dared to ask him any question.

The Question about David's Son

³⁵While Jesus was teaching in the temple, he said, 'How can the scribes say that the Messiah^v is the son of David? ³⁶David himself, by the Holy Spirit, declared,

"The Lord said to my Lord,
  'Sit at my right hand,
    until I put your enemies under your feet.' "

³⁷David himself calls him Lord; so how can he be his son?' And the large crowd was listening to him with delight.

Jesus Denounces the Scribes

³⁸As he taught, he said, 'Beware of the scribes, who like to walk around in long robes, and to be greeted with respect in the market-places, ³⁹and to have the best seats in the synagogues and places of honour at banquets! ⁴⁰They devour widows' houses and for the sake of appearance say long prayers. They will receive the greater condemnation.'

The Widow's Offering

⁴¹He sat down opposite the treasury, and watched the crowd putting money into the treasury. Many rich people put in large sums. ⁴²A poor widow came and put in two small copper coins, which are worth a penny. ⁴³Then he called his disciples and said to them, 'Truly I tell you, this poor widow has put in more than all those who are contributing to the treasury. ⁴⁴For all of them have contributed out of their abundance; but she out of her poverty has put in everything she had, all she had to live on.'

The Destruction of the Temple Foretold

13 As he came out of the temple, one of his disciples said to him, 'Look, Teacher, what large stones and what large buildings!' ²Then Jesus asked him, 'Do you see these great

---

v Or the Christ

buildings? Not one stone will be left here upon another; all will be thrown down.'

³When he was sitting on the Mount of Olives opposite the temple, Peter, James, John, and Andrew asked him privately, ⁴'Tell us, when will this be, and what will be the sign that all these things are about to be accomplished?' ⁵Then Jesus began to say to them, 'Beware that no one leads you astray. ⁶Many will come in my name and say, "I am he!"ʷ and they will lead many astray. ⁷When you hear of wars and rumours of wars, do not be alarmed; this must take place, but the end is still to come. ⁸For nation will rise against nation, and kingdom against kingdom; there will be earthquakes in various places; there will be famines. This is but the beginning of the birth pangs.

Persecution Foretold

⁹'As for yourselves, beware; for they will hand you over to councils; and you will be beaten in synagogues; and you will stand before governors and kings because of me, as a testimony to them. ¹⁰And the good newsˣ must first be proclaimed to all nations. ¹¹When they bring youᵗ to trial and hand you over, do not worry beforehand about what you are to say; but say whatever is given you at that time, for it is not you who speak, but the Holy Spirit. ¹²Brother will betray brother to death, and a father his child, and children will rise against parents and have them put to death; ¹³and you will be hated by all because of my name. But the one who endures to the end will be saved.

The Desolating Sacrilege

¹⁴'But when you see the desolating sacrilege set up where it ought not to be (let the reader understand), then those in Judea must flee to the mountains; ¹⁵someone on the housetop must not go down or enter the house to take anything away; ¹⁶someone in the field must not turn back to get a coat. ¹⁷Woe to those who are pregnant and to those who are nursing infants in those days! ¹⁸Pray that it may not be in winter. ¹⁹For in those days there will be suffering, such as has not been from the beginning of the creation that God created until now, no, and never will be. ²⁰And

---

w Gk *I am*   x Gk *gospel*

if the Lord had not cut short those days, no one would be saved; but for the sake of the elect, whom he chose, he has cut short those days. ²¹And if anyone says to you at that time, "Look! Here is the Messiah!"ʸ or "Look! There he is!"—do not believe it. ²²False messiahsᶻ and false prophets will appear and produce signs and omens, to lead astray, if possible, the elect. ²³But be alert; I have already told you everything.

The Coming of the Son of Man

²⁴ 'But in those days, after that suffering,
the sun will be darkened,
and the moon will not give its light,
²⁵ and the stars will be falling from heaven,
and the powers in the heavens will be shaken.
²⁶Then they will see "the Son of Man coming in clouds" with great power and glory. ²⁷Then he will send out the angels, and gather his elect from the four winds, from the ends of the earth to the ends of heaven.

The Lesson of the Fig Tree

²⁸'From the fig tree learn its lesson: as soon as its branch becomes tender and puts forth its leaves, you know that summer is near. ²⁹So also, when you see these things taking place, you know that heᵃ is near, at the very gates. ³⁰Truly I tell you, this generation will not pass away until all these things have taken place. ³¹Heaven and earth will pass away, but my words will not pass away.

The Necessity for Watchfulness

³²'But about that day or hour no one knows, neither the angels in heaven, nor the Son, but only the Father. ³³Beware, keep alert;ᵇ for you do not know when the time will come. ³⁴It is like a man going on a journey, when he leaves home and puts his slaves in charge, each with his work, and commands the doorkeeper to be on the watch. ³⁵Therefore, keep awake—for you do not know when the master of the house will come, in the evening, or at midnight, or at cockcrow, or at dawn, ³⁶or else he may find you

---

y Or *the Christ*   z Or *christs*   a Or *it*   b Other ancient authorities add *and pray*

asleep when he comes suddenly. ³⁷And what I say to you I say to all: Keep awake.'

The Plot to Kill Jesus

14 It was two days before the Passover and the festival of Unleavened Bread. The chief priests and the scribes were looking for a way to arrest Jesus^c by stealth and kill him; ²for they said, 'Not during the festival, or there may be a riot among the people.'

The Anointing at Bethany

³While he was at Bethany in the house of Simon the leper,^d as he sat at the table, a woman came with an alabaster jar of very costly ointment of nard, and she broke open the jar and poured the ointment on his head. ⁴But some were there who said to one another in anger, 'Why was the ointment wasted in this way? ⁵For this ointment could have been sold for more than three hundred denarii,^e and the money given to the poor.' And they scolded her. ⁶But Jesus said, 'Let her alone; why do you trouble her? She has performed a good service for me. ⁷For you always have the poor with you, and you can show kindness to them whenever you wish; but you will not always have me. ⁸She has done what she could; she has anointed my body beforehand for its burial. ⁹Truly I tell you, wherever the good news^f is proclaimed in the whole world, what she has done will be told in remembrance of her.'

Judas Agrees to Betray Jesus

¹⁰Then Judas Iscariot, who was one of the twelve, went to the chief priests in order to betray him to them. ¹¹When they heard it, they were greatly pleased, and promised to give him money. So he began to look for an opportunity to betray him.

The Passover with the Disciples

¹²On the first day of Unleavened Bread, when the Passover lamb is sacrificed, his disciples said to him, 'Where do you want us to go and make the preparations for you to eat the Passover?' ¹³So

---

c Gk *him* d The terms *leper* and *leprosy* can refer to several diseases e The denarius was the usual day's wage for a labourer f Or *gospel*

he sent two of his disciples, saying to them, 'Go into the city, and a man carrying a jar of water will meet you; follow him, ¹⁴and wherever he enters, say to the owner of the house, "The Teacher asks, Where is my guest room where I may eat the Passover with my disciples?" ¹⁵He will show you a large room upstairs, furnished and ready. Make preparations for us there.' ¹⁶So the disciples set out and went to the city, and found everything as he had told them; and they prepared the Passover meal.

¹⁷When it was evening, he came with the twelve. ¹⁸And when they had taken their places and were eating, Jesus said, 'Truly I tell you, one of you will betray me, one who is eating with me.' ¹⁹They began to be distressed and to say to him one after another, 'Surely, not I?' ²⁰He said to them, 'It is one of the twelve, one who is dipping bread*g* into the bowl*h* with me. ²¹For the Son of Man goes as it is written of him, but woe to that one by whom the Son of Man is betrayed! It would have been better for that one not to have been born.'

The Institution of the Lord's Supper

²²While they were eating, he took a loaf of bread, and after blessing it he broke it, gave it to them, and said, 'Take; this is my body.' ²³Then he took a cup, and after giving thanks he gave it to them, and all of them drank from it. ²⁴He said to them, 'This is my blood of the*i* covenant, which is poured out for many. ²⁵Truly I tell you, I will never again drink of the fruit of the vine until that day when I drink it new in the kingdom of God.'

Peter's Denial Foretold

²⁶When they had sung the hymn, they went out to the Mount of Olives. ²⁷And Jesus said to them, 'You will all become deserters; for it is written,

"I will strike the shepherd,
    and the sheep will be scattered."
²⁸But after I am raised up, I will go before you to Galilee.' ²⁹Peter said to him, 'Even though all become deserters, I will not.' ³⁰Jesus said to him, 'Truly I tell you, this day, this very night, before the

---

g Gk lacks *bread*   h Other ancient authorities read *same bowl*   i Other ancient authorities add *new*

cock crows twice, you will deny me three times.' ³¹But he said vehemently, 'Even though I must die with you, I will not deny you.' And all of them said the same.

Jesus Prays in Gethsemane

³²They went to a place called Gethsemane; and he said to his disciples, 'Sit here while I pray.' ³³He took with him Peter and James and John, and began to be distressed and agitated. ³⁴And he said to them, 'I am deeply grieved, even to death; remain here, and keep awake.' ³⁵And going a little farther, he threw himself on the ground and prayed that, if it were possible, the hour might pass from him. ³⁶He said, 'Abba,ʲ Father, for you all things are possible; remove this cup from me; yet, not what I want, but what you want.' ³⁷He came and found them sleeping; and he said to Peter, 'Simon, are you asleep? Could you not keep awake one hour? ³⁸Keep awake and pray that you may not come into the time of trial;ᵏ the spirit indeed is willing, but the flesh is weak.' ³⁹And again he went away and prayed, saying the same words. ⁴⁰And once more he came and found them sleeping, for their eyes were very heavy; and they did not know what to say to him. ⁴¹He came a third time and said to them, 'Are you still sleeping and taking your rest? Enough! The hour has come; the Son of Man is betrayed into the hands of sinners. ⁴²Get up, let us be going. See, my betrayer is at hand.'

The Betrayal and Arrest of Jesus

⁴³Immediately, while he was still speaking, Judas, one of the twelve, arrived; and with him there was a crowd with swords and clubs, from the chief priests, the scribes, and the elders. ⁴⁴Now the betrayer had given them a sign, saying, 'The one I will kiss is the man; arrest him and lead him away under guard.' ⁴⁵So when he came, he went up to him at once and said, 'Rabbi!' and kissed him. ⁴⁶Then they laid hands on him and arrested him. ⁴⁷But one of those who stood near drew his sword and struck the slave of the high priest, cutting off his ear. ⁴⁸Then Jesus said to them, 'Have you come out with swords and clubs to arrest me as though I were a bandit? ⁴⁹Day after day I was with you in the

---

j Aramaic for *Father*   k Or *into temptation*

temple teaching, and you did not arrest me. But let the scriptures be fulfilled.' ⁵⁰All of them deserted him and fled.

⁵¹A certain young man was following him, wearing nothing but a linen cloth. They caught hold of him, ⁵²but he left the linen cloth and ran off naked.

Jesus before the Council

⁵³They took Jesus to the high priest; and all the chief priests, the elders, and the scribes were assembled. ⁵⁴Peter had followed him at a distance, right into the courtyard of the high priest; and he was sitting with the guards, warming himself at the fire. ⁵⁵Now the chief priests and the whole council were looking for testimony against Jesus to put him to death; but they found none. ⁵⁶For many gave false testimony against him, and their testimony did not agree. ⁵⁷Some stood up and gave false testimony against him, saying, ⁵⁸'We heard him say, "I will destroy this temple that is made with hands, and in three days I will build another, not made with hands." ' ⁵⁹But even on this point their testimony did not agree. ⁶⁰Then the high priest stood up before them and asked Jesus, 'Have you no answer? What is it that they testify against you?' ⁶¹But he was silent and did not answer. Again the high priest asked him, 'Are you the Messiah,ᴵ the Son of the Blessed One?' ⁶²Jesus said, 'I am; and

"you will see the Son of Man
    seated at the right hand of the Power",
    and "coming with the clouds of heaven." '

⁶³Then the high priest tore his clothes and said, 'Why do we still need witnesses? ⁶⁴You have heard his blasphemy! What is your decision?' All of them condemned him as deserving death. ⁶⁵Some began to spit on him, to blindfold him, and to strike him, saying to him, 'Prophesy!' The guards also took him over and beat him.

Peter Denies Jesus

⁶⁶While Peter was below in the courtyard, one of the servant-girls of the high priest came by. ⁶⁷When she saw Peter warming himself, she stared at him and said, 'You also were with Jesus, the man from Nazareth.' ⁶⁸But he denied it, saying, 'I do not know

---

ᴵ Or the Christ

or understand what you are talking about.' And he went out
into the forecourt.*m* Then the cock crowed.*n* 69 And the servant-
girl, on seeing him, began again to say to the bystanders, 'This
man is one of them.' 70 But again he denied it. Then after a little
while the bystanders again said to Peter, 'Certainly you are one
of them; for you are a Galilean.' 71 But he began to curse, and he
swore an oath, 'I do not know this man you are talking about.'
72 At that moment the cock crowed for the second time. Then
Peter remembered that Jesus had said to him, 'Before the cock
crows twice, you will deny me three times.' And he broke down
and wept.

Jesus before Pilate

15 As soon as it was morning, the chief priests held
a consultation with the elders and scribes and the whole
council. They bound Jesus, led him away, and handed him over
to Pilate. 2 Pilate asked him, 'Are you the King of the Jews?' He
answered him, 'You say so.' 3 Then the chief priests accused him
of many things. 4 Pilate asked him again, 'Have you no answer?
See how many charges they bring against you.' 5 But Jesus made
no further reply, so that Pilate was amazed.

Pilate Hands Jesus over to Be Crucified

6 Now at the festival he used to release a prisoner for them,
anyone for whom they asked. 7 Now a man called Barabbas was
in prison with the rebels who had committed murder during
the insurrection. 8 So the crowd came and began to ask Pilate to
do for them according to his custom. 9 Then he answered them,
'Do you want me to release for you the King of the Jews?' 10 For
he realized that it was out of jealousy that the chief priests had
handed him over. 11 But the chief priests stirred up the crowd to
have him release Barabbas for them instead. 12 Pilate spoke to
them again, 'Then what do you wish me to do*o* with the man
you call*p* the King of the Jews?' 13 They shouted back, 'Crucify
him!' 14 Pilate asked them, 'Why, what evil has he done?' But they
shouted all the more, 'Crucify him!' 15 So Pilate, wishing to satisfy

---

m Or *gateway*   n Other ancient authorities lack *Then the cock crowed*   o Other ancient
authorities read *what should I do*   p Other ancient authorities lack *the man you call*

the crowd, released Barabbas for them; and after flogging Jesus, he handed him over to be crucified.

The Soldiers Mock Jesus

¹⁶Then the soldiers led him into the courtyard of the palace (that is, the governor's headquarters*q*); and they called together the whole cohort. ¹⁷And they clothed him in a purple cloak; and after twisting some thorns into a crown, they put it on him. ¹⁸And they began saluting him, 'Hail, King of the Jews!' ¹⁹They struck his head with a reed, spat upon him, and knelt down in homage to him. ²⁰After mocking him, they stripped him of the purple cloak and put his own clothes on him. Then they led him out to crucify him.

The Crucifixion of Jesus

²¹They compelled a passer-by, who was coming in from the country, to carry his cross; it was Simon of Cyrene, the father of Alexander and Rufus. ²²Then they brought Jesus*r* to the place called Golgotha (which means the place of a skull). ²³And they offered him wine mixed with myrrh; but he did not take it. ²⁴And they crucified him, and divided his clothes among them, casting lots to decide what each should take.

²⁵It was nine o'clock in the morning when they crucified him. ²⁶The inscription of the charge against him read, 'The King of the Jews.' ²⁷And with him they crucified two bandits, one on his right and one on his left.*s* ²⁹Those who passed by derided*t* him, shaking their heads and saying, 'Aha! You who would destroy the temple and build it in three days, ³⁰save yourself, and come down from the cross!' ³¹In the same way the chief priests, along with the scribes, were also mocking him among themselves and saying, 'He saved others; he cannot save himself. ³²Let the Messiah,*u* the King of Israel, come down from the cross now, so that we may see and believe.' Those who were crucified with him also taunted him.

---

q Gk *the praetorium*   r Gk *him*   s Other ancient authorities add verse 28, *And the scripture was fulfilled that says, 'And he was counted among the lawless.'*   t Or *blasphemed*
u Or *the Christ*

The Death of Jesus

³³When it was noon, darkness came over the whole land^v until three in the afternoon. ³⁴At three o'clock Jesus cried out with a loud voice, 'Eloi, Eloi, lema sabachthani?' which means, 'My God, my God, why have you forsaken me?'^w ³⁵When some of the bystanders heard it, they said, 'Listen, he is calling for Elijah.' ³⁶And someone ran, filled a sponge with sour wine, put it on a stick, and gave it to him to drink, saying, 'Wait, let us see whether Elijah will come to take him down.' ³⁷Then Jesus gave a loud cry and breathed his last. ³⁸And the curtain of the temple was torn in two, from top to bottom. ³⁹Now when the centurion, who stood facing him, saw that in this way he^x breathed his last, he said, 'Truly this man was God's Son!'^y

⁴⁰There were also women looking on from a distance; among them were Mary Magdalene, and Mary the mother of James the younger and of Joses, and Salome. ⁴¹These used to follow him and provided for him when he was in Galilee; and there were many other women who had come up with him to Jerusalem.

The Burial of Jesus

⁴²When evening had come, and since it was the day of Preparation, that is, the day before the sabbath, ⁴³Joseph of Arimathea, a respected member of the council, who was also himself waiting expectantly for the kingdom of God, went boldly to Pilate and asked for the body of Jesus. ⁴⁴Then Pilate wondered if he were already dead; and summoning the centurion, he asked him whether he had been dead for some time. ⁴⁵When he learned from the centurion that he was dead, he granted the body to Joseph. ⁴⁶Then Joseph^z bought a linen cloth, and taking down the body,^a wrapped it in the linen cloth, and laid it in a tomb that had been hewn out of the rock. He then rolled a stone against the door of the tomb. ⁴⁷Mary Magdalene and Mary the mother of Joses saw where the body^a was laid.

The Resurrection of Jesus

16 When the sabbath was over, Mary Magdalene, and Mary the mother of James, and Salome bought spices, so that

---

v Or *earth*   w Other ancient authorities read *made me a reproach*   x Other ancient authorities add *cried out and*   y Or *a son of God*   z Gk *he*   a Gk *it*

they might go and anoint him. ²And very early on the first day of the week, when the sun had risen, they went to the tomb. ³They had been saying to one another, 'Who will roll away the stone for us from the entrance to the tomb?' ⁴When they looked up, they saw that the stone, which was very large, had already been rolled back. ⁵As they entered the tomb, they saw a young man, dressed in a white robe, sitting on the right side; and they were alarmed. ⁶But he said to them, 'Do not be alarmed; you are looking for Jesus of Nazareth, who was crucified. He has been raised; he is not here. Look, there is the place they laid him. ⁷But go, tell his disciples and Peter that he is going ahead of you to Galilee; there you will see him, just as he told you.' ⁸So they went out and fled from the tomb, for terror and amazement had seized them; and they said nothing to anyone, for they were afraid.[b]

THE SHORTER ENDING OF MARK

And all that had been commanded them they told briefly to those around Peter. And afterwards Jesus himself sent out through them, from east to west, the sacred and imperishable proclamation of eternal salvation.[c]

THE LONGER ENDING OF MARK

Jesus Appears to Mary Magdalene

⁹*Now after he rose early on the first day of the week, he appeared first to Mary Magdalene, from whom he had cast out seven demons.* ¹⁰*She went out and told those who had been with him, while they were mourning and weeping.* ¹¹*But when they heard that he was alive and had been seen by her, they would not believe it.*

Jesus Appears to Two Disciples

¹²*After this he appeared in another form to two of them, as they were walking into the country.* ¹³*And they went back and told the rest, but they did not believe them.*

---

b Some of the most ancient authorities bring the book to a close at the end of verse 8. One authority concludes the book with the shorter ending; others include the shorter ending and then continue with verses 9–20. In most authorities verses 9–20 follow immediately after verse 8, though in some of these authorities the passage is marked as being doubtful.
c Other ancient authorities add *Amen*

Jesus Commissions the Disciples

[14] *Later he appeared to the eleven themselves as they were sitting at the table; and he upbraided them for their lack of faith and stubbornness, because they had not believed those who saw him after he had risen.*[d] [15]*And he said to them, 'Go into all the world and proclaim the good news*[e] *to the whole creation.* [16]*The one who believes and is baptized will be saved; but the one who does not believe will be condemned.* [17]*And these signs will accompany those who believe: by using my name they will cast out demons; they will speak in new tongues;* [18]*they will pick up snakes in their hands,*[f] *and if they drink any deadly thing, it will not hurt them; they will lay their hands on the sick, and they will recover.'*

The Ascension of Jesus

[19]*So then the Lord Jesus, after he had spoken to them, was taken up into heaven and sat down at the right hand of God.* [20]*And they went out and proclaimed the good news everywhere, while the Lord worked with them and confirmed the message by the signs that accompanied it.*[g]

---

d Other ancient authorities add, in whole or in part, *And they excused themselves, saying, 'This age of lawlessness and unbelief is under Satan, who does not allow the truth and power of God to prevail over the unclean things of the spirits. Therefore reveal your righteousness now'—thus they spoke to Christ. And Christ replied to them, 'The term of years of Satan's power has been fulfilled, but other terrible things draw near. And for those who have sinned I was handed over to death, that they may return to the truth and sin no more, that they may inherit the spiritual and imperishable glory of righteousness that is in heaven.'* **e** Or *gospel* **f** Other ancient authorities lack *in their hands* **g** Other ancient authorities add *Amen*

The Gospel According to

Luke

Dedication to Theophilus

1 Since many have undertaken to set down an orderly account of the events that have been fulfilled among us, [2] just as they were handed on to us by those who from the beginning were eyewitnesses and servants of the word, [3] I too decided, after investigating everything carefully from the very first,[a] to write an orderly account for you, most excellent Theophilus, [4] so that you may know the truth concerning the things about which you have been instructed.

The Birth of John the Baptist Foretold

[5] In the days of King Herod of Judea, there was a priest named Zechariah, who belonged to the priestly order of Abijah. His wife was a descendant of Aaron, and her name was Elizabeth. [6] Both of them were righteous before God, living blamelessly according to all the commandments and regulations of the Lord. [7] But they had no children, because Elizabeth was barren, and both were getting on in years.

[8] Once when he was serving as priest before God and his section was on duty, [9] he was chosen by lot, according to the custom of the priesthood, to enter the sanctuary of the Lord and offer incense. [10] Now at the time of the incense-offering, the whole assembly of the people was praying outside. [11] Then there appeared to him an angel of the Lord, standing at the right side of the altar of incense. [12] When Zechariah saw him, he was terrified;

---

a Or for a long time

and fear overwhelmed him. ¹³But the angel said to him, 'Do not be afraid, Zechariah, for your prayer has been heard. Your wife Elizabeth will bear you a son, and you will name him John. ¹⁴You will have joy and gladness, and many will rejoice at his birth, ¹⁵for he will be great in the sight of the Lord. He must never drink wine or strong drink; even before his birth he will be filled with the Holy Spirit. ¹⁶He will turn many of the people of Israel to the Lord their God. ¹⁷With the spirit and power of Elijah he will go before him, to turn the hearts of parents to their children, and the disobedient to the wisdom of the righteous, to make ready a people prepared for the Lord.' ¹⁸Zechariah said to the angel, 'How will I know that this is so? For I am an old man, and my wife is getting on in years.' ¹⁹The angel replied, 'I am Gabriel. I stand in the presence of God, and I have been sent to speak to you and to bring you this good news. ²⁰But now, because you did not believe my words, which will be fulfilled in their time, you will become mute, unable to speak, until the day these things occur.'

²¹Meanwhile, the people were waiting for Zechariah, and wondered at his delay in the sanctuary. ²²When he did come out, he could not speak to them, and they realized that he had seen a vision in the sanctuary. He kept motioning to them and remained unable to speak. ²³When his time of service was ended, he went to his home.

²⁴After those days his wife Elizabeth conceived, and for five months she remained in seclusion. She said, ²⁵'This is what the Lord has done for me when he looked favourably on me and took away the disgrace I have endured among my people.'

The Birth of Jesus Foretold

²⁶In the sixth month the angel Gabriel was sent by God to a town in Galilee called Nazareth, ²⁷to a virgin engaged to a man whose name was Joseph, of the house of David. The virgin's name was Mary. ²⁸And he came to her and said, 'Greetings, favoured one! The Lord is with you.'ᵇ ²⁹But she was much perplexed by his words and pondered what sort of greeting this might be. ³⁰The angel said to her, 'Do not be afraid, Mary, for you have found favour with God. ³¹And now, you will conceive in your womb

---

b Other ancient authorities add *Blessed are you among women*

and bear a son, and you will name him Jesus. [32] He will be great, and will be called the Son of the Most High, and the Lord God will give to him the throne of his ancestor David. [33] He will reign over the house of Jacob for ever, and of his kingdom there will be no end.' [34] Mary said to the angel, 'How can this be, since I am a virgin?'[c] [35] The angel said to her, 'The Holy Spirit will come upon you, and the power of the Most High will overshadow you; therefore the child to be born[d] will be holy; he will be called Son of God. [36] And now, your relative Elizabeth in her old age has also conceived a son; and this is the sixth month for her who was said to be barren. [37] For nothing will be impossible with God.' [38] Then Mary said, 'Here am I, the servant of the Lord; let it be with me according to your word.' Then the angel departed from her.

Mary Visits Elizabeth

[39] In those days Mary set out and went with haste to a Judean town in the hill country, [40] where she entered the house of Zechariah and greeted Elizabeth. [41] When Elizabeth heard Mary's greeting, the child leapt in her womb. And Elizabeth was filled with the Holy Spirit [42] and exclaimed with a loud cry, 'Blessed are you among women, and blessed is the fruit of your womb. [43] And why has this happened to me, that the mother of my Lord comes to me? [44] For as soon as I heard the sound of your greeting, the child in my womb leapt for joy. [45] And blessed is she who believed that there would be[e] a fulfilment of what was spoken to her by the Lord.'

Mary's Song of Praise

[46] And Mary[f] said,
  'My soul magnifies the Lord,
[47]   and my spirit rejoices in God my Saviour,
[48] for he has looked with favour on the lowliness of his
        servant.
      Surely, from now on all generations will call me blessed;
[49] for the Mighty One has done great things for me,
        and holy is his name.

---

c Gk *I do not know a man*   d Other ancient authorities add *of you*   e Or *believed, for there will be*   f Other ancient authorities read *Elizabeth*

⁵⁰ His mercy is for those who fear him
>   from generation to generation.
⁵¹ He has shown strength with his arm;
>   he has scattered the proud in the thoughts of their
>   hearts.
⁵² He has brought down the powerful from their thrones,
>   and lifted up the lowly;
⁵³ he has filled the hungry with good things,
>   and sent the rich away empty.
⁵⁴ He has helped his servant Israel,
>   in remembrance of his mercy,
⁵⁵ according to the promise he made to our ancestors,
>   to Abraham and to his descendants for ever.'

⁵⁶And Mary remained with her for about three months and then returned to her home.

The Birth of John the Baptist

⁵⁷Now the time came for Elizabeth to give birth, and she bore a son. ⁵⁸Her neighbours and relatives heard that the Lord had shown his great mercy to her, and they rejoiced with her.

⁵⁹On the eighth day they came to circumcise the child, and they were going to name him Zechariah after his father. ⁶⁰But his mother said, 'No; he is to be called John.' ⁶¹They said to her, 'None of your relatives has this name.' ⁶²Then they began motioning to his father to find out what name he wanted to give him. ⁶³He asked for a writing-tablet and wrote, 'His name is John.' And all of them were amazed. ⁶⁴Immediately his mouth was opened and his tongue freed, and he began to speak, praising God. ⁶⁵Fear came over all their neighbours, and all these things were talked about throughout the entire hill country of Judea. ⁶⁶All who heard them pondered them and said, 'What then will this child become?' For, indeed, the hand of the Lord was with him.

Zechariah's Prophecy

⁶⁷Then his father Zechariah was filled with the Holy Spirit and spoke this prophecy:

⁶⁸ 'Blessed be the Lord God of Israel,
>   for he has looked favourably on his people and redeemed
>   them.

⁶⁹ He has raised up a mighty saviour*g* for us
    in the house of his servant David,
⁷⁰ as he spoke through the mouth of his holy prophets from
    of old,
⁷¹   that we would be saved from our enemies and from the
    hand of all who hate us.
⁷² Thus he has shown the mercy promised to our ancestors,
    and has remembered his holy covenant,
⁷³ the oath that he swore to our ancestor Abraham,
    to grant us ⁷⁴that we, being rescued from the hands of
    our enemies,
  might serve him without fear, ⁷⁵in holiness and
    righteousness
  before him all our days.
⁷⁶ And you, child, will be called the prophet of the Most High;
    for you will go before the Lord to prepare his ways,
⁷⁷ to give knowledge of salvation to his people
    by the forgiveness of their sins.
⁷⁸ By the tender mercy of our God,
    the dawn from on high will break upon*h* us,
⁷⁹ to give light to those who sit in darkness and in the
    shadow of death,
    to guide our feet into the way of peace.'

⁸⁰The child grew and became strong in spirit, and he was in the wilderness until the day he appeared publicly to Israel.

The Birth of Jesus

2 In those days a decree went out from Emperor Augustus that all the world should be registered. ²This was the first registration and was taken while Quirinius was governor of Syria. ³All went to their own towns to be registered. ⁴Joseph also went from the town of Nazareth in Galilee to Judea, to the city of David called Bethlehem, because he was descended from the house and family of David. ⁵He went to be registered with Mary, to whom he was engaged and who was expecting a child. ⁶While they were there, the time came for her to deliver her child. ⁷And she gave birth to her firstborn son and wrapped him in bands

---

g Gk *a horn of salvation*   h Other ancient authorities read *has broken upon*

of cloth, and laid him in a manger, because there was no place for them in the inn.

The Shepherds and the Angels

[8] In that region there were shepherds living in the fields, keeping watch over their flock by night. [9] Then an angel of the Lord stood before them, and the glory of the Lord shone around them, and they were terrified. [10] But the angel said to them, 'Do not be afraid; for see—I am bringing you good news of great joy for all the people: [11] to you is born this day in the city of David a Saviour, who is the Messiah,[i] the Lord. [12] This will be a sign for you: you will find a child wrapped in bands of cloth and lying in a manger.' [13] And suddenly there was with the angel a multitude of the heavenly host,[j] praising God and saying,

[14] 'Glory to God in the highest heaven,
    and on earth peace among those whom he favours!'[k]

[15] When the angels had left them and gone into heaven, the shepherds said to one another, 'Let us go now to Bethlehem and see this thing that has taken place, which the Lord has made known to us.' [16] So they went with haste and found Mary and Joseph, and the child lying in the manger. [17] When they saw this, they made known what had been told them about this child; [18] and all who heard it were amazed at what the shepherds told them. [19] But Mary treasured all these words and pondered them in her heart. [20] The shepherds returned, glorifying and praising God for all they had heard and seen, as it had been told them.

Jesus Is Named

[21] After eight days had passed, it was time to circumcise the child; and he was called Jesus, the name given by the angel before he was conceived in the womb.

Jesus Is Presented in the Temple

[22] When the time came for their purification according to the law of Moses, they brought him up to Jerusalem to present him to the Lord [23] (as it is written in the law of the Lord, 'Every firstborn male shall be designated as holy to the Lord'), [24] and

---

i Or *the Christ*   j Gk *army*   k Other ancient authorities read *peace, goodwill among people*

they offered a sacrifice according to what is stated in the law of the Lord, 'a pair of turtle-doves or two young pigeons.'

²⁵ Now there was a man in Jerusalem whose name was Simeon;[l] this man was righteous and devout, looking forward to the consolation of Israel, and the Holy Spirit rested on him. ²⁶ It had been revealed to him by the Holy Spirit that he would not see death before he had seen the Lord's Messiah.[m] ²⁷ Guided by the Spirit, Simeon[n] came into the temple; and when the parents brought in the child Jesus, to do for him what was customary under the law, ²⁸ Simeon[o] took him in his arms and praised God, saying,

²⁹ 'Master, now you are dismissing your servant[p] in peace,
        according to your word;
³⁰ for my eyes have seen your salvation,
³¹   which you have prepared in the presence of all peoples,
³² a light for revelation to the Gentiles
        and for glory to your people Israel.'

³³ And the child's father and mother were amazed at what was being said about him. ³⁴ Then Simeon[q] blessed them and said to his mother Mary, 'This child is destined for the falling and the rising of many in Israel, and to be a sign that will be opposed ³⁵ so that the inner thoughts of many will be revealed—and a sword will pierce your own soul too.'

³⁶ There was also a prophet, Anna[r] the daughter of Phanuel, of the tribe of Asher. She was of a great age, having lived with her husband for seven years after her marriage, ³⁷ then as a widow to the age of eighty-four. She never left the temple but worshipped there with fasting and prayer night and day. ³⁸ At that moment she came, and began to praise God and to speak about the child[s] to all who were looking for the redemption of Jerusalem.

The Return to Nazareth

³⁹ When they had finished everything required by the law of the Lord, they returned to Galilee, to their own town of Nazareth. ⁴⁰ The child grew and became strong, filled with wisdom; and the favour of God was upon him.

---

l Gk *Symeon*   m Or *the Lord's Christ*   n Gk *In the Spirit, he*   o Gk *he*   p Gk *slave*
q Gk *Symeon*   r Gk *Hanna*   s Gk *him*

The Boy Jesus in the Temple

⁴¹Now every year his parents went to Jerusalem for the festival of the Passover. ⁴²And when he was twelve years old, they went up as usual for the festival. ⁴³When the festival was ended and they started to return, the boy Jesus stayed behind in Jerusalem, but his parents did not know it. ⁴⁴Assuming that he was in the group of travellers, they went a day's journey. Then they started to look for him among their relatives and friends. ⁴⁵When they did not find him, they returned to Jerusalem to search for him. ⁴⁶After three days they found him in the temple, sitting among the teachers, listening to them and asking them questions. ⁴⁷And all who heard him were amazed at his understanding and his answers. ⁴⁸When his parents*t* saw him they were astonished; and his mother said to him, 'Child, why have you treated us like this? Look, your father and I have been searching for you in great anxiety.' ⁴⁹He said to them, 'Why were you searching for me? Did you not know that I must be in my Father's house?'*u* ⁵⁰But they did not understand what he said to them. ⁵¹Then he went down with them and came to Nazareth, and was obedient to them. His mother treasured all these things in her heart.

⁵²And Jesus increased in wisdom and in years,*v* and in divine and human favour.

The Proclamation of John the Baptist

3 In the fifteenth year of the reign of Emperor Tiberius, when Pontius Pilate was governor of Judea, and Herod was ruler*w* of Galilee, and his brother Philip ruler*w* of the region of Ituraea and Trachonitis, and Lysanias ruler*w* of Abilene, ²during the high-priesthood of Annas and Caiaphas, the word of God came to John son of Zechariah in the wilderness. ³He went into all the region around the Jordan, proclaiming a baptism of repentance for the forgiveness of sins, ⁴as it is written in the book of the words of the prophet Isaiah,

'The voice of one crying out in the wilderness:
"Prepare the way of the Lord,
    make his paths straight.

---

t Gk *they*   u Or *be about my Father's interests?*   v Or *in stature*   w Gk *tetrarch*

⁵ Every valley shall be filled,
  and every mountain and hill shall be made low,
 and the crooked shall be made straight,
  and the rough ways made smooth;
⁶ and all flesh shall see the salvation of God." '

⁷John said to the crowds that came out to be baptized by him, 'You brood of vipers! Who warned you to flee from the wrath to come? ⁸Bear fruits worthy of repentance. Do not begin to say to yourselves, "We have Abraham as our ancestor"; for I tell you, God is able from these stones to raise up children to Abraham. ⁹Even now the axe is lying at the root of the trees; every tree therefore that does not bear good fruit is cut down and thrown into the fire.'

¹⁰And the crowds asked him, 'What then should we do?' ¹¹In reply he said to them, 'Whoever has two coats must share with anyone who has none; and whoever has food must do likewise.' ¹²Even tax-collectors came to be baptized, and they asked him, 'Teacher, what should we do?' ¹³He said to them, 'Collect no more than the amount prescribed for you.' ¹⁴Soldiers also asked him, 'And we, what should we do?' He said to them, 'Do not extort money from anyone by threats or false accusation, and be satisfied with your wages.'

¹⁵As the people were filled with expectation, and all were questioning in their hearts concerning John, whether he might be the Messiah,ˣ ¹⁶John answered all of them by saying, 'I baptize you with water; but one who is more powerful than I is coming; I am not worthy to untie the thong of his sandals. He will baptize you withʸ the Holy Spirit and fire. ¹⁷His winnowing-fork is in his hand, to clear his threshing-floor and to gather the wheat into his granary; but the chaff he will burn with unquenchable fire.'

¹⁸So, with many other exhortations, he proclaimed the good news to the people. ¹⁹But Herod the ruler,ᶻ who had been rebuked by him because of Herodias, his brother's wife, and because of all the evil things that Herod had done, ²⁰added to them all by shutting up John in prison.

The Baptism of Jesus

²¹Now when all the people were baptized, and when Jesus also had been baptized and was praying, the heaven was opened,

---

x Or *the Christ*   y Or *in*   z Gk *tetrarch*

²²and the Holy Spirit descended upon him in bodily form like a dove. And a voice came from heaven, 'You are my Son, the Beloved;ᵃ with you I am well pleased.'ᵇ

The Ancestors of Jesus

²³Jesus was about thirty years old when he began his work. He was the son (as was thought) of Joseph son of Heli, ²⁴son of Matthat, son of Levi, son of Melchi, son of Jannai, son of Joseph, ²⁵son of Mattathias, son of Amos, son of Nahum, son of Esli, son of Naggai, ²⁶son of Maath, son of Mattathias, son of Semein, son of Josech, son of Joda, ²⁷son of Joanan, son of Rhesa, son of Zerubbabel, son of Shealtiel,ᶜ son of Neri, ²⁸son of Melchi, son of Addi, son of Cosam, son of Elmadam, son of Er, ²⁹son of Joshua, son of Eliezer, son of Jorim, son of Matthat, son of Levi, ³⁰son of Simeon, son of Judah, son of Joseph, son of Jonam, son of Eliakim, ³¹son of Melea, son of Menna, son of Mattatha, son of Nathan, son of David, ³²son of Jesse, son of Obed, son of Boaz, son of Sala,ᵈ son of Nahshon, ³³son of Amminadab, son of Admin, son of Arni,ᵉ son of Hezron, son of Perez, son of Judah, ³⁴son of Jacob, son of Isaac, son of Abraham, son of Terah, son of Nahor, ³⁵son of Serug, son of Reu, son of Peleg, son of Eber, son of Shelah, ³⁶son of Cainan, son of Arphaxad, son of Shem, son of Noah, son of Lamech, ³⁷son of Methuselah, son of Enoch, son of Jared, son of Mahalaleel, son of Cainan, ³⁸son of Enos, son of Seth, son of Adam, son of God.

The Temptation of Jesus

4 Jesus, full of the Holy Spirit, returned from the Jordan and was led by the Spirit in the wilderness, ²where for forty days he was tempted by the devil. He ate nothing at all during those days, and when they were over, he was famished. ³The devil said to him, 'If you are the Son of God, command this stone to become a loaf of bread.' ⁴Jesus answered him, 'It is written, "One does not live by bread alone." '

⁵Then the devilᶠ led him up and showed him in an instant all the kingdoms of the world. ⁶And the devilᶠ said to him, 'To

---

a Or *my beloved Son*   b Other ancient authorities read *You are my Son, today I have begotten you*   c Gk *Salathiel*   d Other ancient authorities read *Salmon*   e Other ancient authorities read *Amminadab, son of Aram*; others vary widely   f Gk *he*

you I will give their glory and all this authority; for it has been given over to me, and I give it to anyone I please.' ⁷If you, then, will worship me, it will all be yours.' ⁸Jesus answered him, 'It is written,

> "Worship the Lord your God,
>> and serve only him." '

⁹Then the devil ᶠ took him to Jerusalem, and placed him on the pinnacle of the temple, saying to him, 'If you are the Son of God, throw yourself down from here, ¹⁰for it is written,

> "He will command his angels concerning you,
>> to protect you",

¹¹and

> "On their hands they will bear you up,
>> so that you will not dash your foot against a stone." '

¹²Jesus answered him, 'It is said, "Do not put the Lord your God to the test." ' ¹³When the devil had finished every test, he departed from him until an opportune time.

The Beginning of the Galilean Ministry

¹⁴Then Jesus, filled with the power of the Spirit, returned to Galilee, and a report about him spread through all the surrounding country. ¹⁵He began to teach in their synagogues and was praised by everyone.

The Rejection of Jesus at Nazareth

¹⁶When he came to Nazareth, where he had been brought up, he went to the synagogue on the sabbath day, as was his custom. He stood up to read, ¹⁷and the scroll of the prophet Isaiah was given to him. He unrolled the scroll and found the place where it was written:

> ¹⁸ 'The Spirit of the Lord is upon me,
>> because he has anointed me
>> to bring good news to the poor.
> He has sent me to proclaim release to the captives
>> and recovery of sight to the blind,
>> to let the oppressed go free,
> ¹⁹ to proclaim the year of the Lord's favour.'

²⁰And he rolled up the scroll, gave it back to the attendant, and sat down. The eyes of all in the synagogue were fixed on him. ²¹Then

he began to say to them, 'Today this scripture has been fulfilled in your hearing.' ²²All spoke well of him and were amazed at the gracious words that came from his mouth. They said, 'Is not this Joseph's son?' ²³He said to them, 'Doubtless you will quote to me this proverb, "Doctor, cure yourself!" And you will say, "Do here also in your home town the things that we have heard you did at Capernaum." ' ²⁴And he said, 'Truly I tell you, no prophet is accepted in the prophet's home town. ²⁵But the truth is, there were many widows in Israel in the time of Elijah, when the heaven was shut up for three years and six months, and there was a severe famine over all the land; ²⁶yet Elijah was sent to none of them except to a widow at Zarephath in Sidon. ²⁷There were also many lepers^g in Israel in the time of the prophet Elisha, and none of them was cleansed except Naaman the Syrian.' ²⁸When they heard this, all in the synagogue were filled with rage. ²⁹They got up, drove him out of the town, and led him to the brow of the hill on which their town was built, so that they might hurl him off the cliff. ³⁰But he passed through the midst of them and went on his way.

The Man with an Unclean Spirit

³¹He went down to Capernaum, a city in Galilee, and was teaching them on the sabbath. ³²They were astounded at his teaching, because he spoke with authority. ³³In the synagogue there was a man who had the spirit of an unclean demon, and he cried out with a loud voice, ³⁴'Let us alone! What have you to do with us, Jesus of Nazareth? Have you come to destroy us? I know who you are, the Holy One of God.' ³⁵But Jesus rebuked him, saying, 'Be silent, and come out of him!' When the demon had thrown him down before them, he came out of him without having done him any harm. ³⁶They were all amazed and kept saying to one another, 'What kind of utterance is this? For with authority and power he commands the unclean spirits, and out they come!' ³⁷And a report about him began to reach every place in the region.

Healings at Simon's House

³⁸After leaving the synagogue he entered Simon's house. Now Simon's mother-in-law was suffering from a high fever, and they

---

g The terms *leper* and *leprosy* can refer to several diseases

asked him about her. ³⁹Then he stood over her and rebuked the fever, and it left her. Immediately she got up and began to serve them.

⁴⁰As the sun was setting, all those who had any who were sick with various kinds of diseases brought them to him; and he laid his hands on each of them and cured them. ⁴¹Demons also came out of many, shouting, 'You are the Son of God!' But he rebuked them and would not allow them to speak, because they knew that he was the Messiah.ʰ

Jesus Preaches in the Synagogues

⁴²At daybreak he departed and went into a deserted place. And the crowds were looking for him; and when they reached him, they wanted to prevent him from leaving them. ⁴³But he said to them, 'I must proclaim the good news of the kingdom of God to the other cities also; for I was sent for this purpose.' ⁴⁴So he continued proclaiming the message in the synagogues of Judea.ⁱ

Jesus Calls the First Disciples

5 Once while Jesusʲ was standing beside the lake of Gennesaret, and the crowd was pressing in on him to hear the word of God, ²he saw two boats there at the shore of the lake; the fishermen had gone out of them and were washing their nets. ³He got into one of the boats, the one belonging to Simon, and asked him to put out a little way from the shore. Then he sat down and taught the crowds from the boat. ⁴When he had finished speaking, he said to Simon, 'Put out into the deep water and let down your nets for a catch.' ⁵Simon answered, 'Master, we have worked all night long but have caught nothing. Yet if you say so, I will let down the nets.' ⁶When they had done this, they caught so many fish that their nets were beginning to break. ⁷So they signalled to their partners in the other boat to come and help them. And they came and filled both boats, so that they began to sink. ⁸But when Simon Peter saw it, he fell down at Jesus' knees, saying, 'Go away from me, Lord, for I am a sinful man!' ⁹For he and all who were with him were amazed at the catch of fish that they had taken; ¹⁰and so also were James

h Or *the Christ*   i Other ancient authorities read *Galilee*   j Gk *he* and John, sons of Zebedee, who were partners with Simon. Then Jesus said to Simon, 'Do not be afraid; from now on you will be catching people.' 11 When they had brought their boats to shore, they left everything and followed him.

Jesus Cleanses a Leper

12 Once, when he was in one of the cities, there was a man covered with leprosy.[k] When he saw Jesus, he bowed with his face to the ground and begged him, 'Lord, if you choose, you can make me clean.' 13 Then Jesus[l] stretched out his hand, touched him, and said, 'I do choose. Be made clean.' Immediately the leprosy[m] left him. 14 And he ordered him to tell no one. 'Go', he said, 'and show yourself to the priest, and, as Moses commanded, make an offering for your cleansing, for a testimony to them.' 15 But now more than ever the word about Jesus[n] spread abroad; many crowds would gather to hear him and to be cured of their diseases. 16 But he would withdraw to deserted places and pray.

Jesus Heals a Paralytic

17 One day, while he was teaching, Pharisees and teachers of the law were sitting nearby (they had come from every village of Galilee and Judea and from Jerusalem); and the power of the Lord was with him to heal.[o] 18 Just then some men came, carrying a paralysed man on a bed. They were trying to bring him in and lay him before Jesus;[p] 19 but finding no way to bring him in because of the crowd, they went up on the roof and let him down with his bed through the tiles into the middle of the crowd[q] in front of Jesus. 20 When he saw their faith, he said, 'Friend,[r] your sins are forgiven you.' 21 Then the scribes and the Pharisees began to question, 'Who is this who is speaking blasphemies? Who can forgive sins but God alone?' 22 When Jesus perceived their questionings, he answered them, 'Why do you raise such questions in your hearts? 23 Which is easier, to say, "Your sins are forgiven you", or to say, "Stand up and walk"? 24 But so that you may know that the Son of Man has authority on earth to forgive sins'—he said to

---

k The terms *leper* and *leprosy* can refer to several diseases **l** Gk *he* **m** The terms *leper* and *leprosy* can refer to several diseases **n** Gk *him* **o** Other ancient authorities read *was present to heal them* **p** Gk *him* **q** Gk *into the midst* **r** Gk *Man*

the one who was paralysed—'I say to you, stand up and take your bed and go to your home.' ²⁵Immediately he stood up before them, took what he had been lying on, and went to his home, glorifying God. ²⁶Amazement seized all of them, and they glorified God and were filled with awe, saying, 'We have seen strange things today.'

Jesus Calls Levi

²⁷After this he went out and saw a tax-collector named Levi, sitting at the tax booth; and he said to him, 'Follow me.' ²⁸And he got up, left everything, and followed him.

²⁹Then Levi gave a great banquet for him in his house; and there was a large crowd of tax-collectors and others sitting at the table ˢ with them. ³⁰The Pharisees and their scribes were complaining to his disciples, saying, 'Why do you eat and drink with tax-collectors and sinners?' ³¹Jesus answered, 'Those who are well have no need of a physician, but those who are sick; ³²I have come to call not the righteous but sinners to repentance.'

The Question about Fasting

³³Then they said to him, 'John's disciples, like the disciples of the Pharisees, frequently fast and pray, but your disciples eat and drink.' ³⁴Jesus said to them, 'You cannot make wedding-guests fast while the bridegroom is with them, can you? ³⁵The days will come when the bridegroom will be taken away from them, and then they will fast in those days.' ³⁶He also told them a parable: 'No one tears a piece from a new garment and sews it on an old garment; otherwise the new will be torn, and the piece from the new will not match the old. ³⁷And no one puts new wine into old wineskins; otherwise the new wine will burst the skins and will be spilled, and the skins will be destroyed. ³⁸But new wine must be put into fresh wineskins. ³⁹And no one after drinking old wine desires new wine, but says, "The old is good." ' ᵗ

The Question about the Sabbath

6 One sabbath ᵘ while Jesus ᵛ was going through the cornfields, his disciples plucked some heads of grain, rubbed them

---

s Gk *reclining*   t Other ancient authorities read *better*; others lack verse 39   u Other ancient authorities read *On the second first sabbath*   v Gk *he*

in their hands, and ate them. ²But some of the Pharisees said, 'Why are you doing what is not lawful[w] on the sabbath?' ³Jesus answered, 'Have you not read what David did when he and his companions were hungry? ⁴He entered the house of God and took and ate the bread of the Presence, which it is not lawful for any but the priests to eat, and gave some to his companions?' ⁵Then he said to them, 'The Son of Man is lord of the sabbath.'

The Man with a Withered Hand

⁶On another sabbath he entered the synagogue and taught, and there was a man there whose right hand was withered. ⁷The scribes and the Pharisees watched him to see whether he would cure on the sabbath, so that they might find an accusation against him. ⁸Even though he knew what they were thinking, he said to the man who had the withered hand, 'Come and stand here.' He got up and stood there. ⁹Then Jesus said to them, 'I ask you, is it lawful to do good or to do harm on the sabbath, to save life or to destroy it?' ¹⁰After looking around at all of them, he said to him, 'Stretch out your hand.' He did so, and his hand was restored. ¹¹But they were filled with fury and discussed with one another what they might do to Jesus.

Jesus Chooses the Twelve Apostles

¹²Now during those days he went out to the mountain to pray; and he spent the night in prayer to God. ¹³And when day came, he called his disciples and chose twelve of them, whom he also named apostles: ¹⁴Simon, whom he named Peter, and his brother Andrew, and James, and John, and Philip, and Bartholomew, ¹⁵and Matthew, and Thomas, and James son of Alphaeus, and Simon, who was called the Zealot, ¹⁶and Judas son of James, and Judas Iscariot, who became a traitor.

Jesus Teaches and Heals

¹⁷He came down with them and stood on a level place, with a great crowd of his disciples and a great multitude of people from all Judea, Jerusalem, and the coast of Tyre and Sidon. ¹⁸They had come to hear him and to be healed of their diseases; and

---

w Other ancient authorities add *to do*

those who were troubled with unclean spirits were cured. ¹⁹ And all in the crowd were trying to touch him, for power came out from him and healed all of them.

Blessings and Woes

²⁰ Then he looked up at his disciples and said:

'Blessed are you who are poor,
    for yours is the kingdom of God.
²¹ 'Blessed are you who are hungry now,
    for you will be filled.
'Blessed are you who weep now,
    for you will laugh.

²² 'Blessed are you when people hate you, and when they exclude you, revile you, and defame you ˣ on account of the Son of Man. ²³ Rejoice on that day and leap for joy, for surely your reward is great in heaven; for that is what their ancestors did to the prophets.

²⁴ 'But woe to you who are rich,
    for you have received your consolation.
²⁵ 'Woe to you who are full now,
    for you will be hungry.
'Woe to you who are laughing now,
    for you will mourn and weep.

²⁶ 'Woe to you when all speak well of you, for that is what their ancestors did to the false prophets.

Love for Enemies

²⁷ 'But I say to you that listen, Love your enemies, do good to those who hate you, ²⁸ bless those who curse you, pray for those who abuse you. ²⁹ If anyone strikes you on the cheek, offer the other also; and from anyone who takes away your coat do not withhold even your shirt. ³⁰ Give to everyone who begs from you; and if anyone takes away your goods, do not ask for them again. ³¹ Do to others as you would have them do to you.

³² 'If you love those who love you, what credit is that to you? For even sinners love those who love them. ³³ If you do good to those who do good to you, what credit is that to you? For even

---

x Gk *cast out your name as evil*

sinners do the same. ³⁴If you lend to those from whom you hope to receive, what credit is that to you? Even sinners lend to sinners, to receive as much again. ³⁵But love your enemies, do good, and lend, expecting nothing in return.^y Your reward will be great, and you will be children of the Most High; for he is kind to the ungrateful and the wicked. ³⁶Be merciful, just as your Father is merciful.

Judging Others

³⁷'Do not judge, and you will not be judged; do not condemn, and you will not be condemned. Forgive, and you will be forgiven; ³⁸give, and it will be given to you. A good measure, pressed down, shaken together, running over, will be put into your lap; for the measure you give will be the measure you get back.'

³⁹He also told them a parable: 'Can a blind person guide a blind person? Will not both fall into a pit? ⁴⁰A disciple is not above the teacher, but everyone who is fully qualified will be like the teacher. ⁴¹Why do you see the speck in your neighbour's^z eye, but do not notice the log in your own eye? ⁴²Or how can you say to your neighbour,^a "Friend,^a let me take out the speck in your eye", when you yourself do not see the log in your own eye? You hypocrite, first take the log out of your own eye, and then you will see clearly to take the speck out of your neighbour's^b eye.

A Tree and Its Fruit

⁴³'No good tree bears bad fruit, nor again does a bad tree bear good fruit; ⁴⁴for each tree is known by its own fruit. Figs are not gathered from thorns, nor are grapes picked from a bramble bush. ⁴⁵The good person out of the good treasure of the heart produces good, and the evil person out of evil treasure produces evil; for it is out of the abundance of the heart that the mouth speaks.

The Two Foundations

⁴⁶'Why do you call me "Lord, Lord", and do not do what I tell you? ⁴⁷I will show you what someone is like who comes to me, hears my words, and acts on them. ⁴⁸That one is like a man

---

y Other ancient authorities read *despairing of no one*   z Gk *brother's*   a Gk *brother*
b Gk *brother's*

building a house, who dug deeply and laid the foundation on rock; when a flood arose, the river burst against that house but could not shake it, because it had been well built.ᶜ ⁴⁹But the one who hears and does not act is like a man who built a house on the ground without a foundation. When the river burst against it, immediately it fell, and great was the ruin of that house.'

Jesus Heals a Centurion's Servant

7 After Jesusᵈ had finished all his sayings in the hearing of the people, he entered Capernaum. ²A centurion there had a slave whom he valued highly, and who was ill and close to death. ³When he heard about Jesus, he sent some Jewish elders to him, asking him to come and heal his slave. ⁴When they came to Jesus, they appealed to him earnestly, saying, 'He is worthy of having you do this for him, ⁵for he loves our people, and it is he who built our synagogue for us.' ⁶And Jesus went with them, but when he was not far from the house, the centurion sent friends to say to him, 'Lord, do not trouble yourself, for I am not worthy to have you come under my roof; ⁷therefore I did not presume to come to you. But only speak the word, and let my servant be healed. ⁸For I also am a man set under authority, with soldiers under me; and I say to one, "Go", and he goes, and to another, "Come", and he comes, and to my slave, "Do this", and the slave does it.' ⁹When Jesus heard this he was amazed at him, and turning to the crowd that followed him, he said, 'I tell you, not even in Israel have I found such faith.' ¹⁰When those who had been sent returned to the house, they found the slave in good health.

Jesus Raises the Widow's Son at Nain

¹¹Soon afterwardsᵉ he went to a town called Nain, and his disciples and a large crowd went with him. ¹²As he approached the gate of the town, a man who had died was being carried out. He was his mother's only son, and she was a widow; and with her was a large crowd from the town. ¹³When the Lord saw her, he had compassion for her and said to her, 'Do not weep.' ¹⁴Then

---

c Other ancient authorities read *founded upon the rock*   d Gk *he*   e Other ancient authorities read *Next day*

he came forward and touched the bier, and the bearers stood still. And he said, 'Young man, I say to you, rise!' ¹⁵The dead man sat up and began to speak, and Jesus^f gave him to his mother. ¹⁶Fear seized all of them; and they glorified God, saying, 'A great prophet has risen among us!' and 'God has looked favourably on his people!' ¹⁷This word about him spread throughout Judea and all the surrounding country.

Messengers from John the Baptist

¹⁸The disciples of John reported all these things to him. So John summoned two of his disciples ¹⁹and sent them to the Lord to ask, 'Are you the one who is to come, or are we to wait for another?' ²⁰When the men had come to him, they said, 'John the Baptist has sent us to you to ask, "Are you the one who is to come, or are we to wait for another?" ' ²¹Jesus^g had just then cured many people of diseases, plagues, and evil spirits, and had given sight to many who were blind. ²²And he answered them, 'Go and tell John what you have seen and heard: the blind receive their sight, the lame walk, the lepers^h are cleansed, the deaf hear, the dead are raised, the poor have good news brought to them. ²³And blessed is anyone who takes no offence at me.'

²⁴When John's messengers had gone, Jesus^i began to speak to the crowds about John:^j 'What did you go out into the wilderness to look at? A reed shaken by the wind? ²⁵What then did you go out to see? Someone^k dressed in soft robes? Look, those who put on fine clothing and live in luxury are in royal palaces. ²⁶What then did you go out to see? A prophet? Yes, I tell you, and more than a prophet. ²⁷This is the one about whom it is written,

"See, I am sending my messenger ahead of you,
     who will prepare your way before you."

²⁸I tell you, among those born of women no one is greater than John; yet the least in the kingdom of God is greater than he.' ²⁹(And all the people who heard this, including the tax-collectors, acknowledged the justice of God,^l because they had been baptized with John's baptism. ³⁰But by refusing to be baptized by him, the Pharisees and the lawyers rejected God's purpose for themselves.)

---

f Gk he   g Gk He   h The terms *leper* and *leprosy* can refer to several diseases   i Gk he
j Gk him   k Or *Why then did you go out? To see someone*   l Or *praised God*

³¹'To what then will I compare the people of this generation, and what are they like? ³²They are like children sitting in the market-place and calling to one another,

"We played the flute for you, and you did not dance;
we wailed, and you did not weep."

³³For John the Baptist has come eating no bread and drinking no wine, and you say, "He has a demon"; ³⁴the Son of Man has come eating and drinking, and you say, "Look, a glutton and a drunkard, a friend of tax-collectors and sinners!" ³⁵Nevertheless, wisdom is vindicated by all her children.'

A Sinful Woman Forgiven

³⁶One of the Pharisees asked Jesus*m* to eat with him, and he went into the Pharisee's house and took his place at the table. ³⁷And a woman in the city, who was a sinner, having learned that he was eating in the Pharisee's house, brought an alabaster jar of ointment. ³⁸She stood behind him at his feet, weeping, and began to bathe his feet with her tears and to dry them with her hair. Then she continued kissing his feet and anointing them with the ointment. ³⁹Now when the Pharisee who had invited him saw it, he said to himself, 'If this man were a prophet, he would have known who and what kind of woman this is who is touching him—that she is a sinner.' ⁴⁰Jesus spoke up and said to him, 'Simon, I have something to say to you.' 'Teacher,' he replied, 'speak.' ⁴¹'A certain creditor had two debtors; one owed five hundred denarii,*n* and the other fifty. ⁴²When they could not pay, he cancelled the debts for both of them. Now which of them will love him more?' ⁴³Simon answered, 'I suppose the one for whom he cancelled the greater debt.' And Jesus*o* said to him, 'You have judged rightly.' ⁴⁴Then turning towards the woman, he said to Simon, 'Do you see this woman? I entered your house; you gave me no water for my feet, but she has bathed my feet with her tears and dried them with her hair. ⁴⁵You gave me no kiss, but from the time I came in she has not stopped kissing my feet. ⁴⁶You did not anoint my head with oil, but she has anointed my feet with ointment. ⁴⁷Therefore, I tell you, her sins, which were many, have been forgiven; hence she has shown great love. But

---

m Gk *him*   n The denarius was the usual day's wage for a labourer   o Gk *he*

the one to whom little is forgiven, loves little.' ⁴⁸Then he said to her, 'Your sins are forgiven.' ⁴⁹But those who were at the table with him began to say among themselves, 'Who is this who even forgives sins?' ⁵⁰And he said to the woman, 'Your faith has saved you; go in peace.'

Some Women Accompany Jesus

8 Soon afterwards he went on through cities and villages, proclaiming and bringing the good news of the kingdom of God. The twelve were with him, ²as well as some women who had been cured of evil spirits and infirmities: Mary, called Magdalene, from whom seven demons had gone out, ³and Joanna, the wife of Herod's steward Chuza, and Susanna, and many others, who provided for them*ᵖ* out of their resources.

The Parable of the Sower

⁴When a great crowd gathered and people from town after town came to him, he said in a parable: ⁵'A sower went out to sow his seed; and as he sowed, some fell on the path and was trampled on, and the birds of the air ate it up. ⁶Some fell on the rock; and as it grew up, it withered for lack of moisture. ⁷Some fell among thorns, and the thorns grew with it and choked it. ⁸Some fell into good soil, and when it grew, it produced a hundredfold.' As he said this, he called out, 'Let anyone with ears to hear listen!'

The Purpose of the Parables

⁹Then his disciples asked him what this parable meant. ¹⁰He said, 'To you it has been given to know the secrets* q* of the kingdom of God; but to others I speak*ʳ* in parables, so that
"looking they may not perceive,
     and listening they may not understand."

The Parable of the Sower Explained

¹¹'Now the parable is this: The seed is the word of God. ¹²The ones on the path are those who have heard; then the devil comes and takes away the word from their hearts, so that they may

---

p Other ancient authorities read *him*   q Or *mysteries*   r Gk lacks *I speak*

not believe and be saved. [13] The ones on the rock are those who, when they hear the word, receive it with joy. But these have no root; they believe only for a while and in a time of testing fall away. [14] As for what fell among the thorns, these are the ones who hear; but as they go on their way, they are choked by the cares and riches and pleasures of life, and their fruit does not mature. [15] But as for that in the good soil, these are the ones who, when they hear the word, hold it fast in an honest and good heart, and bear fruit with patient endurance.

A Lamp under a Jar

[16] 'No one after lighting a lamp hides it under a jar, or puts it under a bed, but puts it on a lampstand, so that those who enter may see the light. [17] For nothing is hidden that will not be disclosed, nor is anything secret that will not become known and come to light. [18] Then pay attention to how you listen; for to those who have, more will be given; and from those who do not have, even what they seem to have will be taken away.'

The True Kindred of Jesus

[19] Then his mother and his brothers came to him, but they could not reach him because of the crowd. [20] And he was told, 'Your mother and your brothers are standing outside, wanting to see you.' [21] But he said to them, 'My mother and my brothers are those who hear the word of God and do it.'

Jesus Calms a Storm

[22] One day he got into a boat with his disciples, and he said to them, 'Let us go across to the other side of the lake.' So they put out, [23] and while they were sailing he fell asleep. A gale swept down on the lake, and the boat was filling with water, and they were in danger. [24] They went to him and woke him up, shouting, 'Master, Master, we are perishing!' And he woke up and rebuked the wind and the raging waves; they ceased, and there was a calm. [25] He said to them, 'Where is your faith?' They were afraid and amazed, and said to one another, 'Who then is this, that he commands even the winds and the water, and they obey him?'

Jesus Heals the Gerasene Demoniac

²⁶Then they arrived at the country of the Gerasenes,ˢ which is opposite Galilee. ²⁷As he stepped out on land, a man of the city who had demons met him. For a long time he had wornᵗ no clothes, and he did not live in a house but in the tombs. ²⁸When he saw Jesus, he fell down before him and shouted at the top of his voice, 'What have you to do with me, Jesus, Son of the Most High God? I beg you, do not torment me'— ²⁹for Jesusᵘ had commanded the unclean spirit to come out of the man. (For many times it had seized him; he was kept under guard and bound with chains and shackles, but he would break the bonds and be driven by the demon into the wilds.) ³⁰Jesus then asked him, 'What is your name?' He said, 'Legion'; for many demons had entered him. ³¹They begged him not to order them to go back into the abyss.

³²Now there on the hillside a large herd of swine was feeding; and the demonsᵛ begged Jesusʷ to let them enter these. So he gave them permission. ³³Then the demons came out of the man and entered the swine, and the herd rushed down the steep bank into the lake and was drowned.

³⁴When the swineherds saw what had happened, they ran off and told it in the city and in the country. ³⁵Then people came out to see what had happened, and when they came to Jesus, they found the man from whom the demons had gone sitting at the feet of Jesus, clothed and in his right mind. And they were afraid. ³⁶Those who had seen it told them how the one who had been possessed by demons had been healed. ³⁷Then all the people of the surrounding country of the Gerasenesˣ asked Jesusʸ to leave them; for they were seized with great fear. So he got into the boat and returned. ³⁸The man from whom the demons had gone begged that he might be with him; but Jesusᶻ sent him away, saying, ³⁹'Return to your home, and declare how much God has done for you.' So he went away, proclaiming throughout the city how much Jesus had done for him.

---

s Other ancient authorities read *Gadarenes*; others, *Gergesenes*   t Other ancient authorities read *a man of the city who had had demons for a long time met him. He wore*   u Gk *he*
v Gk *they*   w Gk *him*   x Other ancient authorities read *Gadarenes*; others, *Gergesenes*
y Gk *him*   z Gk *he*

A Girl Restored to Life and a Woman Healed

40 Now when Jesus returned, the crowd welcomed him, for they were all waiting for him. 41 Just then there came a man named Jairus, a leader of the synagogue. He fell at Jesus' feet and begged him to come to his house, 42 for he had an only daughter, about twelve years old, who was dying.

As he went, the crowds pressed in on him. 43 Now there was a woman who had been suffering from haemorrhages for twelve years; and though she had spent all she had on physicians,*a* no one could cure her. 44 She came up behind him and touched the fringe of his clothes, and immediately her haemorrhage stopped. 45 Then Jesus asked, 'Who touched me?' When all denied it, Peter*b* said, 'Master, the crowds surround you and press in on you.' 46 But Jesus said, 'Someone touched me; for I noticed that power had gone out from me.' 47 When the woman saw that she could not remain hidden, she came trembling; and falling down before him, she declared in the presence of all the people why she had touched him, and how she had been immediately healed. 48 He said to her, 'Daughter, your faith has made you well; go in peace.'

49 While he was still speaking, someone came from the leader's house to say, 'Your daughter is dead; do not trouble the teacher any longer.' 50 When Jesus heard this, he replied, 'Do not fear. Only believe, and she will be saved.' 51 When he came to the house, he did not allow anyone to enter with him, except Peter, John, and James, and the child's father and mother. 52 They were all weeping and wailing for her; but he said, 'Do not weep; for she is not dead but sleeping.' 53 And they laughed at him, knowing that she was dead. 54 But he took her by the hand and called out, 'Child, get up!' 55 Her spirit returned, and she got up at once. Then he directed them to give her something to eat. 56 Her parents were astounded; but he ordered them to tell no one what had happened.

The Mission of the Twelve

9 Then Jesus*c* called the twelve together and gave them power and authority over all demons and to cure diseases,

---

a Other ancient authorities lack *and though she had spent all she had on physicians*   b Other ancient authorities add *and those who were with him*   c Gk *he*

²and he sent them out to proclaim the kingdom of God and to heal. ³He said to them, 'Take nothing for your journey, no staff, nor bag, nor bread, nor money—not even an extra tunic. ⁴Whatever house you enter, stay there, and leave from there. ⁵Wherever they do not welcome you, as you are leaving that town shake the dust off your feet as a testimony against them.' ⁶They departed and went through the villages, bringing the good news and curing diseases everywhere.

Herod's Perplexity

⁷Now Herod the ruler*d* heard about all that had taken place, and he was perplexed, because it was said by some that John had been raised from the dead, ⁸by some that Elijah had appeared, and by others that one of the ancient prophets had arisen. ⁹Herod said, 'John I beheaded; but who is this about whom I hear such things?' And he tried to see him.

Feeding the Five Thousand

¹⁰On their return the apostles told Jesus*e* all they had done. He took them with him and withdrew privately to a city called Bethsaida. ¹¹When the crowds found out about it, they followed him; and he welcomed them, and spoke to them about the kingdom of God, and healed those who needed to be cured. ¹²The day was drawing to a close, and the twelve came to him and said, 'Send the crowd away, so that they may go into the surrounding villages and countryside, to lodge and get provisions; for we are here in a deserted place.' ¹³But he said to them, 'You give them something to eat.' They said, 'We have no more than five loaves and two fish—unless we are to go and buy food for all these people.' ¹⁴For there were about five thousand men. And he said to his disciples, 'Make them sit down in groups of about fifty each.' ¹⁵They did so and made them all sit down. ¹⁶And taking the five loaves and the two fish, he looked up to heaven, and blessed and broke them, and gave them to the disciples to set before the crowd. ¹⁷And all ate and were filled. What was left over was gathered up, twelve baskets of broken pieces.

---

d Gk *tetrarch*   e Gk *him*

Peter's Declaration about Jesus

18 Once when Jesus*f* was praying alone, with only the disciples near him, he asked them, 'Who do the crowds say that I am?' 19 They answered, 'John the Baptist; but others, Elijah; and still others, that one of the ancient prophets has arisen.' 20 He said to them, 'But who do you say that I am?' Peter answered, 'The Messiah*g* of God.'

Jesus Foretells His Death and Resurrection

21 He sternly ordered and commanded them not to tell anyone, 22 saying, 'The Son of Man must undergo great suffering, and be rejected by the elders, chief priests, and scribes, and be killed, and on the third day be raised.'

23 Then he said to them all, 'If any want to become my followers, let them deny themselves and take up their cross daily and follow me. 24 For those who want to save their life will lose it, and those who lose their life for my sake will save it. 25 What does it profit them if they gain the whole world, but lose or forfeit themselves? 26 Those who are ashamed of me and of my words, of them the Son of Man will be ashamed when he comes in his glory and the glory of the Father and of the holy angels. 27 But truly I tell you, there are some standing here who will not taste death before they see the kingdom of God.'

The Transfiguration

28 Now about eight days after these sayings Jesus*h* took with him Peter and John and James, and went up on the mountain to pray. 29 And while he was praying, the appearance of his face changed, and his clothes became dazzling white. 30 Suddenly they saw two men, Moses and Elijah, talking to him. 31 They appeared in glory and were speaking of his departure, which he was about to accomplish at Jerusalem. 32 Now Peter and his companions were weighed down with sleep; but since they had stayed awake,*i* they saw his glory and the two men who stood with him. 33 Just as they were leaving him, Peter said to Jesus, 'Master, it is good for us to be here; let us make three dwellings,*j* one for you, one for Moses, and one for Elijah'—not knowing what he said. 34 While

---

f Gk *he*   g Or *The Christ*   h Gk *he*   i Or *but when they were fully awake*   j Or *tents*

he was saying this, a cloud came and overshadowed them; and they were terrified as they entered the cloud. ³⁵Then from the cloud came a voice that said, 'This is my Son, my Chosen;ᵏ listen to him!' ³⁶When the voice had spoken, Jesus was found alone. And they kept silent and in those days told no one any of the things they had seen.

Jesus Heals a Boy with a Demon

³⁷On the next day, when they had come down from the mountain, a great crowd met him. ³⁸Just then a man from the crowd shouted, 'Teacher, I beg you to look at my son; he is my only child. ³⁹Suddenly a spirit seizes him, and all at once heˡ shrieks. It throws him into convulsions until he foams at the mouth; it mauls him and will scarcely leave him. ⁴⁰I begged your disciples to cast it out, but they could not.' ⁴¹Jesus answered, 'You faithless and perverse generation, how much longer must I be with you and bear with you? Bring your son here.' ⁴²While he was coming, the demon dashed him to the ground in convulsions. But Jesus rebuked the unclean spirit, healed the boy, and gave him back to his father. ⁴³And all were astounded at the greatness of God.

Jesus Again Foretells His Death

While everyone was amazed at all that he was doing, he said to his disciples, ⁴⁴'Let these words sink into your ears: The Son of Man is going to be betrayed into human hands.' ⁴⁵But they did not understand this saying; its meaning was concealed from them, so that they could not perceive it. And they were afraid to ask him about this saying.

True Greatness

⁴⁶An argument arose among them as to which one of them was the greatest. ⁴⁷But Jesus, aware of their inner thoughts, took a little child and put it by his side, ⁴⁸and said to them, 'Whoever welcomes this child in my name welcomes me, and whoever welcomes me welcomes the one who sent me; for the least among all of you is the greatest.'

---

k Other ancient authorities read *my Beloved*   l Or *it*

Another Exorcist

⁴⁹John answered, 'Master, we saw someone casting out demons in your name, and we tried to stop him, because he does not follow with us.' ⁵⁰But Jesus said to him, 'Do not stop him; for whoever is not against you is for you.'

A Samaritan Village Refuses to Receive Jesus

⁵¹When the days drew near for him to be taken up, he set his face to go to Jerusalem. ⁵²And he sent messengers ahead of him. On their way they entered a village of the Samaritans to make ready for him; ⁵³but they did not receive him, because his face was set towards Jerusalem. ⁵⁴When his disciples James and John saw it, they said, 'Lord, do you want us to command fire to come down from heaven and consume them?'ᵐ ⁵⁵But he turned and rebuked them. ⁵⁶Thenⁿ they went on to another village.

Would-Be Followers of Jesus

⁵⁷As they were going along the road, someone said to him, 'I will follow you wherever you go.' ⁵⁸And Jesus said to him, 'Foxes have holes, and birds of the air have nests; but the Son of Man has nowhere to lay his head.' ⁵⁹To another he said, 'Follow me.' But he said, 'Lord, first let me go and bury my father.' ⁶⁰But Jesusᵒ said to him, 'Let the dead bury their own dead; but as for you, go and proclaim the kingdom of God.' ⁶¹Another said, 'I will follow you, Lord; but let me first say farewell to those at my home.' ⁶²Jesus said to him, 'No one who puts a hand to the plough and looks back is fit for the kingdom of God.'

The Mission of the Seventy

10 After this the Lord appointed seventyᵖ others and sent them on ahead of him in pairs to every town and place where he himself intended to go. ²He said to them, 'The harvest is plentiful, but the labourers are few; therefore ask the Lord of the harvest to send out labourers into his harvest. ³Go on

---

m Other ancient authorities add *as Elijah did*   n Other ancient authorities read *rebuked them, and said, 'You do not know what spirit you are of,* ⁵⁶ *for the Son of Man has not come to destroy the lives of human beings but to save them.' Then*   o Gk *he*   p Other ancient authorities read *seventy-two*

your way. See, I am sending you out like lambs into the midst of wolves. [4]Carry no purse, no bag, no sandals; and greet no one on the road. [5]Whatever house you enter, first say, "Peace to this house!" [6]And if anyone is there who shares in peace, your peace will rest on that person; but if not, it will return to you. [7]Remain in the same house, eating and drinking whatever they provide, for the labourer deserves to be paid. Do not move about from house to house. [8]Whenever you enter a town and its people welcome you, eat what is set before you; [9]cure the sick who are there, and say to them, "The kingdom of God has come near to you."[q] [10]But whenever you enter a town and they do not welcome you, go out into its streets and say, [11]"Even the dust of your town that clings to our feet, we wipe off in protest against you. Yet know this: the kingdom of God has come near."[r] [12]I tell you, on that day it will be more tolerable for Sodom than for that town.

Woes to Unrepentant Cities

[13]'Woe to you, Chorazin! Woe to you, Bethsaida! For if the deeds of power done in you had been done in Tyre and Sidon, they would have repented long ago, sitting in sackcloth and ashes. [14]But at the judgement it will be more tolerable for Tyre and Sidon than for you.

[15] And you, Capernaum,
      will you be exalted to heaven?
         No, you will be brought down to Hades.

[16]'Whoever listens to you listens to me, and whoever rejects you rejects me, and whoever rejects me rejects the one who sent me.'

The Return of the Seventy

[17]The seventy[s] returned with joy, saying, 'Lord, in your name even the demons submit to us!' [18]He said to them, 'I watched Satan fall from heaven like a flash of lightning. [19]See, I have given you authority to tread on snakes and scorpions, and over all the power of the enemy; and nothing will hurt you. [20]Nevertheless, do not rejoice at this, that the spirits submit to you, but rejoice that your names are written in heaven.'

---

q Or *is at hand for you*   r Or *is at hand*   s Other ancient authorities read *seventy-two*

Jesus Rejoices

²¹At that same hour Jesusᵗ rejoiced in the Holy Spiritᵘ and said, 'I thankᵛ you, Father, Lord of heaven and earth, because you have hidden these things from the wise and the intelligent and have revealed them to infants; yes, Father, for such was your gracious will.ʷ ²²All things have been handed over to me by my Father; and no one knows who the Son is except the Father, or who the Father is except the Son and anyone to whom the Son chooses to reveal him.'

²³Then turning to the disciples, Jesusˣ said to them privately, 'Blessed are the eyes that see what you see! ²⁴For I tell you that many prophets and kings desired to see what you see, but did not see it, and to hear what you hear, but did not hear it.'

The Parable of the Good Samaritan

²⁵Just then a lawyer stood up to test Jesus.ʸ 'Teacher,' he said, 'what must I do to inherit eternal life?' ²⁶He said to him, 'What is written in the law? What do you read there?' ²⁷He answered, 'You shall love the Lord your God with all your heart, and with all your soul, and with all your strength, and with all your mind; and your neighbour as yourself.' ²⁸And he said to him, 'You have given the right answer; do this, and you will live.'

²⁹But wanting to justify himself, he asked Jesus, 'And who is my neighbour?' ³⁰Jesus replied, 'A man was going down from Jerusalem to Jericho, and fell into the hands of robbers, who stripped him, beat him, and went away, leaving him half dead. ³¹Now by chance a priest was going down that road; and when he saw him, he passed by on the other side. ³²So likewise a Levite, when he came to the place and saw him, passed by on the other side. ³³But a Samaritan while travelling came near him; and when he saw him, he was moved with pity. ³⁴He went to him and bandaged his wounds, having poured oil and wine on them. Then he put him on his own animal, brought him to an inn, and took care of him. ³⁵The next day he took out two denarii,ᶻ gave them to the innkeeper, and said, "Take care of him; and when I come

---

t Gk *he*   u Other authorities read *in the spirit*   v Or *praise*   w Or *for so it was well-pleasing in your sight*   x Gk *he*   y Gk *him*   z The denarius was the usual day's wage for a labourer

back, I will repay you whatever more you spend." ³⁶Which of these three, do you think, was a neighbour to the man who fell into the hands of the robbers?' ³⁷He said, 'The one who showed him mercy.' Jesus said to him, 'Go and do likewise.'

Jesus Visits Martha and Mary

³⁸Now as they went on their way, he entered a certain village, where a woman named Martha welcomed him into her home. ³⁹She had a sister named Mary, who sat at the Lord's feet and listened to what he was saying. ⁴⁰But Martha was distracted by her many tasks; so she came to him and asked, 'Lord, do you not care that my sister has left me to do all the work by myself? Tell her then to help me.' ⁴¹But the Lord answered her, 'Martha, Martha, you are worried and distracted by many things; ⁴²there is need of only one thing.ᵃ Mary has chosen the better part, which will not be taken away from her.'

The Lord's Prayer

11 He was praying in a certain place, and after he had finished, one of his disciples said to him, 'Lord, teach us to pray, as John taught his disciples.' ²He said to them, 'When you pray, say:
Father,ᵇ hallowed be your name.
Your kingdom come.ᶜ
³ Give us each day our daily bread.ᵈ
⁴ And forgive us our sins,
for we ourselves forgive everyone indebted to us.
And do not bring us to the time of trial.'ᵉ

Perseverance in Prayer

⁵And he said to them, 'Suppose one of you has a friend, and you go to him at midnight and say to him, "Friend, lend me three loaves of bread; ⁶for a friend of mine has arrived, and I have nothing to set before him." ⁷And he answers from within, "Do not bother me; the door has already been locked, and my children

---

a Other ancient authorities read *few things are necessary, or only one*   b Other ancient authorities read *Our Father in heaven*   c A few ancient authorities read *Your Holy Spirit come upon us and cleanse us.* Other ancient authorities add *Your will be done, on earth as in heaven*   d Or *our bread for tomorrow*   e Or *us into temptation.* Other ancient authorities add *but rescue us from the evil one* (or *from evil*)

are with me in bed; I cannot get up and give you anything.'
⁸I tell you, even though he will not get up and give him anything because he is his friend, at least because of his persistence he will get up and give him whatever he needs.

⁹'So I say to you, Ask, and it will be given to you; search, and you will find; knock, and the door will be opened for you. ¹⁰For everyone who asks receives, and everyone who searches finds, and for everyone who knocks, the door will be opened. ¹¹Is there anyone among you who, if your child asks for*f* a fish, will give a snake instead of a fish? ¹²Or if the child asks for an egg, will give a scorpion? ¹³If you then, who are evil, know how to give good gifts to your children, how much more will the heavenly Father give the Holy Spirit*g* to those who ask him!'

Jesus and Beelzebul

¹⁴Now he was casting out a demon that was mute; when the demon had gone out, the one who had been mute spoke, and the crowds were amazed. ¹⁵But some of them said, 'He casts out demons by Beelzebul, the ruler of the demons.' ¹⁶Others, to test him, kept demanding from him a sign from heaven. ¹⁷But he knew what they were thinking and said to them, 'Every kingdom divided against itself becomes a desert, and house falls on house. ¹⁸If Satan also is divided against himself, how will his kingdom stand?—for you say that I cast out the demons by Beelzebul. ¹⁹Now if I cast out the demons by Beelzebul, by whom do your exorcists*h* cast them out? Therefore they will be your judges. ²⁰But if it is by the finger of God that I cast out the demons, then the kingdom of God has come to you. ²¹When a strong man, fully armed, guards his castle, his property is safe. ²²But when one stronger than he attacks him and overpowers him, he takes away his armour in which he trusted and divides his plunder. ²³Whoever is not with me is against me, and whoever does not gather with me scatters.

The Return of the Unclean Spirit

²⁴'When the unclean spirit has gone out of a person, it wanders through waterless regions looking for a resting-place, but not

---

f Other ancient authorities add *bread, will give a stone; or if your child asks for*   g Other ancient authorities read *the Father give the Holy Spirit from heaven*   h Gk *sons*

finding any, it says, "I will return to my house from which I came."
²⁵When it comes, it finds it swept and put in order. ²⁶Then it goes
and brings seven other spirits more evil than itself, and they
enter and live there; and the last state of that person is worse
than the first.'

True Blessedness

²⁷While he was saying this, a woman in the crowd raised her
voice and said to him, 'Blessed is the womb that bore you and
the breasts that nursed you!' ²⁸But he said, 'Blessed rather are
those who hear the word of God and obey it!'

The Sign of Jonah

²⁹When the crowds were increasing, he began to say, 'This
generation is an evil generation; it asks for a sign, but no sign will
be given to it except the sign of Jonah. ³⁰For just as Jonah became
a sign to the people of Nineveh, so the Son of Man will be to this
generation. ³¹The queen of the South will rise at the judgement with
the people of this generation and condemn them, because she came
from the ends of the earth to listen to the wisdom of Solomon,
and see, something greater than Solomon is here! ³²The people of
Nineveh will rise up at the judgement with this generation and
condemn it, because they repented at the proclamation of Jonah,
and see, something greater than Jonah is here!

The Light of the Body

³³'No one after lighting a lamp puts it in a cellar,ⁱ but on the
lampstand so that those who enter may see the light. ³⁴Your eye
is the lamp of your body. If your eye is healthy, your whole body
is full of light; but if it is not healthy, your body is full of darkness.
³⁵Therefore consider whether the light in you is not darkness. ³⁶If
then your whole body is full of light, with no part of it in darkness,
it will be as full of light as when a lamp gives you light with its rays.'

Jesus Denounces Pharisees and Lawyers

³⁷While he was speaking, a Pharisee invited him to dine with
him; so he went in and took his place at the table. ³⁸The Pharisee

---

i Other ancient authorities add *or under the bushel basket*

was amazed to see that he did not first wash before dinner. [39]Then the Lord said to him, 'Now you Pharisees clean the outside of the cup and of the dish, but inside you are full of greed and wickedness. [40]You fools! Did not the one who made the outside make the inside also? [41]So give for alms those things that are within; and see, everything will be clean for you.

[42]'But woe to you Pharisees! For you tithe mint and rue and herbs of all kinds, and neglect justice and the love of God; it is these you ought to have practised, without neglecting the others. [43]Woe to you Pharisees! For you love to have the seat of honour in the synagogues and to be greeted with respect in the market-places. [44]Woe to you! For you are like unmarked graves, and people walk over them without realizing it.'

[45]One of the lawyers answered him, 'Teacher, when you say these things, you insult us too.' [46]And he said, 'Woe also to you lawyers! For you load people with burdens hard to bear, and you yourselves do not lift a finger to ease them. [47]Woe to you! For you build the tombs of the prophets whom your ancestors killed. [48]So you are witnesses and approve of the deeds of your ancestors; for they killed them, and you build their tombs. [49]Therefore also the Wisdom of God said, "I will send them prophets and apostles, some of whom they will kill and persecute", [50]so that this generation may be charged with the blood of all the prophets shed since the foundation of the world, [51]from the blood of Abel to the blood of Zechariah, who perished between the altar and the sanctuary. Yes, I tell you, it will be charged against this generation. [52]Woe to you lawyers! For you have taken away the key of knowledge; you did not enter yourselves, and you hindered those who were entering.'

[53]When he went outside, the scribes and the Pharisees began to be very hostile towards him and to cross-examine him about many things, [54]lying in wait for him, to catch him in something he might say.

A Warning against Hypocrisy

12 Meanwhile, when the crowd gathered in thousands, so that they trampled on one another, he began to speak first to his disciples, 'Beware of the yeast of the Pharisees, that is, their hypocrisy. [2]Nothing is covered up that will not be uncovered, and nothing secret that will not become known. ³Therefore whatever you have said in the dark will be heard in the light, and what you have whispered behind closed doors will be proclaimed from the housetops.

Exhortation to Fearless Confession

⁴'I tell you, my friends, do not fear those who kill the body, and after that can do nothing more. ⁵But I will warn you whom to fear: fear him who, after he has killed, has authorityʲ to cast into hell.ᵏ Yes, I tell you, fear him! ⁶Are not five sparrows sold for two pennies? Yet not one of them is forgotten in God's sight. ⁷But even the hairs of your head are all counted. Do not be afraid; you are of more value than many sparrows.

⁸'And I tell you, everyone who acknowledges me before others, the Son of Man also will acknowledge before the angels of God; ⁹but whoever denies me before others will be denied before the angels of God. ¹⁰And everyone who speaks a word against the Son of Man will be forgiven; but whoever blasphemes against the Holy Spirit will not be forgiven. ¹¹When they bring you before the synagogues, the rulers, and the authorities, do not worry about howˡ you are to defend yourselves or what you are to say; ¹²for the Holy Spirit will teach you at that very hour what you ought to say.'

The Parable of the Rich Fool

¹³Someone in the crowd said to him, 'Teacher, tell my brother to divide the family inheritance with me.' ¹⁴But he said to him, 'Friend, who set me to be a judge or arbitrator over you?' ¹⁵And he said to them, 'Take care! Be on your guard against all kinds of greed; for one's life does not consist in the abundance of possessions.' ¹⁶Then he told them a parable: 'The land of a rich man produced abundantly. ¹⁷And he thought to himself, "What should I do, for I have no place to store my crops?" ¹⁸Then he said, "I will do this: I will pull down my barns and build larger ones, and there I will store all my grain and my goods. ¹⁹And I will say to my soul, Soul, you have ample goods laid up for many years; relax, eat, drink, be merry." ²⁰But God said to him,

---

j Or *power*   k Gk *Gehenna*   l Other ancient authorities add *or what*

"You fool! This very night your life is being demanded of you. And the things you have prepared, whose will they be?" 21So it is with those who store up treasures for themselves but are not rich towards God.'

Do Not Worry

22He said to his disciples, 'Therefore I tell you, do not worry about your life, what you will eat, or about your body, what you will wear. 23For life is more than food, and the body more than clothing. 24Consider the ravens: they neither sow nor reap, they have neither storehouse nor barn, and yet God feeds them. Of how much more value are you than the birds! 25And can any of you by worrying add a single hour to your span of life?*m* 26If then you are not able to do so small a thing as that, why do you worry about the rest? 27Consider the lilies, how they grow: they neither toil nor spin;*n* yet I tell you, even Solomon in all his glory was not clothed like one of these. 28But if God so clothes the grass of the field, which is alive today and tomorrow is thrown into the oven, how much more will he clothe you—you of little faith! 29And do not keep striving for what you are to eat and what you are to drink, and do not keep worrying. 30For it is the nations of the world that strive after all these things, and your Father knows that you need them. 31Instead, strive for his*o* kingdom, and these things will be given to you as well.

32'Do not be afraid, little flock, for it is your Father's good pleasure to give you the kingdom. 33Sell your possessions, and give alms. Make purses for yourselves that do not wear out, an unfailing treasure in heaven, where no thief comes near and no moth destroys. 34For where your treasure is, there your heart will be also.

Watchful Slaves

35'Be dressed for action and have your lamps lit; 36be like those who are waiting for their master to return from the wedding banquet, so that they may open the door for him as soon as he comes and knocks. 37Blessed are those slaves whom the master

---

m Or *add a cubit to your stature*   n Other ancient authorities read *Consider the lilies; they neither spin nor weave*   o Other ancient authorities read *God's*

finds alert when he comes; truly I tell you, he will fasten his belt
and have them sit down to eat, and he will come and serve them.
38 If he comes during the middle of the night, or near dawn, and
finds them so, blessed are those slaves.
39 'But know this: if the owner of the house had known at what
hour the thief was coming, he[p] would not have let his house
be broken into. 40 You also must be ready, for the Son of Man is
coming at an unexpected hour.'

The Faithful or the Unfaithful Slave

41 Peter said, 'Lord, are you telling this parable for us or for
everyone?' 42 And the Lord said, 'Who then is the faithful and
prudent manager whom his master will put in charge of his
slaves, to give them their allowance of food at the proper time?
43 Blessed is that slave whom his master will find at work when
he arrives. 44 Truly I tell you, he will put that one in charge of all
his possessions. 45 But if that slave says to himself, "My master
is delayed in coming", and if he begins to beat the other slaves,
men and women, and to eat and drink and get drunk, 46 the
master of that slave will come on a day when he does not expect
him and at an hour that he does not know, and will cut him in
pieces,[q] and put him with the unfaithful. 47 That slave who knew
what his master wanted, but did not prepare himself or do what
was wanted, will receive a severe beating. 48 But one who did
not know and did what deserved a beating will receive a light
beating. From everyone to whom much has been given, much will
be required; and from one to whom much has been entrusted,
even more will be demanded.

Jesus the Cause of Division

49 'I came to bring fire to the earth, and how I wish it were
already kindled! 50 I have a baptism with which to be baptized,
and what stress I am under until it is completed! 51 Do you think
that I have come to bring peace to the earth? No, I tell you, but
rather division! 52 From now on, five in one household will be
divided, three against two and two against three; 53 they will
be divided:

---

p Other ancient authorities add *would have watched and* q Or *cut him off*

>   father against son
>   and son against father,
>   mother against daughter
>   and daughter against mother,
>   mother-in-law against her daughter-in-law
>   and daughter-in-law against mother-in-law.'

Interpreting the Time

⁵⁴He also said to the crowds, 'When you see a cloud rising in the west, you immediately say, "It is going to rain"; and so it happens. ⁵⁵And when you see the south wind blowing, you say, "There will be scorching heat"; and it happens. ⁵⁶You hypocrites! You know how to interpret the appearance of earth and sky, but why do you not know how to interpret the present time?

Settling with Your Opponent

⁵⁷'And why do you not judge for yourselves what is right? ⁵⁸Thus, when you go with your accuser before a magistrate, on the way make an effort to settle the case,ʳ or you may be dragged before the judge, and the judge hand you over to the officer, and the officer throw you in prison. ⁵⁹I tell you, you will never get out until you have paid the very last penny.'

Repent or Perish

13 At that very time there were some present who told him about the Galileans whose blood Pilate had mingled with their sacrifices. ²He asked them, 'Do you think that because these Galileans suffered in this way they were worse sinners than all other Galileans? ³No, I tell you; but unless you repent, you will all perish as they did. ⁴Or those eighteen who were killed when the tower of Siloam fell on them—do you think that they were worse offenders than all the others living in Jerusalem? ⁵No, I tell you; but unless you repent, you will all perish just as they did.'

The Parable of the Barren Fig Tree

⁶Then he told this parable: 'A man had a fig tree planted in his vineyard; and he came looking for fruit on it and found none.

---

r Gk *settle with him*

⁷So he said to the gardener, "See here! For three years I have come looking for fruit on this fig tree, and still I find none. Cut it down! Why should it be wasting the soil?" ⁸He replied, "Sir, let it alone for one more year, until I dig round it and put manure on it. ⁹If it bears fruit next year, well and good; but if not, you can cut it down." '

Jesus Heals a Crippled Woman

¹⁰Now he was teaching in one of the synagogues on the sabbath. ¹¹And just then there appeared a woman with a spirit that had crippled her for eighteen years. She was bent over and was quite unable to stand up straight. ¹²When Jesus saw her, he called her over and said, 'Woman, you are set free from your ailment.' ¹³When he laid his hands on her, immediately she stood up straight and began praising God. ¹⁴But the leader of the synagogue, indignant because Jesus had cured on the sabbath, kept saying to the crowd, 'There are six days on which work ought to be done; come on those days and be cured, and not on the sabbath day.' ¹⁵But the Lord answered him and said, 'You hypocrites! Does not each of you on the sabbath untie his ox or his donkey from the manger, and lead it away to give it water? ¹⁶And ought not this woman, a daughter of Abraham whom Satan bound for eighteen long years, be set free from this bondage on the sabbath day?' ¹⁷When he said this, all his opponents were put to shame; and the entire crowd was rejoicing at all the wonderful things that he was doing.

The Parable of the Mustard Seed

¹⁸He said therefore, 'What is the kingdom of God like? And to what should I compare it? ¹⁹It is like a mustard seed that someone took and sowed in the garden; it grew and became a tree, and the birds of the air made nests in its branches.'

The Parable of the Yeast

²⁰And again he said, 'To what should I compare the kingdom of God? ²¹It is like yeast that a woman took and mixed in withˢ three measures of flour until all of it was leavened.'

---

s Gk *hid in*

The Narrow Door

²²Jesus[t] went through one town and village after another, teaching as he made his way to Jerusalem. ²³Someone asked him, 'Lord, will only a few be saved?' He said to them, ²⁴'Strive to enter through the narrow door; for many, I tell you, will try to enter and will not be able. ²⁵When once the owner of the house has got up and shut the door, and you begin to stand outside and to knock at the door, saying, "Lord, open to us", then in reply he will say to you, "I do not know where you come from." ²⁶Then you will begin to say, "We ate and drank with you, and you taught in our streets." ²⁷But he will say, "I do not know where you come from; go away from me, all you evildoers!" ²⁸There will be weeping and gnashing of teeth when you see Abraham and Isaac and Jacob and all the prophets in the kingdom of God, and you yourselves thrown out. ²⁹Then people will come from east and west, from north and south, and will eat in the kingdom of God. ³⁰Indeed, some are last who will be first, and some are first who will be last.'

The Lament over Jerusalem

³¹At that very hour some Pharisees came and said to him, 'Get away from here, for Herod wants to kill you.' ³²He said to them, 'Go and tell that fox for me,[u] "Listen, I am casting out demons and performing cures today and tomorrow, and on the third day I finish my work. ³³Yet today, tomorrow, and the next day I must be on my way, because it is impossible for a prophet to be killed away from Jerusalem." ³⁴Jerusalem, Jerusalem, the city that kills the prophets and stones those who are sent to it! How often have I desired to gather your children together as a hen gathers her brood under her wings, and you were not willing! ³⁵See, your house is left to you. And I tell you, you will not see me until the time comes when[v] you say, "Blessed is the one who comes in the name of the Lord." '

Jesus Heals the Man with Dropsy

14 On one occasion when Jesus[w] was going to the house of a leader of the Pharisees to eat a meal on the sabbath,

---

t Gk *He*   u Gk lacks *for me*   v Other ancient authorities lack *the time comes when*
w Gk *he*

they were watching him closely. ²Just then, in front of him, there was a man who had dropsy. ³And Jesus asked the lawyers and Pharisees, 'Is it lawful to cure people on the sabbath, or not?' ⁴But they were silent. So Jesusʷ took him and healed him, and sent him away. ⁵Then he said to them, 'If one of you has a childˣ or an ox that has fallen into a well, will you not immediately pull it out on a sabbath day?' ⁶And they could not reply to this.

Humility and Hospitality

⁷When he noticed how the guests chose the places of honour, he told them a parable. ⁸'When you are invited by someone to a wedding banquet, do not sit down at the place of honour, in case someone more distinguished than you has been invited by your host; ⁹and the host who invited both of you may come and say to you, "Give this person your place", and then in disgrace you would start to take the lowest place. ¹⁰But when you are invited, go and sit down at the lowest place, so that when your host comes, he may say to you, "Friend, move up higher"; then you will be honoured in the presence of all who sit at the table with you. ¹¹For all who exalt themselves will be humbled, and those who humble themselves will be exalted.'

¹²He said also to the one who had invited him, 'When you give a luncheon or a dinner, do not invite your friends or your brothers or your relatives or rich neighbours, in case they may invite you in return, and you would be repaid. ¹³But when you give a banquet, invite the poor, the crippled, the lame, and the blind. ¹⁴And you will be blessed, because they cannot repay you, for you will be repaid at the resurrection of the righteous.'

The Parable of the Great Dinner

¹⁵One of the dinner guests, on hearing this, said to him, 'Blessed is anyone who will eat bread in the kingdom of God!' ¹⁶Then Jesusʸ said to him, 'Someone gave a great dinner and invited many. ¹⁷At the time for the dinner he sent his slave to say to those who had been invited, "Come; for everything is ready now." ¹⁸But they all alike began to make excuses. The first said to him, "I have bought a piece of land, and I must

---

w Gk he   x Other ancient authorities read *a donkey*   y Gk he

go out and see it; please accept my apologies." [19]Another said, "I have bought five yoke of oxen, and I am going to try them out; please accept my apologies." [20]Another said, "I have just been married, and therefore I cannot come." [21]So the slave returned and reported this to his master. Then the owner of the house became angry and said to his slave, "Go out at once into the streets and lanes of the town and bring in the poor, the crippled, the blind, and the lame." [22]And the slave said, "Sir, what you ordered has been done, and there is still room." [23]Then the master said to the slave, "Go out into the roads and lanes, and compel people to come in, so that my house may be filled. [24]For I tell you,[z] none of those who were invited will taste my dinner." '

The Cost of Discipleship

[25]Now large crowds were travelling with him; and he turned and said to them, [26]'Whoever comes to me and does not hate father and mother, wife and children, brothers and sisters, yes, and even life itself, cannot be my disciple. [27]Whoever does not carry the cross and follow me cannot be my disciple. [28]For which of you, intending to build a tower, does not first sit down and estimate the cost, to see whether he has enough to complete it? [29]Otherwise, when he has laid a foundation and is not able to finish, all who see it will begin to ridicule him, [30]saying, "This fellow began to build and was not able to finish." [31]Or what king, going out to wage war against another king, will not sit down first and consider whether he is able with ten thousand to oppose the one who comes against him with twenty thousand? [32]If he cannot, then, while the other is still far away, he sends a delegation and asks for the terms of peace. [33]So therefore, none of you can become my disciple if you do not give up all your possessions.

About Salt

[34]'Salt is good; but if salt has lost its taste, how can its saltiness be restored?[a] [35]It is fit neither for the soil nor for the manure heap; they throw it away. Let anyone with ears to hear listen!'

---

z The Greek word for *you* here is plural   a Or *how can it be used for seasoning?*

The Parable of the Lost Sheep

15 Now all the tax-collectors and sinners were coming near to listen to him. [2]And the Pharisees and the scribes were grumbling and saying, 'This fellow welcomes sinners and eats with them.'

[3]So he told them this parable: [4]'Which one of you, having a hundred sheep and losing one of them, does not leave the ninety-nine in the wilderness and go after the one that is lost until he finds it? [5]When he has found it, he lays it on his shoulders and rejoices. [6]And when he comes home, he calls together his friends and neighbours, saying to them, "Rejoice with me, for I have found my sheep that was lost." [7]Just so, I tell you, there will be more joy in heaven over one sinner who repents than over ninety-nine righteous people who need no repentance.

The Parable of the Lost Coin

[8]'Or what woman having ten silver coins,[b] if she loses one of them, does not light a lamp, sweep the house, and search carefully until she finds it? [9]When she has found it, she calls together her friends and neighbours, saying, "Rejoice with me, for I have found the coin that I had lost." [10]Just so, I tell you, there is joy in the presence of the angels of God over one sinner who repents.'

The Parable of the Prodigal and His Brother

[11]Then Jesus[c] said, 'There was a man who had two sons. [12]The younger of them said to his father, "Father, give me the share of the property that will belong to me." So he divided his property between them. [13]A few days later the younger son gathered all he had and travelled to a distant country, and there he squandered his property in dissolute living. [14]When he had spent everything, a severe famine took place throughout that country, and he began to be in need. [15]So he went and hired himself out to one of the citizens of that country, who sent him to his fields to feed the pigs. [16]He would gladly have filled himself with[d] the pods that the pigs were eating; and no one gave him anything. [17]But

---

b Gk *drachmas*, each worth about a day's wage for a labourer   **c** Gk *he*   **d** Other ancient authorities read *filled his stomach with*

when he came to himself he said, "How many of my father's hired hands have bread enough and to spare, but here I am dying of hunger! ¹⁸I will get up and go to my father, and I will say to him, 'Father, I have sinned against heaven and before you; ¹⁹I am no longer worthy to be called your son; treat me like one of your hired hands.' " ²⁰So he set off and went to his father. But while he was still far off, his father saw him and was filled with compassion; he ran and put his arms around him and kissed him. ²¹Then the son said to him, "Father, I have sinned against heaven and before you; I am no longer worthy to be called your son."ᵉ ²²But the father said to his slaves, "Quickly, bring out a robe—the best one—and put it on him; put a ring on his finger and sandals on his feet. ²³And get the fatted calf and kill it, and let us eat and celebrate; ²⁴for this son of mine was dead and is alive again; he was lost and is found!" And they began to celebrate.

²⁵'Now his elder son was in the field; and when he came and approached the house, he heard music and dancing. ²⁶He called one of the slavesᵍ and asked what was going on. ²⁷He replied, "Your brother has come, and your father has killed the fatted calf, because he has got him back safe and sound." ²⁸Then he became angry and refused to go in. His father came out and began to plead with him. ²⁹But he answered his father, "Listen! For all these years I have been working like a slave for you, and I have never disobeyed your command; yet you have never given me even a young goat so that I might celebrate with my friends. ³⁰But when this son of yours came back, who has devoured your property with prostitutes, you killed the fatted calf for him!" ³¹Then the fatherᶠ said to him, "Son, you are always with me, and all that is mine is yours. ³²But we had to celebrate and rejoice, because this brother of yours was dead and has come to life; he was lost and has been found." '

The Parable of the Dishonest Manager

16 Then Jesusᵍ said to the disciples, 'There was a rich man who had a manager, and charges were brought to him that this man was squandering his property. ²So he summoned him and said to him, "What is this that I hear about you? Give me an account of

---

e Other ancient authorities add *Treat me like one of your hired servants*   f Gk *he*   g Gk *he*

your management, because you cannot be my manager any longer."
³Then the manager said to himself, "What will I do, now that my
master is taking the position away from me? I am not strong
enough to dig, and I am ashamed to beg. ⁴I have decided what to
do so that, when I am dismissed as manager, people may welcome
me into their homes." ⁵So, summoning his master's debtors one by
one, he asked the first, "How much do you owe my master?" ⁶He
answered, "A hundred jugs of olive oil." He said to him, "Take your
bill, sit down quickly, and make it fifty." ⁷Then he asked another,
"And how much do you owe?" He replied, "A hundred containers of
wheat." He said to him, "Take your bill and make it eighty." ⁸And
his master commended the dishonest manager because he had
acted shrewdly; for the children of this age are more shrewd in
dealing with their own generation than are the children of light.
⁹And I tell you, make friends for yourselves by means of dishonest
wealth*h* so that when it is gone, they may welcome you into the
eternal homes.*i*

¹⁰'Whoever is faithful in a very little is faithful also in much;
and whoever is dishonest in a very little is dishonest also in much.
¹¹If then you have not been faithful with the dishonest wealth,*j*
who will entrust to you the true riches? ¹²And if you have not
been faithful with what belongs to another, who will give you
what is your own? ¹³No slave can serve two masters; for a slave
will either hate the one and love the other, or be devoted to the
one and despise the other. You cannot serve God and wealth.'*j*

The Law and the Kingdom of God

¹⁴The Pharisees, who were lovers of money, heard all this, and
they ridiculed him. ¹⁵So he said to them, 'You are those who
justify yourselves in the sight of others; but God knows your
hearts; for what is prized by human beings is an abomination
in the sight of God.

¹⁶'The law and the prophets were in effect until John came;
since then the good news of the kingdom of God is proclaimed,
and everyone tries to enter it by force.*k* ¹⁷But it is easier for
heaven and earth to pass away, than for one stroke of a letter
in the law to be dropped.

---

h Gk *mammon*   i Gk *tents*   j Gk *mammon*   k Or *everyone is strongly urged to enter it*

18 'Anyone who divorces his wife and marries another commits adultery, and whoever marries a woman divorced from her husband commits adultery.

The Rich Man and Lazarus

19 'There was a rich man who was dressed in purple and fine linen and who feasted sumptuously every day. 20 And at his gate lay a poor man named Lazarus, covered with sores, 21 who longed to satisfy his hunger with what fell from the rich man's table; even the dogs would come and lick his sores. 22 The poor man died and was carried away by the angels to be with Abraham. *l* The rich man also died and was buried. 23 In Hades, where he was being tormented, he looked up and saw Abraham far away with Lazarus by his side. *m* 24 He called out, "Father Abraham, have mercy on me, and send Lazarus to dip the tip of his finger in water and cool my tongue; for I am in agony in these flames." 25 But Abraham said, "Child, remember that during your lifetime you received your good things, and Lazarus in like manner evil things; but now he is comforted here, and you are in agony. 26 Besides all this, between you and us a great chasm has been fixed, so that those who might want to pass from here to you cannot do so, and no one can cross from there to us." 27 He said, "Then, father, I beg you to send him to my father's house— 28 for I have five brothers—that he may warn them, so that they will not also come into this place of torment." 29 Abraham replied, "They have Moses and the prophets; they should listen to them." 30 He said, "No, father Abraham; but if someone goes to them from the dead, they will repent." 31 He said to him, "If they do not listen to Moses and the prophets, neither will they be convinced even if someone rises from the dead." '

Some Sayings of Jesus

17 Jesus *n* said to his disciples, 'Occasions for stumbling are bound to come, but woe to anyone by whom they come! 2 It would be better for you if a millstone were hung around your neck and you were thrown into the sea than for you to cause one of these little ones to stumble. 3 Be on your guard!

---

l Gk *to Abraham's bosom*   **m** Gk *in his bosom*   **n** Gk *He*

If another disciple^o sins, you must rebuke the offender, and if there is repentance, you must forgive. ⁴And if the same person sins against you seven times a day, and turns back to you seven times and says, "I repent", you must forgive.'

⁵The apostles said to the Lord, 'Increase our faith!' ⁶The Lord replied, 'If you had faith the size of a^p mustard seed, you could say to this mulberry tree, "Be uprooted and planted in the sea", and it would obey you.

⁷'Who among you would say to your slave who has just come in from ploughing or tending sheep in the field, "Come here at once and take your place at the table"? ⁸Would you not rather say to him, "Prepare supper for me, put on your apron and serve me while I eat and drink; later you may eat and drink"? ⁹Do you thank the slave for doing what was commanded? ¹⁰So you also, when you have done all that you were ordered to do, say, "We are worthless slaves; we have done only what we ought to have done!" '

Jesus Cleanses Ten Lepers

¹¹On the way to Jerusalem Jesus^q was going through the region between Samaria and Galilee. ¹²As he entered a village, ten lepers^r approached him. Keeping their distance, ¹³they called out, saying, 'Jesus, Master, have mercy on us!' ¹⁴When he saw them, he said to them, 'Go and show yourselves to the priests.' And as they went, they were made clean. ¹⁵Then one of them, when he saw that he was healed, turned back, praising God with a loud voice. ¹⁶He prostrated himself at Jesus'^s feet and thanked him. And he was a Samaritan. ¹⁷Then Jesus asked, 'Were not ten made clean? But the other nine, where are they? ¹⁸Was none of them found to return and give praise to God except this foreigner?' ¹⁹Then he said to him, 'Get up and go on your way; your faith has made you well.'

The Coming of the Kingdom

²⁰Once Jesus^t was asked by the Pharisees when the kingdom of God was coming, and he answered, 'The kingdom of God is

---

o Gk *your brother*   p Gk *faith as a grain of*   q Gk *he*   r The terms *leper* and *leprosy* can refer to several diseases   s Gk *his*   t Gk *he*

not coming with things that can be observed; ²¹nor will they say, "Look, here it is!" or "There it is!" For, in fact, the kingdom of God is among*u* you.'

²²Then he said to the disciples, 'The days are coming when you will long to see one of the days of the Son of Man, and you will not see it. ²³They will say to you, "Look there!" or "Look here!" Do not go, do not set off in pursuit. ²⁴For as the lightning flashes and lights up the sky from one side to the other, so will the Son of Man be in his day.*v* ²⁵But first he must endure much suffering and be rejected by this generation. ²⁶Just as it was in the days of Noah, so too it will be in the days of the Son of Man. ²⁷They were eating and drinking, and marrying and being given in marriage, until the day Noah entered the ark, and the flood came and destroyed all of them. ²⁸Likewise, just as it was in the days of Lot: they were eating and drinking, buying and selling, planting and building, ²⁹but on the day that Lot left Sodom, it rained fire and sulphur from heaven and destroyed all of them— ³⁰it will be like that on the day that the Son of Man is revealed. ³¹On that day, anyone on the housetop who has belongings in the house must not come down to take them away; and likewise anyone in the field must not turn back. ³²Remember Lot's wife. ³³Those who try to make their life secure will lose it, but those who lose their life will keep it. ³⁴I tell you, on that night there will be two in one bed; one will be taken and the other left. ³⁵There will be two women grinding meal together; one will be taken and the other left.'*w* ³⁷Then they asked him, 'Where, Lord?' He said to them, 'Where the corpse is, there the vultures will gather.'

The Parable of the Widow and the Unjust Judge

18 Then Jesus*x* told them a parable about their need to pray always and not to lose heart. ²He said, 'In a certain city there was a judge who neither feared God nor had respect for people. ³In that city there was a widow who kept coming to him and saying, "Grant me justice against my opponent." ⁴For a while he refused; but later he said to himself, "Though I have

---

u Or *within*   v Other ancient authorities lack *in his day*   w Other ancient authorities add verse 36, *'Two will be in the field; one will be taken and the other left.'*   x Gk *he*

no fear of God and no respect for anyone, 5yet because this widow keeps bothering me, I will grant her justice, so that she may not wear me out by continually coming." 'y 6And the Lord said, 'Listen to what the unjust judge says. 7And will not God grant justice to his chosen ones who cry to him day and night? Will he delay long in helping them? 8I tell you, he will quickly grant justice to them. And yet, when the Son of Man comes, will he find faith on earth?'

The Parable of the Pharisee and the Tax-Collector

9He also told this parable to some who trusted in themselves that they were righteous and regarded others with contempt: 10'Two men went up to the temple to pray, one a Pharisee and the other a tax-collector. 11The Pharisee, standing by himself, was praying thus, "God, I thank you that I am not like other people: thieves, rogues, adulterers, or even like this tax-collector. 12I fast twice a week; I give a tenth of all my income." 13But the tax-collector, standing far off, would not even look up to heaven, but was beating his breast and saying, "God, be merciful to me, a sinner!" 14I tell you, this man went down to his home justified rather than the other; for all who exalt themselves will be humbled, but all who humble themselves will be exalted.'

Jesus Blesses Little Children

15People were bringing even infants to him that he might touch them; and when the disciples saw it, they sternly ordered them not to do it. 16But Jesus called for them and said, 'Let the little children come to me, and do not stop them; for it is to such as these that the kingdom of God belongs. 17Truly I tell you, whoever does not receive the kingdom of God as a little child will never enter it.'

The Rich Ruler

18A certain ruler asked him, 'Good Teacher, what must I do to inherit eternal life?' 19Jesus said to him, 'Why do you call me good? No one is good but God alone. 20You know the commandments:

---

y Or *so that she may not finally come and slap me in the face*

"You shall not commit adultery; You shall not murder; You shall not steal; You shall not bear false witness; Honour your father and mother." ' ²¹He replied, 'I have kept all these since my youth.' ²²When Jesus heard this, he said to him, 'There is still one thing lacking. Sell all that you own and distribute the money* to the poor, and you will have treasure in heaven; then come, follow me.' ²³But when he heard this, he became sad; for he was very rich. ²⁴Jesus looked at him and said, 'How hard it is for those who have wealth to enter the kingdom of God! ²⁵Indeed, it is easier for a camel to go through the eye of a needle than for someone who is rich to enter the kingdom of God.'

²⁶Those who heard it said, 'Then who can be saved?' ²⁷He replied, 'What is impossible for mortals is possible for God.'

²⁸Then Peter said, 'Look, we have left our homes and followed you.' ²⁹And he said to them, 'Truly I tell you, there is no one who has left house or wife or brothers or parents or children, for the sake of the kingdom of God, ³⁰who will not get back very much more in this age, and in the age to come eternal life.'

A Third Time Jesus Foretells His Death and Resurrection

³¹Then he took the twelve aside and said to them, 'See, we are going up to Jerusalem, and everything that is written about the Son of Man by the prophets will be accomplished. ³²For he will be handed over to the Gentiles; and he will be mocked and insulted and spat upon. ³³After they have flogged him, they will kill him, and on the third day he will rise again.' ³⁴But they understood nothing about all these things; in fact, what he said was hidden from them, and they did not grasp what was said.

Jesus Heals a Blind Beggar Near Jericho

³⁵As he approached Jericho, a blind man was sitting by the roadside begging. ³⁶When he heard a crowd going by, he asked what was happening. ³⁷They told him, 'Jesus of Nazareth* is passing by.' ³⁸Then he shouted, 'Jesus, Son of David, have mercy on me!' ³⁹Those who were in front sternly ordered him to be quiet; but he shouted even more loudly, 'Son of David, have mercy on me!' ⁴⁰Jesus stood still and ordered the man to be brought to

---

z Gk lacks *the money*   a Gk *the Nazorean*

him; and when he came near, he asked him, ⁴¹'What do you want me to do for you?' He said, 'Lord, let me see again.' ⁴²Jesus said to him, 'Receive your sight; your faith has saved you.' ⁴³Immediately he regained his sight and followed him, glorifying God; and all the people, when they saw it, praised God.

Jesus and Zacchaeus

19 He entered Jericho and was passing through it. ²A man was there named Zacchaeus; he was a chief tax-collector and was rich. ³He was trying to see who Jesus was, but on account of the crowd he could not, because he was short in stature. ⁴So he ran ahead and climbed a sycamore tree to see him, because he was going to pass that way. ⁵When Jesus came to the place, he looked up and said to him, 'Zacchaeus, hurry and come down; for I must stay at your house today.' ⁶So he hurried down and was happy to welcome him. ⁷All who saw it began to grumble and said, 'He has gone to be the guest of one who is a sinner.' ⁸Zacchaeus stood there and said to the Lord, 'Look, half of my possessions, Lord, I will give to the poor; and if I have defrauded anyone of anything, I will pay back four times as much.' ⁹Then Jesus said to him, 'Today salvation has come to this house, because he too is a son of Abraham. ¹⁰For the Son of Man came to seek out and to save the lost.'

The Parable of the Ten Pounds

¹¹As they were listening to this, he went on to tell a parable, because he was near Jerusalem, and because they supposed that the kingdom of God was to appear immediately. ¹²So he said, 'A nobleman went to a distant country to get royal power for himself and then return. ¹³He summoned ten of his slaves, and gave them ten pounds,^b and said to them, "Do business with these until I come back." ¹⁴But the citizens of his country hated him and sent a delegation after him, saying, "We do not want this man to rule over us." ¹⁵When he returned, having received royal power, he ordered these slaves, to whom he had given the money, to be summoned so that he might find out what they had gained by trading. ¹⁶The first came forward and said, "Lord,

---

b The mina, rendered here by *pound*, was about three months' wages for a labourer

your pound has made ten more pounds." ¹⁷He said to him, "Well done, good slave! Because you have been trustworthy in a very small thing, take charge of ten cities." ¹⁸Then the second came, saying, "Lord, your pound has made five pounds." ¹⁹He said to him, "And you, rule over five cities." ²⁰Then the other came, saying, "Lord, here is your pound. I wrapped it up in a piece of cloth, ²¹for I was afraid of you, because you are a harsh man; you take what you did not deposit, and reap what you did not sow." ²²He said to him, "I will judge you by your own words, you wicked slave! You knew, did you, that I was a harsh man, taking what I did not deposit and reaping what I did not sow? ²³Why then did you not put my money into the bank? Then when I returned, I could have collected it with interest." ²⁴He said to the bystanders, "Take the pound from him and give it to the one who has ten pounds." ²⁵(And they said to him, "Lord, he has ten pounds!") ²⁶"I tell you, to all those who have, more will be given; but from those who have nothing, even what they have will be taken away. ²⁷But as for these enemies of mine who did not want me to be king over them—bring them here and slaughter them in my presence." '

Jesus' Triumphal Entry into Jerusalem

²⁸After he had said this, he went on ahead, going up to Jerusalem.

²⁹When he had come near Bethphage and Bethany, at the place called the Mount of Olives, he sent two of the disciples, ³⁰saying, 'Go into the village ahead of you, and as you enter it you will find tied there a colt that has never been ridden. Untie it and bring it here. ³¹If anyone asks you, "Why are you untying it?" just say this: "The Lord needs it." ' ³²So those who were sent departed and found it as he had told them. ³³As they were untying the colt, its owners asked them, 'Why are you untying the colt?' ³⁴They said, 'The Lord needs it.' ³⁵Then they brought it to Jesus; and after throwing their cloaks on the colt, they set Jesus on it. ³⁶As he rode along, people kept spreading their cloaks on the road. ³⁷As he was now approaching the path down from the Mount of Olives, the whole multitude of the disciples began to praise God joyfully with a loud voice for all the deeds of power that they had seen, ³⁸saying,

'Blessed is the king
    who comes in the name of the Lord!
  Peace in heaven,
    and glory in the highest heaven!'

39 Some of the Pharisees in the crowd said to him, 'Teacher, order your disciples to stop.' 40 He answered, 'I tell you, if these were silent, the stones would shout out.'

Jesus Weeps over Jerusalem

41 As he came near and saw the city, he wept over it, 42 saying, 'If you, even you, had only recognized on this day the things that make for peace! But now they are hidden from your eyes. 43 Indeed, the days will come upon you, when your enemies will set up ramparts around you and surround you, and hem you in on every side. 44 They will crush you to the ground, you and your children within you, and they will not leave within you one stone upon another; because you did not recognize the time of your visitation from God.'c

Jesus Cleanses the Temple

45 Then he entered the temple and began to drive out those who were selling things there; 46 and he said, 'It is written,

    "My house shall be a house of prayer";
      but you have made it a den of robbers.'

47 Every day he was teaching in the temple. The chief priests, the scribes, and the leaders of the people kept looking for a way to kill him; 48 but they did not find anything they could do, for all the people were spellbound by what they heard.

The Authority of Jesus Questioned

20 One day, as he was teaching the people in the temple and telling the good news, the chief priests and the scribes came with the elders 2 and said to him, 'Tell us, by what authority are you doing these things? Who is it who gave you this authority?' 3 He answered them, 'I will also ask you a question, and you tell me: 4 Did the baptism of John come from heaven, or was it of human origin?' 5 They discussed it with one another,

---

c Gk lacks *from God*

saying, 'If we say, "From heaven", he will say, "Why did you not believe him?" ⁶But if we say, "Of human origin", all the people will stone us; for they are convinced that John was a prophet.' ⁷So they answered that they did not know where it came from. ⁸Then Jesus said to them, 'Neither will I tell you by what authority I am doing these things.'

The Parable of the Wicked Tenants

⁹He began to tell the people this parable: 'A man planted a vineyard, and leased it to tenants, and went to another country for a long time. ¹⁰When the season came, he sent a slave to the tenants in order that they might give him his share of the produce of the vineyard; but the tenants beat him and sent him away empty-handed. ¹¹Next he sent another slave; that one also they beat and insulted and sent away empty-handed. ¹²And he sent yet a third; this one also they wounded and threw out. ¹³Then the owner of the vineyard said, "What shall I do? I will send my beloved son; perhaps they will respect him." ¹⁴But when the tenants saw him, they discussed it among themselves and said, "This is the heir; let us kill him so that the inheritance may be ours." ¹⁵So they threw him out of the vineyard and killed him. What then will the owner of the vineyard do to them? ¹⁶He will come and destroy those tenants and give the vineyard to others.' When they heard this, they said, 'Heaven forbid!' ¹⁷But he looked at them and said, 'What then does this text mean:

"The stone that the builders rejected
    has become the cornerstone"?ᵈ

¹⁸Everyone who falls on that stone will be broken to pieces; and it will crush anyone on whom it falls.' ¹⁹When the scribes and chief priests realized that he had told this parable against them, they wanted to lay hands on him at that very hour, but they feared the people.

The Question about Paying Taxes

²⁰So they watched him and sent spies who pretended to be honest, in order to trap him by what he said, so as to hand him over to the jurisdiction and authority of the governor. ²¹So they

---

d Or keystone

asked him, 'Teacher, we know that you are right in what you say and teach, and you show deference to no one, but teach the way of God in accordance with truth. ²²Is it lawful for us to pay taxes to the emperor, or not?' ²³But he perceived their craftiness and said to them, ²⁴'Show me a denarius. Whose head and whose title does it bear?' They said, 'The emperor's.' ²⁵He said to them, 'Then give to the emperor the things that are the emperor's, and to God the things that are God's.' ²⁶And they were not able in the presence of the people to trap him by what he said; and being amazed by his answer, they became silent.

The Question about the Resurrection

²⁷Some Sadducees, those who say there is no resurrection, came to him ²⁸and asked him a question, 'Teacher, Moses wrote for us that if a man's brother dies, leaving a wife but no children, the man*e* shall marry the widow and raise up children for his brother. ²⁹Now there were seven brothers; the first married, and died childless; ³⁰then the second ³¹and the third married her, and so in the same way all seven died childless. ³²Finally the woman also died. ³³In the resurrection, therefore, whose wife will the woman be? For the seven had married her.'

³⁴Jesus said to them, 'Those who belong to this age marry and are given in marriage; ³⁵but those who are considered worthy of a place in that age and in the resurrection from the dead neither marry nor are given in marriage. ³⁶Indeed they cannot die any more, because they are like angels and are children of God, being children of the resurrection. ³⁷And the fact that the dead are raised Moses himself showed, in the story about the bush, where he speaks of the Lord as the God of Abraham, the God of Isaac, and the God of Jacob. ³⁸Now he is God not of the dead, but of the living; for to him all of them are alive.' ³⁹Then some of the scribes answered, 'Teacher, you have spoken well.' ⁴⁰For they no longer dared to ask him another question.

The Question about David's Son

⁴¹Then he said to them, 'How can they say that the Messiah*f* is David's son? ⁴²For David himself says in the book of Psalms,

---

e Gk *his brother*   f Or *the Christ*

"The Lord said to my Lord,
  'Sit at my right hand,
43   until I make your enemies your footstool.' "
44David thus calls him Lord; so how can he be his son?'

Jesus Denounces the Scribes

45In the hearing of all the people he said to theᵍ disciples,
46'Beware of the scribes, who like to walk around in long robes,
and love to be greeted with respect in the market-places, and
to have the best seats in the synagogues and places of honour
at banquets. 47They devour widows' houses and for the sake
of appearance say long prayers. They will receive the greater
condemnation.'

The Widow's Offering

21 He looked up and saw rich people putting their gifts into
the treasury; 2he also saw a poor widow put in two small
copper coins. 3He said, 'Truly I tell you, this poor widow has put
in more than all of them; 4for all of them have contributed out
of their abundance, but she out of her poverty has put in all she
had to live on.'

The Destruction of the Temple Foretold

5When some were speaking about the temple, how it was
adorned with beautiful stones and gifts dedicated to God, he
said, 6'As for these things that you see, the days will come when
not one stone will be left upon another; all will be thrown down.'

Signs and Persecutions

7They asked him, 'Teacher, when will this be, and what will be
the sign that this is about to take place?' 8And he said, 'Beware
that you are not led astray; for many will come in my name and
say, "I am he!"ʰ and, "The time is near!"ⁱ Do not go after them.
9'When you hear of wars and insurrections, do not be
terrified; for these things must take place first, but the end
will not follow immediately.' 10Then he said to them, 'Nation
will rise against nation, and kingdom against kingdom; 11there

g Other ancient authorities read *his*   h Gk *I am*   i Or *at hand* will be great earthquakes, and in various places famines and plagues; and there will be dreadful portents and great signs from heaven.

¹²'But before all this occurs, they will arrest you and persecute you; they will hand you over to synagogues and prisons, and you will be brought before kings and governors because of my name. ¹³This will give you an opportunity to testify. ¹⁴So make up your minds not to prepare your defence in advance; ¹⁵for I will give you words^j and a wisdom that none of your opponents will be able to withstand or contradict. ¹⁶You will be betrayed even by parents and brothers, by relatives and friends; and they will put some of you to death. ¹⁷You will be hated by all because of my name. ¹⁸But not a hair of your head will perish. ¹⁹By your endurance you will gain your souls.

The Destruction of Jerusalem Foretold

²⁰'When you see Jerusalem surrounded by armies, then know that its desolation has come near.^k ²¹Then those in Judea must flee to the mountains, and those inside the city must leave it, and those out in the country must not enter it; ²²for these are days of vengeance, as a fulfilment of all that is written. ²³Woe to those who are pregnant and to those who are nursing infants in those days! For there will be great distress on the earth and wrath against this people; ²⁴they will fall by the edge of the sword and be taken away as captives among all nations; and Jerusalem will be trampled on by the Gentiles, until the times of the Gentiles are fulfilled.

The Coming of the Son of Man

²⁵'There will be signs in the sun, the moon, and the stars, and on the earth distress among nations confused by the roaring of the sea and the waves. ²⁶People will faint from fear and foreboding of what is coming upon the world, for the powers of the heavens will be shaken. ²⁷Then they will see "the Son of Man coming in a cloud" with power and great glory. ²⁸Now when these things begin to take place, stand up and raise your heads, because your redemption is drawing near.'

---

j Gk *a mouth*   k Or *is at hand*

The Lesson of the Fig Tree

²⁹ Then he told them a parable: 'Look at the fig tree and all the trees; ³⁰ as soon as they sprout leaves you can see for yourselves and know that summer is already near. ³¹ So also, when you see these things taking place, you know that the kingdom of God is near. ³² Truly I tell you, this generation will not pass away until all things have taken place. ³³ Heaven and earth will pass away, but my words will not pass away.

Exhortation to Watch

³⁴ 'Be on guard so that your hearts are not weighed down with dissipation and drunkenness and the worries of this life, and that day does not catch you unexpectedly, ³⁵ like a trap. For it will come upon all who live on the face of the whole earth. ³⁶ Be alert at all times, praying that you may have the strength to escape all these things that will take place, and to stand before the Son of Man.'

³⁷ Every day he was teaching in the temple, and at night he would go out and spend the night on the Mount of Olives, as it was called. ³⁸ And all the people would get up early in the morning to listen to him in the temple.

The Plot to Kill Jesus

22 Now the festival of Unleavened Bread, which is called the Passover, was near. ² The chief priests and the scribes were looking for a way to put Jesus[l] to death, for they were afraid of the people.

³ Then Satan entered into Judas called Iscariot, who was one of the twelve; ⁴ he went away and conferred with the chief priests and officers of the temple police about how he might betray him to them. ⁵ They were greatly pleased and agreed to give him money. ⁶ So he consented and began to look for an opportunity to betray him to them when no crowd was present.

The Preparation of the Passover

⁷ Then came the day of Unleavened Bread, on which the Passover lamb had to be sacrificed. ⁸ So Jesus[m] sent Peter and

---

l Gk *him*   m Gk *he*

John, saying, 'Go and prepare the Passover meal for us that we may eat it.' ⁹They asked him, 'Where do you want us to make preparations for it?' ¹⁰'Listen,' he said to them, 'when you have entered the city, a man carrying a jar of water will meet you; follow him into the house he enters ¹¹and say to the owner of the house, "The teacher asks you, 'Where is the guest room, where I may eat the Passover with my disciples?' " ¹²He will show you a large room upstairs, already furnished. Make preparations for us there.' ¹³So they went and found everything as he had told them; and they prepared the Passover meal.

The Institution of the Lord's Supper

¹⁴When the hour came, he took his place at the table, and the apostles with him. ¹⁵He said to them, 'I have eagerly desired to eat this Passover with you before I suffer; ¹⁶for I tell you, I will not eat it*ⁿ* until it is fulfilled in the kingdom of God.' ¹⁷Then he took a cup, and after giving thanks he said, 'Take this and divide it among yourselves; ¹⁸for I tell you that from now on I will not drink of the fruit of the vine until the kingdom of God comes.' ¹⁹Then he took a loaf of bread, and when he had given thanks, he broke it and gave it to them, saying, 'This is my body, which is given for you. Do this in remembrance of me.' ²⁰And he did the same with the cup after supper, saying, 'This cup that is poured out for you is the new covenant in my blood.*º* ²¹But see, the one who betrays me is with me, and his hand is on the table. ²²For the Son of Man is going as it has been determined, but woe to that one by whom he is betrayed!' ²³Then they began to ask one another which one of them it could be who would do this.

The Dispute about Greatness

²⁴A dispute also arose among them as to which one of them was to be regarded as the greatest. ²⁵But he said to them, 'The kings of the Gentiles lord it over them; and those in authority over them are called benefactors. ²⁶But not so with you; rather the greatest among you must become like the youngest, and the leader like one who serves. ²⁷For who is greater, the one who is

---

n Other ancient authorities read *never eat it again*   o Other ancient authorities lack, in whole or in part, verses 19b-20 (*which is given...in my blood*)

at the table or the one who serves? Is it not the one at the table? But I am among you as one who serves.

28 'You are those who have stood by me in my trials; 29 and I confer on you, just as my Father has conferred on me, a kingdom, 30 so that you may eat and drink at my table in my kingdom, and you will sit on thrones judging the twelve tribes of Israel.

Jesus Predicts Peter's Denial

31 'Simon, Simon, listen! Satan has demanded*p* to sift all of you like wheat, 32 but I have prayed for you that your own faith may not fail; and you, when once you have turned back, strengthen your brothers.' 33 And he said to him, 'Lord, I am ready to go with you to prison and to death!' 34 Jesus*q* said, 'I tell you, Peter, the cock will not crow this day, until you have denied three times that you know me.'

Purse, Bag, and Sword

35 He said to them, 'When I sent you out without a purse, bag, or sandals, did you lack anything?' They said, 'No, not a thing.' 36 He said to them, 'But now, the one who has a purse must take it, and likewise a bag. And the one who has no sword must sell his cloak and buy one. 37 For I tell you, this scripture must be fulfilled in me, "And he was counted among the lawless"; and indeed what is written about me is being fulfilled.' 38 They said, 'Lord, look, here are two swords.' He replied, 'It is enough.'

Jesus Prays on the Mount of Olives

39 He came out and went, as was his custom, to the Mount of Olives; and the disciples followed him. 40 When he reached the place, he said to them, 'Pray that you may not come into the time of trial.'*r* 41 Then he withdrew from them about a stone's throw, knelt down, and prayed, 42 'Father, if you are willing, remove this cup from me; yet, not my will but yours be done.' [43 Then an angel from heaven appeared to him and gave him strength. 44 In his anguish he prayed more earnestly, and his sweat became like great drops of blood falling down on the ground.]*s* 45 When he got

---

p Or *has obtained permission*   q Gk *He*   r Or *into temptation*   s Other ancient authorities lack verses 43 and 44

up from prayer, he came to the disciples and found them sleeping because of grief, ⁴⁶and he said to them, 'Why are you sleeping? Get up and pray that you may not come into the time of trial.'ᵗ

The Betrayal and Arrest of Jesus

⁴⁷While he was still speaking, suddenly a crowd came, and the one called Judas, one of the twelve, was leading them. He approached Jesus to kiss him; ⁴⁸but Jesus said to him, 'Judas, is it with a kiss that you are betraying the Son of Man?' ⁴⁹When those who were around him saw what was coming, they asked, 'Lord, should we strike with the sword?' ⁵⁰Then one of them struck the slave of the high priest and cut off his right ear. ⁵¹But Jesus said, 'No more of this!' And he touched his ear and healed him. ⁵²Then Jesus said to the chief priests, the officers of the temple police, and the elders who had come for him, 'Have you come out with swords and clubs as if I were a bandit? ⁵³When I was with you day after day in the temple, you did not lay hands on me. But this is your hour, and the power of darkness!'

Peter Denies Jesus

⁵⁴Then they seized him and led him away, bringing him into the high priest's house. But Peter was following at a distance. ⁵⁵When they had kindled a fire in the middle of the courtyard and sat down together, Peter sat among them. ⁵⁶Then a servant-girl, seeing him in the firelight, stared at him and said, 'This man also was with him.' ⁵⁷But he denied it, saying, 'Woman, I do not know him.' ⁵⁸A little later someone else, on seeing him, said, 'You also are one of them.' But Peter said, 'Man, I am not!' ⁵⁹Then about an hour later yet another kept insisting, 'Surely this man also was with him; for he is a Galilean.' ⁶⁰But Peter said, 'Man, I do not know what you are talking about!' At that moment, while he was still speaking, the cock crowed. ⁶¹The Lord turned and looked at Peter. Then Peter remembered the word of the Lord, how he had said to him, 'Before the cock crows today, you will deny me three times.' ⁶²And he went out and wept bitterly.

---

t Or *into temptation*

The Mocking and Beating of Jesus

⁶³Now the men who were holding Jesus began to mock him and beat him; ⁶⁴they also blindfolded him and kept asking him, 'Prophesy! Who is it that struck you?' ⁶⁵They kept heaping many other insults on him.

Jesus before the Council

⁶⁶When day came, the assembly of the elders of the people, both chief priests and scribes, gathered together, and they brought him to their council. ⁶⁷They said, 'If you are the Messiah,ᵘ tell us.' He replied, 'If I tell you, you will not believe; ⁶⁸and if I question you, you will not answer. ⁶⁹But from now on the Son of Man will be seated at the right hand of the power of God.' ⁷⁰All of them asked, 'Are you, then, the Son of God?' He said to them, 'You say that I am.' ⁷¹Then they said, 'What further testimony do we need? We have heard it ourselves from his own lips!'

Jesus before Pilate

23 Then the assembly rose as a body and brought Jesusᵛ before Pilate. ²They began to accuse him, saying, 'We found this man perverting our nation, forbidding us to pay taxes to the emperor, and saying that he himself is the Messiah, a king.'ʷ ³Then Pilate asked him, 'Are you the king of the Jews?' He answered, 'You say so.' ⁴Then Pilate said to the chief priests and the crowds, 'I find no basis for an accusation against this man.' ⁵But they were insistent and said, 'He stirs up the people by teaching throughout all Judea, from Galilee where he began even to this place.'

Jesus before Herod

⁶When Pilate heard this, he asked whether the man was a Galilean. ⁷And when he learned that he was under Herod's jurisdiction, he sent him off to Herod, who was himself in Jerusalem at that time. ⁸When Herod saw Jesus, he was very glad, for he had been wanting to see him for a long time, because he had heard about him and was hoping to see him perform some sign. ⁹He questioned him at some length, but Jesusˣ gave

---

u Or the Christ   v Gk him   w Or is an anointed king   x Gk he

him no answer. ¹⁰The chief priests and the scribes stood by, vehemently accusing him. ¹¹Even Herod with his soldiers treated him with contempt and mocked him; then he put an elegant robe on him, and sent him back to Pilate. ¹²That same day Herod and Pilate became friends with each other; before this they had been enemies.

Jesus Sentenced to Death

¹³Pilate then called together the chief priests, the leaders, and the people, ¹⁴and said to them, 'You brought me this man as one who was perverting the people; and here I have examined him in your presence and have not found this man guilty of any of your charges against him. ¹⁵Neither has Herod, for he sent him back to us. Indeed, he has done nothing to deserve death. ¹⁶I will therefore have him flogged and release him.'ʸ

¹⁸Then they all shouted out together, 'Away with this fellow! Release Barabbas for us!' ¹⁹(This was a man who had been put in prison for an insurrection that had taken place in the city, and for murder.) ²⁰Pilate, wanting to release Jesus, addressed them again; ²¹but they kept shouting, 'Crucify, crucify him!' ²²A third time he said to them, 'Why, what evil has he done? I have found in him no ground for the sentence of death; I will therefore have him flogged and then release him.' ²³But they kept urgently demanding with loud shouts that he should be crucified; and their voices prevailed. ²⁴So Pilate gave his verdict that their demand should be granted. ²⁵He released the man they asked for, the one who had been put in prison for insurrection and murder, and he handed Jesus over as they wished.

The Crucifixion of Jesus

²⁶As they led him away, they seized a man, Simon of Cyrene, who was coming from the country, and they laid the cross on him, and made him carry it behind Jesus. ²⁷A great number of the people followed him, and among them were women who were beating their breasts and wailing for him. ²⁸But Jesus turned to them and said, 'Daughters of Jerusalem, do not weep for me, but

---

y Here, or after verse 19, other ancient authorities add verse 17, *Now he was obliged to release someone for them at the festival*

weep for yourselves and for your children. 29 For the days are surely coming when they will say, "Blessed are the barren, and the wombs that never bore, and the breasts that never nursed." 30 Then they will begin to say to the mountains, "Fall on us"; and to the hills, "Cover us." 31 For if they do this when the wood is green, what will happen when it is dry?'

32 Two others also, who were criminals, were led away to be put to death with him. 33 When they came to the place that is called The Skull, they crucified Jesus*z* there with the criminals, one on his right and one on his left. 34 Then Jesus said, 'Father, forgive them; for they do not know what they are doing.'*a* And they cast lots to divide his clothing. 35 And the people stood by, watching; but the leaders scoffed at him, saying, 'He saved others; let him save himself if he is the Messiah*b* of God, his chosen one!' 36 The soldiers also mocked him, coming up and offering him sour wine, 37 and saying, 'If you are the King of the Jews, save yourself!' 38 There was also an inscription over him,*c* 'This is the King of the Jews.'

39 One of the criminals who were hanged there kept deriding*d* him and saying, 'Are you not the Messiah?*e* Save yourself and us!' 40 But the other rebuked him, saying, 'Do you not fear God, since you are under the same sentence of condemnation? 41 And we indeed have been condemned justly, for we are getting what we deserve for our deeds, but this man has done nothing wrong.' 42 Then he said, 'Jesus, remember me when you come into*f* your kingdom.' 43 He replied, 'Truly I tell you, today you will be with me in Paradise.'

The Death of Jesus

44 It was now about noon, and darkness came over the whole land*g* until three in the afternoon, 45 while the sun's light failed;*h* and the curtain of the temple was torn in two. 46 Then Jesus, crying with a loud voice, said, 'Father, into your hands I commend my spirit.' Having said this, he breathed his last. 47 When the centurion saw what had taken place, he praised God and said,

---

z Gk *him*   a Other ancient authorities lack the sentence *Then Jesus...what they are doing*
b Or *the Christ*   c Other ancient authorities add *written in Greek and Latin and Hebrew* (that is, *Aramaic*)   d Or *blaspheming*   e Or *the Christ*   f Other ancient authorities read *in*
g Or *earth*   h Or *the sun was eclipsed.* Other ancient authorities read *the sun was darkened*

'Certainly this man was innocent.'[i] 48 And when all the crowds who had gathered there for this spectacle saw what had taken place, they returned home, beating their breasts. 49 But all his acquaintances, including the women who had followed him from Galilee, stood at a distance, watching these things.

The Burial of Jesus

50 Now there was a good and righteous man named Joseph, who, though a member of the council, 51 had not agreed to their plan and action. He came from the Jewish town of Arimathea, and he was waiting expectantly for the kingdom of God. 52 This man went to Pilate and asked for the body of Jesus. 53 Then he took it down, wrapped it in a linen cloth, and laid it in a rock-hewn tomb where no one had ever been laid. 54 It was the day of Preparation, and the sabbath was beginning.[j] 55 The women who had come with him from Galilee followed, and they saw the tomb and how his body was laid. 56 Then they returned, and prepared spices and ointments.

On the sabbath they rested according to the commandment.

The Resurrection of Jesus

24 But on the first day of the week, at early dawn, they came to the tomb, taking the spices that they had prepared. 2 They found the stone rolled away from the tomb, 3 but when they went in, they did not find the body.[k] 4 While they were perplexed about this, suddenly two men in dazzling clothes stood beside them. 5 The women[l] were terrified and bowed their faces to the ground, but the men[m] said to them, 'Why do you look for the living among the dead? He is not here, but has risen.[n] 6 Remember how he told you, while he was still in Galilee, 7 that the Son of Man must be handed over to sinners, and be crucified, and on the third day rise again.' 8 Then they remembered his words, 9 and returning from the tomb, they told all this to the eleven and to all the rest. 10 Now it was Mary Magdalene, Joanna, Mary the mother of James, and the other women with them who told this to the apostles. 11 But these words seemed to them

---

i Or *righteous*   j Gk *was dawning*   k Other ancient authorities add *of the Lord Jesus*
l Gk *They*   m Gk *but they*   n Other ancient authorities lack *He is not here, but has risen*

an idle tale, and they did not believe them. [12]But Peter got up and ran to the tomb; stooping and looking in, he saw the linen cloths by themselves; then he went home, amazed at what had happened.[o]

The Walk to Emmaus

[13]Now on that same day two of them were going to a village called Emmaus, about seven miles[p] from Jerusalem, [14]and talking with each other about all these things that had happened. [15]While they were talking and discussing, Jesus himself came near and went with them, [16]but their eyes were kept from recognizing him. [17]And he said to them, 'What are you discussing with each other while you walk along?' They stood still, looking sad.[q] [18]Then one of them, whose name was Cleopas, answered him, 'Are you the only stranger in Jerusalem who does not know the things that have taken place there in these days?' [19]He asked them, 'What things?' They replied, 'The things about Jesus of Nazareth,[r] who was a prophet mighty in deed and word before God and all the people, [20]and how our chief priests and leaders handed him over to be condemned to death and crucified him. [21]But we had hoped that he was the one to redeem Israel.[s] Yes, and besides all this, it is now the third day since these things took place. [22]Moreover, some women of our group astounded us. They were at the tomb early this morning, [23]and when they did not find his body there, they came back and told us that they had indeed seen a vision of angels who said that he was alive. [24]Some of those who were with us went to the tomb and found it just as the women had said; but they did not see him.' [25]Then he said to them, 'Oh, how foolish you are, and how slow of heart to believe all that the prophets have declared! [26]Was it not necessary that the Messiah[t] should suffer these things and then enter into his glory?' [27]Then beginning with Moses and all the prophets, he interpreted to them the things about himself in all the scriptures.

[28]As they came near the village to which they were going, he walked ahead as if he were going on. [29]But they urged him

---

o Other ancient authorities lack verse 12   p Gk *sixty stadia*; other ancient authorities read *a hundred and sixty stadia*   q Other ancient authorities read *walk along, looking sad?'*
r Other ancient authorities read *Jesus the Nazorean*   s Or *to set Israel free*   t Or *the Christ*

strongly, saying, 'Stay with us, because it is almost evening and the day is now nearly over.' So he went in to stay with them. ³⁰When he was at the table with them, he took bread, blessed and broke it, and gave it to them. ³¹Then their eyes were opened, and they recognized him; and he vanished from their sight. ³²They said to each other, 'Were not our hearts burning within us*u* while he was talking to us on the road, while he was opening the scriptures to us?' ³³That same hour they got up and returned to Jerusalem; and they found the eleven and their companions gathered together. ³⁴They were saying, 'The Lord has risen indeed, and he has appeared to Simon!' ³⁵Then they told what had happened on the road, and how he had been made known to them in the breaking of the bread.

Jesus Appears to His Disciples

³⁶While they were talking about this, Jesus himself stood among them and said to them, 'Peace be with you.'*v* ³⁷They were startled and terrified, and thought that they were seeing a ghost. ³⁸He said to them, 'Why are you frightened, and why do doubts arise in your hearts? ³⁹Look at my hands and my feet; see that it is I myself. Touch me and see; for a ghost does not have flesh and bones as you see that I have.' ⁴⁰And when he had said this, he showed them his hands and his feet.*w* ⁴¹While in their joy they were disbelieving and still wondering, he said to them, 'Have you anything here to eat?' ⁴²They gave him a piece of broiled fish, ⁴³and he took it and ate in their presence.

⁴⁴Then he said to them, 'These are my words that I spoke to you while I was still with you—that everything written about me in the law of Moses, the prophets, and the psalms must be fulfilled.' ⁴⁵Then he opened their minds to understand the scriptures, ⁴⁶and he said to them, 'Thus it is written, that the Messiah*x* is to suffer and to rise from the dead on the third day, ⁴⁷and that repentance and forgiveness of sins is to be proclaimed in his name to all nations, beginning from Jerusalem. ⁴⁸You are witnesses*y* of these things. ⁴⁹And see, I am sending upon you

---

u Other ancient authorities lack *within us*   v Other ancient authorities lack *and said to them, 'Peace be with you.'*   w Other ancient authorities lack verse 40   x Or *the Christ*   y Or *nations. Beginning from Jerusalem* ⁴⁸ *you are witnesses*

what my Father promised; so stay here in the city until you have been clothed with power from on high.'

The Ascension of Jesus

⁵⁰Then he led them out as far as Bethany, and, lifting up his hands, he blessed them. ⁵¹While he was blessing them, he withdrew from them and was carried up into heaven.ᶻ ⁵²And they worshipped him, andᵃ returned to Jerusalem with great joy; ⁵³and they were continually in the temple blessing God.ᵇ

---

z Other ancient authorities lack *and was carried up into heaven*   a Other ancient authorities lack *worshipped him, and*   b Other ancient authorities add *Amen*

The Gospel According to

John

The Word Became Flesh

1 In the beginning was the Word, and the Word was with God, and the Word was God. [2] He was in the beginning with God. [3] All things came into being through him, and without him not one thing came into being. What has come into being [4] in him was life,[a] and the life was the light of all people. [5] The light shines in the darkness, and the darkness did not overcome it.

[6] There was a man sent from God, whose name was John. [7] He came as a witness to testify to the light, so that all might believe through him. [8] He himself was not the light, but he came to testify to the light. [9] The true light, which enlightens everyone, was coming into the world.[b]

[10] He was in the world, and the world came into being through him; yet the world did not know him. [11] He came to what was his own,[c] and his own people did not accept him. [12] But to all who received him, who believed in his name, he gave power to become children of God, [13] who were born, not of blood or of the will of the flesh or of the will of man, but of God.

[14] And the Word became flesh and lived among us, and we have seen his glory, the glory as of a father's only son,[d] full of grace and truth. [15] (John testified to him and cried out, 'This was he of whom I said, "He who comes after me ranks ahead of me because he was before me." ') [16] From his fullness we have all received,

---

a Or [3] *through him. And without him not one thing came into being that has come into being.*
[4] *In him was life*   b Or *He was the true light that enlightens everyone coming into the world*
c Or *to his own home*   d Or *the Father's only Son*

grace upon grace. ¹⁷The law indeed was given through Moses; grace and truth came through Jesus Christ. ¹⁸No one has ever seen God. It is God the only Son,ᵉ who is close to the Father's heart,ᶠ who has made him known.

The Testimony of John the Baptist

¹⁹This is the testimony given by John when the Jews sent priests and Levites from Jerusalem to ask him, 'Who are you?' ²⁰He confessed and did not deny it, but confessed, 'I am not the Messiah.'ᵍ ²¹And they asked him, 'What then? Are you Elijah?' He said, 'I am not.' 'Are you the prophet?' He answered, 'No.' ²²Then they said to him, 'Who are you? Let us have an answer for those who sent us. What do you say about yourself?' ²³He said,

'I am the voice of one crying out in the wilderness,
   "Make straight the way of the Lord" ',

as the prophet Isaiah said.

²⁴Now they had been sent from the Pharisees. ²⁵They asked him, 'Why then are you baptizing if you are neither the Messiah,ᵍ nor Elijah, nor the prophet?' ²⁶John answered them, 'I baptize with water. Among you stands one whom you do not know, ²⁷the one who is coming after me; I am not worthy to untie the thong of his sandal.' ²⁸This took place in Bethany across the Jordan where John was baptizing.

The Lamb of God

²⁹The next day he saw Jesus coming towards him and declared, 'Here is the Lamb of God who takes away the sin of the world! ³⁰This is he of whom I said, "After me comes a man who ranks ahead of me because he was before me." ³¹I myself did not know him; but I came baptizing with water for this reason, that he might be revealed to Israel.' ³²And John testified, 'I saw the Spirit descending from heaven like a dove, and it remained on him. ³³I myself did not know him, but the one who sent me to baptize with water said to me, "He on whom you see the Spirit descend and remain is the one who baptizes with the Holy Spirit." ³⁴And I myself have seen and have testified that this is the Son of God.'ʰ

---

e Other ancient authorities read *It is an only Son, God*, or *It is the only Son*   f Gk *bosom*
g Or *the Christ*   h Other ancient authorities read *is God's chosen one*

The First Disciples of Jesus

35 The next day John again was standing with two of his disciples, 36 and as he watched Jesus walk by, he exclaimed, 'Look, here is the Lamb of God!' 37 The two disciples heard him say this, and they followed Jesus. 38 When Jesus turned and saw them following, he said to them, 'What are you looking for?' They said to him, 'Rabbi' (which translated means Teacher), 'where are you staying?' 39 He said to them, 'Come and see.' They came and saw where he was staying, and they remained with him that day. It was about four o'clock in the afternoon. 40 One of the two who heard John speak and followed him was Andrew, Simon Peter's brother. 41 He first found his brother Simon and said to him, 'We have found the Messiah' (which is translated Anointed[i]). 42 He brought Simon[j] to Jesus, who looked at him and said, 'You are Simon son of John. You are to be called Cephas' (which is translated Peter[k]).

Jesus Calls Philip and Nathanael

43 The next day Jesus decided to go to Galilee. He found Philip and said to him, 'Follow me.' 44 Now Philip was from Bethsaida, the city of Andrew and Peter. 45 Philip found Nathanael and said to him, 'We have found him about whom Moses in the law and also the prophets wrote, Jesus son of Joseph from Nazareth.' 46 Nathanael said to him, 'Can anything good come out of Nazareth?' Philip said to him, 'Come and see.' 47 When Jesus saw Nathanael coming towards him, he said of him, 'Here is truly an Israelite in whom there is no deceit!' 48 Nathanael asked him, 'Where did you come to know me?' Jesus answered, 'I saw you under the fig tree before Philip called you.' 49 Nathanael replied, 'Rabbi, you are the Son of God! You are the King of Israel!' 50 Jesus answered, 'Do you believe because I told you that I saw you under the fig tree? You will see greater things than these.' 51 And he said to him, 'Very truly, I tell you,[l] you will see heaven opened and the angels of God ascending and descending upon the Son of Man.'

---

i Or Christ   j Gk him   k From the word for rock in Aramaic (kepha) and Greek (petra), respectively   l Both instances of the Greek word for you in this verse are plural

The Wedding at Cana

2 On the third day there was a wedding in Cana of Galilee, and the mother of Jesus was there. ²Jesus and his disciples had also been invited to the wedding. ³When the wine gave out, the mother of Jesus said to him, 'They have no wine.' ⁴And Jesus said to her, 'Woman, what concern is that to you and to me? My hour has not yet come.' ⁵His mother said to the servants, 'Do whatever he tells you.' ⁶Now standing there were six stone water-jars for the Jewish rites of purification, each holding twenty or thirty gallons. ⁷Jesus said to them, 'Fill the jars with water.' And they filled them up to the brim. ⁸He said to them, 'Now draw some out, and take it to the chief steward.' So they took it. ⁹When the steward tasted the water that had become wine, and did not know where it came from (though the servants who had drawn the water knew), the steward called the bridegroom ¹⁰and said to him, 'Everyone serves the good wine first, and then the inferior wine after the guests have become drunk. But you have kept the good wine until now.' ¹¹Jesus did this, the first of his signs, in Cana of Galilee, and revealed his glory; and his disciples believed in him.

¹²After this he went down to Capernaum with his mother, his brothers, and his disciples; and they remained there for a few days.

Jesus Cleanses the Temple

¹³The Passover of the Jews was near, and Jesus went up to Jerusalem. ¹⁴In the temple he found people selling cattle, sheep, and doves, and the money-changers seated at their tables. ¹⁵Making a whip of cords, he drove all of them out of the temple, both the sheep and the cattle. He also poured out the coins of the money-changers and overturned their tables. ¹⁶He told those who were selling the doves, 'Take these things out of here! Stop making my Father's house a market-place!' ¹⁷His disciples remembered that it was written, 'Zeal for your house will consume me.' ¹⁸The Jews then said to him, 'What sign can you show us for doing this?' ¹⁹Jesus answered them, 'Destroy this temple, and in three days I will raise it up.' ²⁰The Jews then said, 'This temple has been under construction for forty-six years, and will you raise it up in three days?' ²¹But he was

speaking of the temple of his body. ²²After he was raised from the dead, his disciples remembered that he had said this; and they believed the scripture and the word that Jesus had spoken.

²³When he was in Jerusalem during the Passover festival, many believed in his name because they saw the signs that he was doing. ²⁴But Jesus on his part would not entrust himself to them, because he knew all people ²⁵and needed no one to testify about anyone; for he himself knew what was in everyone.

Nicodemus Visits Jesus

3 Now there was a Pharisee named Nicodemus, a leader of the Jews. ²He came to Jesus[m] by night and said to him, 'Rabbi, we know that you are a teacher who has come from God; for no one can do these signs that you do apart from the presence of God.' ³Jesus answered him, 'Very truly, I tell you, no one can see the kingdom of God without being born from above.'[n] ⁴Nicodemus said to him, 'How can anyone be born after having grown old? Can one enter a second time into the mother's womb and be born?' ⁵Jesus answered, 'Very truly, I tell you, no one can enter the kingdom of God without being born of water and Spirit. ⁶What is born of the flesh is flesh, and what is born of the Spirit is spirit.[o] ⁷Do not be astonished that I said to you, "You[p] must be born from above."[q] ⁸The wind[r] blows where it chooses, and you hear the sound of it, but you do not know where it comes from or where it goes. So it is with everyone who is born of the Spirit.' ⁹Nicodemus said to him, 'How can these things be?' ¹⁰Jesus answered him, 'Are you a teacher of Israel, and yet you do not understand these things?

¹¹'Very truly, I tell you, we speak of what we know and testify to what we have seen; yet you[s] do not receive our testimony. ¹²If I have told you about earthly things and you do not believe, how can you believe if I tell you about heavenly things? ¹³No one has ascended into heaven except the one who descended from heaven, the Son of Man.[t] ¹⁴And just as Moses lifted up the

---

m Gk *him*   n Or *born anew*   o The same Greek word means both *wind* and *spirit*   p The Greek word for *you* here is plural   q Or *anew*   r The same Greek word means both *wind* and *spirit*   s The Greek word for *you* here and in verse 12 is plural   t Other ancient authorities add *who is in heaven*

serpent in the wilderness, so must the Son of Man be lifted up, ¹⁵that whoever believes in him may have eternal life.ᵘ

¹⁶'For God so loved the world that he gave his only Son, so that everyone who believes in him may not perish but may have eternal life.

¹⁷'Indeed, God did not send the Son into the world to condemn the world, but in order that the world might be saved through him. ¹⁸Those who believe in him are not condemned; but those who do not believe are condemned already, because they have not believed in the name of the only Son of God. ¹⁹And this is the judgement, that the light has come into the world, and people loved darkness rather than light because their deeds were evil. ²⁰For all who do evil hate the light and do not come to the light, so that their deeds may not be exposed. ²¹But those who do what is true come to the light, so that it may be clearly seen that their deeds have been done in God.'ᵘ

Jesus and John the Baptist

²²After this Jesus and his disciples went into the Judean countryside, and he spent some time there with them and baptized. ²³John also was baptizing at Aenon near Salim because water was abundant there; and people kept coming and were being baptized— ²⁴John, of course, had not yet been thrown into prison.

²⁵Now a discussion about purification arose between John's disciples and a Jew.ᵛ ²⁶They came to John and said to him, 'Rabbi, the one who was with you across the Jordan, to whom you testified, here he is baptizing, and all are going to him.' ²⁷John answered, 'No one can receive anything except what has been given from heaven. ²⁸You yourselves are my witnesses that I said, "I am not the Messiah,ʷ but I have been sent ahead of him." ²⁹He who has the bride is the bridegroom. The friend of the bridegroom, who stands and hears him, rejoices greatly at the bridegroom's voice. For this reason my joy has been fulfilled. ³⁰He must increase, but I must decrease.'ˣ

---

u Some interpreters hold that the quotation concludes with verse 15   v Other ancient authorities read *the Jews*   w Or *the Christ*   x Some interpreters hold that the quotation continues to the end of verse 36

The One Who Comes from Heaven

³¹The one who comes from above is above all; the one who is of the earth belongs to the earth and speaks about earthly things. The one who comes from heaven is above all. ³²He testifies to what he has seen and heard, yet no one accepts his testimony. ³³Whoever has accepted his testimony has certified[y] this, that God is true. ³⁴He whom God has sent speaks the words of God, for he gives the Spirit without measure. ³⁵The Father loves the Son and has placed all things in his hands. ³⁶Whoever believes in the Son has eternal life; whoever disobeys the Son will not see life, but must endure God's wrath.

Jesus and the Woman of Samaria

4 Now when Jesus[z] learned that the Pharisees had heard, 'Jesus is making and baptizing more disciples than John'— ²although it was not Jesus himself but his disciples who baptized— ³he left Judea and started back to Galilee. ⁴But he had to go through Samaria. ⁵So he came to a Samaritan city called Sychar, near the plot of ground that Jacob had given to his son Joseph. ⁶Jacob's well was there, and Jesus, tired out by his journey, was sitting by the well. It was about noon.

⁷A Samaritan woman came to draw water, and Jesus said to her, 'Give me a drink'. ⁸(His disciples had gone to the city to buy food.) ⁹The Samaritan woman said to him, 'How is it that you, a Jew, ask a drink of me, a woman of Samaria?' (Jews do not share things in common with Samaritans.)[a] ¹⁰Jesus answered her, 'If you knew the gift of God, and who it is that is saying to you, "Give me a drink", you would have asked him, and he would have given you living water.' ¹¹The woman said to him, 'Sir, you have no bucket, and the well is deep. Where do you get that living water? ¹²Are you greater than our ancestor Jacob, who gave us the well, and with his sons and his flocks drank from it?' ¹³Jesus said to her, 'Everyone who drinks of this water will be thirsty again, ¹⁴but those who drink of the water that I will give them will never be thirsty. The water that I will give will become in them a spring of water gushing up to eternal life.' ¹⁵The woman

---

y Gk *set a seal to*   z Other ancient authorities read *the Lord*   a Other ancient authorities lack this sentence

said to him, 'Sir, give me this water, so that I may never be thirsty or have to keep coming here to draw water.'

¹⁶Jesus said to her, 'Go, call your husband, and come back.' ¹⁷The woman answered him, 'I have no husband.' Jesus said to her, 'You are right in saying, "I have no husband"; ¹⁸for you have had five husbands, and the one you have now is not your husband. What you have said is true!' ¹⁹The woman said to him, 'Sir, I see that you are a prophet. ²⁰Our ancestors worshipped on this mountain, but you*ᵇ* say that the place where people must worship is in Jerusalem.' ²¹Jesus said to her, 'Woman, believe me, the hour is coming when you will worship the Father neither on this mountain nor in Jerusalem. ²²You worship what you do not know; we worship what we know, for salvation is from the Jews. ²³But the hour is coming, and is now here, when the true worshippers will worship the Father in spirit and truth, for the Father seeks such as these to worship him. ²⁴God is spirit, and those who worship him must worship in spirit and truth.' ²⁵The woman said to him, 'I know that Messiah is coming' (who is called Christ). 'When he comes, he will proclaim all things to us.' ²⁶Jesus said to her, 'I am he,ᶜ the one who is speaking to you.'

²⁷Just then his disciples came. They were astonished that he was speaking with a woman, but no one said, 'What do you want?' or, 'Why are you speaking with her?' ²⁸Then the woman left her water-jar and went back to the city. She said to the people, ²⁹'Come and see a man who told me everything I have ever done! He cannot be the Messiah,ᵈ can he?' ³⁰They left the city and were on their way to him.

³¹Meanwhile the disciples were urging him, 'Rabbi, eat something.' ³²But he said to them, 'I have food to eat that you do not know about.' ³³So the disciples said to one another, 'Surely no one has brought him something to eat?' ³⁴Jesus said to them, 'My food is to do the will of him who sent me and to complete his work. ³⁵Do you not say, "Four months more, then comes the harvest"? But I tell you, look around you, and see how the fields are ripe for harvesting. ³⁶The reaper is already receivingᵉ wages and is gathering fruit for eternal life, so that sower and reaper

---

b The Greek word for *you* here and in verses 21 and 22 is plural   c Gk *I am*   d Or *the Christ*   e Or ³⁵ ... *the fields are already ripe for harvesting.* ³⁶ *The reaper is receiving*

may rejoice together. ³⁷For here the saying holds true, "One sows and another reaps." ³⁸I sent you to reap that for which you did not labour. Others have laboured, and you have entered into their labour.'

³⁹Many Samaritans from that city believed in him because of the woman's testimony, 'He told me everything I have ever done.' ⁴⁰So when the Samaritans came to him, they asked him to stay with them; and he stayed there for two days. ⁴¹And many more believed because of his word. ⁴²They said to the woman, 'It is no longer because of what you said that we believe, for we have heard for ourselves, and we know that this is truly the Saviour of the world.'

Jesus Returns to Galilee

⁴³When the two days were over, he went from that place to Galilee ⁴⁴(for Jesus himself had testified that a prophet has no honour in the prophet's own country). ⁴⁵When he came to Galilee, the Galileans welcomed him, since they had seen all that he had done in Jerusalem at the festival; for they too had gone to the festival.

Jesus Heals an Official's Son

⁴⁶Then he came again to Cana in Galilee where he had changed the water into wine. Now there was a royal official whose son lay ill in Capernaum. ⁴⁷When he heard that Jesus had come from Judea to Galilee, he went and begged him to come down and heal his son, for he was at the point of death. ⁴⁸Then Jesus said to him, 'Unless you^f see signs and wonders you will not believe.' ⁴⁹The official said to him, 'Sir, come down before my little boy dies.' ⁵⁰Jesus said to him, 'Go; your son will live.' The man believed the word that Jesus spoke to him and started on his way. ⁵¹As he was going down, his slaves met him and told him that his child was alive. ⁵²So he asked them the hour when he began to recover, and they said to him, 'Yesterday at one in the afternoon the fever left him.' ⁵³The father realized that this was the hour when Jesus had said to him, 'Your son will live.' So he himself believed, along with his whole household. ⁵⁴Now this was the second sign that Jesus did after coming from Judea to Galilee.

---

f Both instances of the Greek word for *you* in this verse are plural

Jesus Heals on the Sabbath

5 After this there was a festival of the Jews, and Jesus went up to Jerusalem.

² Now in Jerusalem by the Sheep Gate there is a pool, called in Hebrew[g] Beth-zatha,[h] which has five porticoes. ³ In these lay many invalids—blind, lame, and paralysed.[i] ⁵ One man was there who had been ill for thirty-eight years. ⁶ When Jesus saw him lying there and knew that he had been there a long time, he said to him, 'Do you want to be made well?' ⁷ The sick man answered him, 'Sir, I have no one to put me into the pool when the water is stirred up; and while I am making my way, someone else steps down ahead of me.' ⁸ Jesus said to him, 'Stand up, take your mat and walk.' ⁹ At once the man was made well, and he took up his mat and began to walk.

Now that day was a sabbath. ¹⁰ So the Jews said to the man who had been cured, 'It is the sabbath; it is not lawful for you to carry your mat.' ¹¹ But he answered them, 'The man who made me well said to me, "Take up your mat and walk." ' ¹² They asked him, 'Who is the man who said to you, "Take it up and walk"?' ¹³ Now the man who had been healed did not know who it was, for Jesus had disappeared in[j] the crowd that was there. ¹⁴ Later Jesus found him in the temple and said to him, 'See, you have been made well! Do not sin any more, so that nothing worse happens to you.' ¹⁵ The man went away and told the Jews that it was Jesus who had made him well. ¹⁶ Therefore the Jews started persecuting Jesus, because he was doing such things on the sabbath. ¹⁷ But Jesus answered them, 'My Father is still working, and I also am working.' ¹⁸ For this reason the Jews were seeking all the more to kill him, because he was not only breaking the sabbath, but was also calling God his own Father, thereby making himself equal to God.

The Authority of the Son

¹⁹ Jesus said to them, 'Very truly, I tell you, the Son can do nothing on his own, but only what he sees the Father doing; for

---

g That is, *Aramaic*   h Other ancient authorities read *Bethesda*, others *Bethsaida*   i Other ancient authorities add, wholly or in part, *waiting for the stirring of the water;* ⁴ *for an angel of the Lord went down at certain seasons into the pool, and stirred up the water; whoever stepped in first after the stirring of the water was made well from whatever disease that person had.*
j Or *had left because of*

whatever the Father[k] does, the Son does likewise. 20The Father loves the Son and shows him all that he himself is doing; and he will show him greater works than these, so that you will be astonished. 21Indeed, just as the Father raises the dead and gives them life, so also the Son gives life to whomsoever he wishes. 22The Father judges no one but has given all judgement to the Son, 23so that all may honour the Son just as they honour the Father. Anyone who does not honour the Son does not honour the Father who sent him. 24Very truly, I tell you, anyone who hears my word and believes him who sent me has eternal life, and does not come under judgement, but has passed from death to life.

25'Very truly, I tell you, the hour is coming, and is now here, when the dead will hear the voice of the Son of God, and those who hear will live. 26For just as the Father has life in himself, so he has granted the Son also to have life in himself; 27and he has given him authority to execute judgement, because he is the Son of Man. 28Do not be astonished at this; for the hour is coming when all who are in their graves will hear his voice 29and will come out—those who have done good, to the resurrection of life, and those who have done evil, to the resurrection of condemnation.

Witnesses to Jesus

30'I can do nothing on my own. As I hear, I judge; and my judgement is just, because I seek to do not my own will but the will of him who sent me.

31'If I testify about myself, my testimony is not true. 32There is another who testifies on my behalf, and I know that his testimony to me is true. 33You sent messengers to John, and he testified to the truth. 34Not that I accept such human testimony, but I say these things so that you may be saved. 35He was a burning and shining lamp, and you were willing to rejoice for a while in his light. 36But I have a testimony greater than John's. The works that the Father has given me to complete, the very works that I am doing, testify on my behalf that the Father has sent me. 37And the Father who sent me has himself testified on my behalf. You have never heard his voice or seen his form, 38and you do not

---

k Gk that one

have his word abiding in you, because you do not believe him whom he has sent.

39'You search the scriptures because you think that in them you have eternal life; and it is they that testify on my behalf. 40Yet you refuse to come to me to have life. 41I do not accept glory from human beings. 42But I know that you do not have the love of God in[l] you. 43I have come in my Father's name, and you do not accept me; if another comes in his own name, you will accept him. 44How can you believe when you accept glory from one another and do not seek the glory that comes from the one who alone is God? 45Do not think that I will accuse you before the Father; your accuser is Moses, on whom you have set your hope. 46If you believed Moses, you would believe me, for he wrote about me. 47But if you do not believe what he wrote, how will you believe what I say?'

Feeding the Five Thousand

6 After this Jesus went to the other side of the Sea of Galilee, also called the Sea of Tiberias.[m] 2A large crowd kept following him, because they saw the signs that he was doing for the sick. 3Jesus went up the mountain and sat down there with his disciples. 4Now the Passover, the festival of the Jews, was near. 5When he looked up and saw a large crowd coming towards him, Jesus said to Philip, 'Where are we to buy bread for these people to eat?' 6He said this to test him, for he himself knew what he was going to do. 7Philip answered him, 'Six months' wages[n] would not buy enough bread for each of them to get a little.' 8One of his disciples, Andrew, Simon Peter's brother, said to him, 9'There is a boy here who has five barley loaves and two fish. But what are they among so many people?' 10Jesus said, 'Make the people sit down.' Now there was a great deal of grass in the place; so they[o] sat down, about five thousand in all. 11Then Jesus took the loaves, and when he had given thanks, he distributed them to those who were seated; so also the fish, as much as they wanted. 12When they were satisfied, he told his disciples, 'Gather up the fragments left over, so that nothing may be lost.' 13So they

---

l Or among   m Gk of Galilee of Tiberias   n Gk Two hundred denarii; the denarius was the usual day's wage for a labourer   o Gk the men

gathered them up, and from the fragments of the five barley loaves, left by those who had eaten, they filled twelve baskets. [14]When the people saw the sign that he had done, they began to say, 'This is indeed the prophet who is to come into the world.'

[15]When Jesus realized that they were about to come and take him by force to make him king, he withdrew again to the mountain by himself.

Jesus Walks on the Water

[16]When evening came, his disciples went down to the lake, [17]got into a boat, and started across the lake to Capernaum. It was now dark, and Jesus had not yet come to them. [18]The lake became rough because a strong wind was blowing. [19]When they had rowed about three or four miles,[p] they saw Jesus walking on the lake and coming near the boat, and they were terrified. [20]But he said to them, 'It is I;[q] do not be afraid.' [21]Then they wanted to take him into the boat, and immediately the boat reached the land towards which they were going.

The Bread from Heaven

[22]The next day the crowd that had stayed on the other side of the lake saw that there had been only one boat there. They also saw that Jesus had not got into the boat with his disciples, but that his disciples had gone away alone. [23]Then some boats from Tiberias came near the place where they had eaten the bread after the Lord had given thanks.[r] [24]So when the crowd saw that neither Jesus nor his disciples were there, they themselves got into the boats and went to Capernaum looking for Jesus.

[25]When they found him on the other side of the lake, they said to him, 'Rabbi, when did you come here?' [26]Jesus answered them, 'Very truly, I tell you, you are looking for me, not because you saw signs, but because you ate your fill of the loaves. [27]Do not work for the food that perishes, but for the food that endures for eternal life, which the Son of Man will give you. For it is on him that God the Father has set his seal.' [28]Then they said to him, 'What must we do to perform the works of God?' [29]Jesus

---

p Gk *about twenty-five or thirty stadia*   q Gk *I am*   r Other ancient authorities lack *after the Lord had given thanks*

answered them, 'This is the work of God, that you believe in him whom he has sent.' ³⁰So they said to him, 'What sign are you going to give us then, so that we may see it and believe you? What work are you performing? ³¹Our ancestors ate the manna in the wilderness; as it is written, "He gave them bread from heaven to eat." ' ³²Then Jesus said to them, 'Very truly, I tell you, it was not Moses who gave you the bread from heaven, but it is my Father who gives you the true bread from heaven. ³³For the bread of God is that which[s] comes down from heaven and gives life to the world.' ³⁴They said to him, 'Sir, give us this bread always.'

³⁵Jesus said to them, 'I am the bread of life. Whoever comes to me will never be hungry, and whoever believes in me will never be thirsty. ³⁶But I said to you that you have seen me and yet do not believe. ³⁷Everything that the Father gives me will come to me, and anyone who comes to me I will never drive away; ³⁸for I have come down from heaven, not to do my own will, but the will of him who sent me. ³⁹And this is the will of him who sent me, that I should lose nothing of all that he has given me, but raise it up on the last day. ⁴⁰This is indeed the will of my Father, that all who see the Son and believe in him may have eternal life; and I will raise them up on the last day.'

⁴¹Then the Jews began to complain about him because he said, 'I am the bread that came down from heaven.' ⁴²They were saying, 'Is not this Jesus, the son of Joseph, whose father and mother we know? How can he now say, "I have come down from heaven"?' ⁴³Jesus answered them, 'Do not complain among yourselves. ⁴⁴No one can come to me unless drawn by the Father who sent me; and I will raise that person up on the last day. ⁴⁵It is written in the prophets, "And they shall all be taught by God." Everyone who has heard and learned from the Father comes to me. ⁴⁶Not that anyone has seen the Father except the one who is from God; he has seen the Father. ⁴⁷Very truly, I tell you, whoever believes has eternal life. ⁴⁸I am the bread of life. ⁴⁹Your ancestors ate the manna in the wilderness, and they died. ⁵⁰This is the bread that comes down from heaven, so that one may eat of it and not die. ⁵¹I am the living bread that came down from heaven. Whoever eats of this bread will live for ever; and the bread that I will give for the life of the world is my flesh.'

---

s Or *he who*

⁵²The Jews then disputed among themselves, saying, 'How can this man give us his flesh to eat?' ⁵³So Jesus said to them, 'Very truly, I tell you, unless you eat the flesh of the Son of Man and drink his blood, you have no life in you. ⁵⁴Those who eat my flesh and drink my blood have eternal life, and I will raise them up on the last day; ⁵⁵for my flesh is true food and my blood is true drink. ⁵⁶Those who eat my flesh and drink my blood abide in me, and I in them. ⁵⁷Just as the living Father sent me, and I live because of the Father, so whoever eats me will live because of me. ⁵⁸This is the bread that came down from heaven, not like that which your ancestors ate, and they died. But the one who eats this bread will live for ever.' ⁵⁹He said these things while he was teaching in the synagogue at Capernaum.

The Words of Eternal Life

⁶⁰When many of his disciples heard it, they said, 'This teaching is difficult; who can accept it?' ⁶¹But Jesus, being aware that his disciples were complaining about it, said to them, 'Does this offend you? ⁶²Then what if you were to see the Son of Man ascending to where he was before? ⁶³It is the spirit that gives life; the flesh is useless. The words that I have spoken to you are spirit and life. ⁶⁴But among you there are some who do not believe.' For Jesus knew from the first who were the ones that did not believe, and who was the one that would betray him. ⁶⁵And he said, 'For this reason I have told you that no one can come to me unless it is granted by the Father.'

⁶⁶Because of this many of his disciples turned back and no longer went about with him. ⁶⁷So Jesus asked the twelve, 'Do you also wish to go away?' ⁶⁸Simon Peter answered him, 'Lord, to whom can we go? You have the words of eternal life. ⁶⁹We have come to believe and know that you are the Holy One of God.'ᵗ ⁷⁰Jesus answered them, 'Did I not choose you, the twelve? Yet one of you is a devil.' ⁷¹He was speaking of Judas son of Simon Iscariot,ᵘ for he, though one of the twelve, was going to betray him.

---

t Other ancient authorities read *the Christ, the Son of the living God*   u Other ancient authorities read *Judas Iscariot son of Simon*; others, *Judas son of Simon from Karyot* (Kerioth)

The Unbelief of Jesus' Brothers

7 After this Jesus went about in Galilee. He did not wish[v] to go about in Judea because the Jews were looking for an opportunity to kill him. ²Now the Jewish festival of Booths[w] was near. ³So his brothers said to him, 'Leave here and go to Judea so that your disciples also may see the works you are doing; ⁴for no one who wants[x] to be widely known acts in secret. If you do these things, show yourself to the world.' ⁵(For not even his brothers believed in him.) ⁶Jesus said to them, 'My time has not yet come, but your time is always here. ⁷The world cannot hate you, but it hates me because I testify against it that its works are evil. ⁸Go to the festival yourselves. I am not[y] going to this festival, for my time has not yet fully come.' ⁹After saying this, he remained in Galilee.

Jesus at the Festival of Booths

¹⁰But after his brothers had gone to the festival, then he also went, not publicly but as it were[z] in secret. ¹¹The Jews were looking for him at the festival and saying, 'Where is he?' ¹²And there was considerable complaining about him among the crowds. While some were saying, 'He is a good man', others were saying, 'No, he is deceiving the crowd.' ¹³Yet no one would speak openly about him for fear of the Jews.

¹⁴About the middle of the festival Jesus went up into the temple and began to teach. ¹⁵The Jews were astonished at it, saying, 'How does this man have such learning,[a] when he has never been taught?' ¹⁶Then Jesus answered them, 'My teaching is not mine but his who sent me. ¹⁷Anyone who resolves to do the will of God will know whether the teaching is from God or whether I am speaking on my own. ¹⁸Those who speak on their own seek their own glory; but the one who seeks the glory of him who sent him is true, and there is nothing false in him.

¹⁹'Did not Moses give you the law? Yet none of you keeps the law. Why are you looking for an opportunity to kill me?' ²⁰The crowd answered, 'You have a demon! Who is trying to kill you?'

---

v Other ancient authorities read *was not at liberty*   w Or *Tabernacles*   x Other ancient authorities read *wants it*   y Other ancient authorities add *yet*   z Other ancient authorities lack *as it were*   a Or *this man know his letters*

²¹Jesus answered them, 'I performed one work, and all of you are astonished. ²²Moses gave you circumcision (it is, of course, not from Moses, but from the patriarchs), and you circumcise a man on the sabbath. ²³If a man receives circumcision on the sabbath in order that the law of Moses may not be broken, are you angry with me because I healed a man's whole body on the sabbath? ²⁴Do not judge by appearances, but judge with right judgement.'

Is This the Christ?

²⁵Now some of the people of Jerusalem were saying, 'Is not this the man whom they are trying to kill? ²⁶And here he is, speaking openly, but they say nothing to him! Can it be that the authorities really know that this is the Messiah?ᵇ ²⁷Yet we know where this man is from; but when the Messiahᵇ comes, no one will know where he is from.' ²⁸Then Jesus cried out as he was teaching in the temple, 'You know me, and you know where I am from. I have not come on my own. But the one who sent me is true, and you do not know him. ²⁹I know him, because I am from him, and he sent me.' ³⁰Then they tried to arrest him, but no one laid hands on him, because his hour had not yet come. ³¹Yet many in the crowd believed in him and were saying, 'When the Messiahᵇ comes, will he do more signs than this man has done?'ᶜ

Officers Are Sent to Arrest Jesus

³²The Pharisees heard the crowd muttering such things about him, and the chief priests and Pharisees sent temple police to arrest him. ³³Jesus then said, 'I will be with you a little while longer, and then I am going to him who sent me. ³⁴You will search for me, but you will not find me; and where I am, you cannot come.' ³⁵The Jews said to one another, 'Where does this man intend to go that we will not find him? Does he intend to go to the Dispersion among the Greeks and teach the Greeks? ³⁶What does he mean by saying, "You will search for me and you will not find me" and, "Where I am, you cannot come"?'

---

b Or *the Christ* c Other ancient authorities read *is doing*

Rivers of Living Water

³⁷On the last day of the festival, the great day, while Jesus was standing there, he cried out, 'Let anyone who is thirsty come to me, ³⁸and let the one who believes in me drink. As*ᵈ* the scripture has said, "Out of the believer's heart*ᵉ* shall flow rivers of living water." ' ³⁹Now he said this about the Spirit, which believers in him were to receive; for as yet there was no Spirit,*ᶠ* because Jesus was not yet glorified.

Division among the People

⁴⁰When they heard these words, some in the crowd said, 'This is really the prophet.' ⁴¹Others said, 'This is the Messiah.'*ᵍ* But some asked, 'Surely the Messiah*ᵍ* does not come from Galilee, does he? ⁴²Has not the scripture said that the Messiah*ᵍ* is descended from David and comes from Bethlehem, the village where David lived?' ⁴³So there was a division in the crowd because of him. ⁴⁴Some of them wanted to arrest him, but no one laid hands on him.

The Unbelief of Those in Authority

⁴⁵Then the temple police went back to the chief priests and Pharisees, who asked them, 'Why did you not arrest him?' ⁴⁶The police answered, 'Never has anyone spoken like this!' ⁴⁷Then the Pharisees replied, 'Surely you have not been deceived too, have you? ⁴⁸Has any one of the authorities or of the Pharisees believed in him? ⁴⁹But this crowd, which does not know the law—they are accursed.' ⁵⁰Nicodemus, who had gone to Jesus*ʰ* before, and who was one of them, asked, ⁵¹'Our law does not judge people without first giving them a hearing to find out what they are doing, does it?' ⁵²They replied, 'Surely you are not also from Galilee, are you? Search and you will see that no prophet is to arise from Galilee.'

The Woman Caught in Adultery

⁵³*Then each of them went home,*

8 *while Jesus went to the Mount of Olives. ²Early in the morning he came again to the temple. All the people came to him and he sat down and began to teach them. ³The scribes and the Pharisees*

---

d Or *come to me and drink.* ³⁸ *The one who believes in me, as*   e Gk *out of his belly*   f Other ancient authorities read *for as yet the Spirit* (others, *Holy Spirit*) *had not been given*   g Or *the Christ*   h Gk *him*

brought a woman who had been caught in adultery; and making her stand before all of them, ⁴they said to him, 'Teacher, this woman was caught in the very act of committing adultery. ⁵Now in the law Moses commanded us to stone such women. Now what do you say?' ⁶They said this to test him, so that they might have some charge to bring against him. Jesus bent down and wrote with his finger on the ground. ⁷When they kept on questioning him, he straightened up and said to them, 'Let anyone among you who is without sin be the first to throw a stone at her.' ⁸And once again he bent down and wrote on the ground.ⁱ ⁹When they heard it, they went away, one by one, beginning with the elders; and Jesus was left alone with the woman standing before him. ¹⁰Jesus straightened up and said to her, 'Woman, where are they? Has no one condemned you?' ¹¹She said, 'No one, sir.'ʲ And Jesus said, 'Neither do I condemn you. Go your way, and from now on do not sin again.'ᵏ

Jesus the Light of the World

¹²Again Jesus spoke to them, saying, 'I am the light of the world. Whoever follows me will never walk in darkness but will have the light of life.' ¹³Then the Pharisees said to him, 'You are testifying on your own behalf; your testimony is not valid.' ¹⁴Jesus answered, 'Even if I testify on my own behalf, my testimony is valid because I know where I have come from and where I am going, but you do not know where I come from or where I am going. ¹⁵You judge by human standards;ˡ I judge no one. ¹⁶Yet even if I do judge, my judgement is valid; for it is not I alone who judge, but I and the Fatherᵐ who sent me. ¹⁷In your law it is written that the testimony of two witnesses is valid. ¹⁸I testify on my own behalf, and the Father who sent me testifies on my behalf.' ¹⁹Then they said to him, 'Where is your Father?' Jesus answered, 'You know neither me nor my Father. If you knew me, you would know my Father also.' ²⁰He spoke these words while he was teaching in the treasury of the temple, but no one arrested him, because his hour had not yet come.

---

i Other ancient authorities add *the sins of each of them*   j Or *Lord*   k The most ancient authorities lack 7.53–8.11; other authorities add the passage here or after 7.36 or after 21.25 or after Lk 21.38, with variations of text; some mark the passage as doubtful   l Gk *according to the flesh*   m Other ancient authorities read *he*

Jesus Foretells His Death

[21]Again he said to them, 'I am going away, and you will search
for me, but you will die in your sin. Where I am going, you cannot
come.' [22]Then the Jews said, 'Is he going to kill himself? Is that
what he means by saying, "Where I am going, you cannot come"?'
[23]He said to them, 'You are from below, I am from above; you
are of this world, I am not of this world. [24]I told you that you
would die in your sins, for you will die in your sins unless you
believe that I am he.'[n] [25]They said to him, 'Who are you?' Jesus
said to them, 'Why do I speak to you at all?[o] [26]I have much to
say about you and much to condemn; but the one who sent me
is true, and I declare to the world what I have heard from him.'
[27]They did not understand that he was speaking to them about
the Father. [28]So Jesus said, 'When you have lifted up the Son of
Man, then you will realize that I am he,[p] and that I do nothing
on my own, but I speak these things as the Father instructed me.
[29]And the one who sent me is with me; he has not left me alone,
for I always do what is pleasing to him.' [30]As he was saying these
things, many believed in him.

True Disciples

[31]Then Jesus said to the Jews who had believed in him, 'If
you continue in my word, you are truly my disciples; [32]and you
will know the truth, and the truth will make you free.' [33]They
answered him, 'We are descendants of Abraham and have never
been slaves to anyone. What do you mean by saying, "You will
be made free"?'

[34]Jesus answered them, 'Very truly, I tell you, everyone
who commits sin is a slave to sin. [35]The slave does not have
a permanent place in the household; the son has a place there
for ever. [36]So if the Son makes you free, you will be free
indeed. [37]I know that you are descendants of Abraham; yet
you look for an opportunity to kill me, because there is no
place in you for my word. [38]I declare what I have seen in the
Father's presence; as for you, you should do what you have
heard from the Father.'[q]

---

n Gk *I am* o Or *What I have told you from the beginning* p Gk *I am* q Other ancient authorities read *you do what you have heard from your father*

Jesus and Abraham

³⁹They answered him, 'Abraham is our father.' Jesus said to them, 'If you were Abraham's children, you would be doing^r what Abraham did, ⁴⁰but now you are trying to kill me, a man who has told you the truth that I heard from God. This is not what Abraham did. ⁴¹You are indeed doing what your father does.' They said to him, 'We are not illegitimate children; we have one father, God himself.' ⁴²Jesus said to them, 'If God were your Father, you would love me, for I came from God and now I am here. I did not come on my own, but he sent me. ⁴³Why do you not understand what I say? It is because you cannot accept my word. ⁴⁴You are from your father the devil, and you choose to do your father's desires. He was a murderer from the beginning and does not stand in the truth, because there is no truth in him. When he lies, he speaks according to his own nature, for he is a liar and the father of lies. ⁴⁵But because I tell the truth, you do not believe me. ⁴⁶Which of you convicts me of sin? If I tell the truth, why do you not believe me? ⁴⁷Whoever is from God hears the words of God. The reason you do not hear them is that you are not from God.'

⁴⁸The Jews answered him, 'Are we not right in saying that you are a Samaritan and have a demon?' ⁴⁹Jesus answered, 'I do not have a demon; but I honour my Father, and you dishonour me. ⁵⁰Yet I do not seek my own glory; there is one who seeks it and he is the judge. ⁵¹Very truly, I tell you, whoever keeps my word will never see death.' ⁵²The Jews said to him, 'Now we know that you have a demon. Abraham died, and so did the prophets; yet you say, "Whoever keeps my word will never taste death." ⁵³Are you greater than our father Abraham, who died? The prophets also died. Who do you claim to be?' ⁵⁴Jesus answered, 'If I glorify myself, my glory is nothing. It is my Father who glorifies me, he of whom you say, "He is our God", ⁵⁵though you do not know him. But I know him; if I were to say that I do not know him, I would be a liar like you. But I do know him and I keep his word. ⁵⁶Your ancestor Abraham rejoiced that he would see my day; he saw it and was glad.' ⁵⁷Then the Jews said to him, 'You are not yet fifty years old, and have you seen Abraham?'^{s} ⁵⁸Jesus said to them, 'Very truly, I tell you, before

---

r Other ancient authorities read *If you are Abraham's children, then do*   s Other ancient authorities read *has Abraham seen you?*

Abraham was, I am.' ⁵⁹ So they picked up stones to throw at him, but Jesus hid himself and went out of the temple.

A Man Born Blind Receives Sight

9 As he walked along, he saw a man blind from birth. ² His disciples asked him, 'Rabbi, who sinned, this man or his parents, that he was born blind?' ³ Jesus answered, 'Neither this man nor his parents sinned; he was born blind so that God's works might be revealed in him. ⁴ We[t] must work the works of him who sent me[u] while it is day; night is coming when no one can work. ⁵ As long as I am in the world, I am the light of the world.' ⁶ When he had said this, he spat on the ground and made mud with the saliva and spread the mud on the man's eyes, ⁷ saying to him, 'Go, wash in the pool of Siloam' (which means Sent). Then he went and washed and came back able to see. ⁸ The neighbours and those who had seen him before as a beggar began to ask, 'Is this not the man who used to sit and beg?' ⁹ Some were saying, 'It is he.' Others were saying, 'No, but it is someone like him.' He kept saying, 'I am the man.' ¹⁰ But they kept asking him, 'Then how were your eyes opened?' ¹¹ He answered, 'The man called Jesus made mud, spread it on my eyes, and said to me, "Go to Siloam and wash." Then I went and washed and received my sight.' ¹² They said to him, 'Where is he?' He said, 'I do not know.'

The Pharisees Investigate the Healing

¹³ They brought to the Pharisees the man who had formerly been blind. ¹⁴ Now it was a sabbath day when Jesus made the mud and opened his eyes. ¹⁵ Then the Pharisees also began to ask him how he had received his sight. He said to them, 'He put mud on my eyes. Then I washed, and now I see.' ¹⁶ Some of the Pharisees said, 'This man is not from God, for he does not observe the sabbath.' But others said, 'How can a man who is a sinner perform such signs?' And they were divided. ¹⁷ So they said again to the blind man, 'What do you say about him? It was your eyes he opened.' He said, 'He is a prophet.'

¹⁸ The Jews did not believe that he had been blind and had received his sight until they called the parents of the man who

---

t Other ancient authorities read *I*   u Other ancient authorities read *us* had received his sight ¹⁹and asked them, 'Is this your son, who you say was born blind? How then does he now see?' ²⁰His parents answered, 'We know that this is our son, and that he was born blind; ²¹but we do not know how it is that now he sees, nor do we know who opened his eyes. Ask him; he is of age. He will speak for himself.' ²²His parents said this because they were afraid of the Jews; for the Jews had already agreed that anyone who confessed Jesusᵛ to be the Messiahʷ would be put out of the synagogue. ²³Therefore his parents said, 'He is of age; ask him.'

²⁴So for the second time they called the man who had been blind, and they said to him, 'Give glory to God! We know that this man is a sinner.' ²⁵He answered, 'I do not know whether he is a sinner. One thing I do know, that though I was blind, now I see.' ²⁶They said to him, 'What did he do to you? How did he open your eyes?' ²⁷He answered them, 'I have told you already, and you would not listen. Why do you want to hear it again? Do you also want to become his disciples?' ²⁸Then they reviled him, saying, 'You are his disciple, but we are disciples of Moses. ²⁹We know that God has spoken to Moses, but as for this man, we do not know where he comes from.' ³⁰The man answered, 'Here is an astonishing thing! You do not know where he comes from, and yet he opened my eyes. ³¹We know that God does not listen to sinners, but he does listen to one who worships him and obeys his will. ³²Never since the world began has it been heard that anyone opened the eyes of a person born blind. ³³If this man were not from God, he could do nothing.' ³⁴They answered him, 'You were born entirely in sins, and are you trying to teach us?' And they drove him out.

Spiritual Blindness

³⁵Jesus heard that they had driven him out, and when he found him, he said, 'Do you believe in the Son of Man?'ˣ ³⁶He answered, 'And who is he, sir?ʸ Tell me, so that I may believe in him.' ³⁷Jesus said to him, 'You have seen him, and the one speaking with you is he.' ³⁸He said, 'Lord,ʸ I believe.' And he worshipped him. ³⁹Jesus said, 'I came into this world for judgement so that those who

---

v Gk *him*   w Or *the Christ*   x Other ancient authorities read *the Son of God*   y *Sir* and *Lord* translate the same Greek word

do not see may see, and those who do see may become blind.' ⁴⁰Some of the Pharisees near him heard this and said to him, 'Surely we are not blind, are we?' ⁴¹Jesus said to them, 'If you were blind, you would not have sin. But now that you say, "We see", your sin remains.

Jesus the Good Shepherd

10 'Very truly, I tell you, anyone who does not enter the sheepfold by the gate but climbs in by another way is a thief and a bandit. ²The one who enters by the gate is the shepherd of the sheep. ³The gatekeeper opens the gate for him, and the sheep hear his voice. He calls his own sheep by name and leads them out. ⁴When he has brought out all his own, he goes ahead of them, and the sheep follow him because they know his voice. ⁵They will not follow a stranger, but they will run from him because they do not know the voice of strangers.' ⁶Jesus used this figure of speech with them, but they did not understand what he was saying to them.

⁷So again Jesus said to them, 'Very truly, I tell you, I am the gate for the sheep. ⁸All who came before me are thieves and bandits; but the sheep did not listen to them. ⁹I am the gate. Whoever enters by me will be saved, and will come in and go out and find pasture. ¹⁰The thief comes only to steal and kill and destroy. I came that they may have life, and have it abundantly.

¹¹'I am the good shepherd. The good shepherd lays down his life for the sheep. ¹²The hired hand, who is not the shepherd and does not own the sheep, sees the wolf coming and leaves the sheep and runs away—and the wolf snatches them and scatters them. ¹³The hired hand runs away because a hired hand does not care for the sheep. ¹⁴I am the good shepherd. I know my own and my own know me, ¹⁵just as the Father knows me and I know the Father. And I lay down my life for the sheep. ¹⁶I have other sheep that do not belong to this fold. I must bring them also, and they will listen to my voice. So there will be one flock, one shepherd. ¹⁷For this reason the Father loves me, because I lay down my life in order to take it up again. ¹⁸No one takes^z it from me, but I lay it down of my own accord. I have power to lay it

---

z Other ancient authorities read *has taken*

down, and I have power to take it up again. I have received this command from my Father.'

¹⁹Again the Jews were divided because of these words. ²⁰Many of them were saying, 'He has a demon and is out of his mind. Why listen to him?' ²¹Others were saying, 'These are not the words of one who has a demon. Can a demon open the eyes of the blind?'

Jesus Is Rejected by the Jews

²²At that time the festival of the Dedication took place in Jerusalem. It was winter, ²³and Jesus was walking in the temple, in the portico of Solomon. ²⁴So the Jews gathered around him and said to him, 'How long will you keep us in suspense? If you are the Messiah,ᵃ tell us plainly.' ²⁵Jesus answered, 'I have told you, and you do not believe. The works that I do in my Father's name testify to me; ²⁶but you do not believe, because you do not belong to my sheep. ²⁷My sheep hear my voice. I know them, and they follow me. ²⁸I give me eternal life, and they will never perish. No one will snatch them out of my hand. ²⁹What my Father has given me is greater than all else, and no one can snatch it out of the Father's hand.ᵇ ³⁰The Father and I are one.'

³¹The Jews took up stones again to stone him. ³²Jesus replied, 'I have shown you many good works from the Father. For which of these are you going to stone me?' ³³The Jews answered, 'It is not for a good work that we are going to stone you, but for blasphemy, because you, though only a human being, are making yourself God.' ³⁴Jesus answered, 'Is it not written in your law,ᶜ "I said, you are gods"? ³⁵If those to whom the word of God came were called "gods"—and the scripture cannot be annulled— ³⁶can you say that the one whom the Father has sanctified and sent into the world is blaspheming because I said, "I am God's Son"? ³⁷If I am not doing the works of my Father, then do not believe me. ³⁸But if I do them, even though you do not believe me, believe the works, so that you may know and understandᵈ that the Father is in me and I am in the Father.' ³⁹Then they tried to arrest him again, but he escaped from their hands.

---

a Or *the Christ*   b Other ancient authorities read *My Father who has given them to me is greater than all, and no one can snatch them out of the Father's hand*   c Other ancient authorities read *in the law*   d Other ancient authorities lack *and understand*; others read *and believe*

⁴⁰He went away again across the Jordan to the place where John had been baptizing earlier, and he remained there. ⁴¹Many came to him, and they were saying, 'John performed no sign, but everything that John said about this man was true.' ⁴²And many believed in him there.

The Death of Lazarus

11 Now a certain man was ill, Lazarus of Bethany, the village of Mary and her sister Martha. ²Mary was the one who anointed the Lord with perfume and wiped his feet with her hair; her brother Lazarus was ill. ³So the sisters sent a message to Jesus,ᵉ 'Lord, he whom you love is ill.' ⁴But when Jesus heard it, he said, 'This illness does not lead to death; rather it is for God's glory, so that the Son of God may be glorified through it.' ⁵Accordingly, though Jesus loved Martha and her sister and Lazarus, ⁶after having heard that Lazarusᶠ was ill, he stayed two days longer in the place where he was.

⁷Then after this he said to the disciples, 'Let us go to Judea again.' ⁸The disciples said to him, 'Rabbi, the Jews were just now trying to stone you, and are you going there again?' ⁹Jesus answered, 'Are there not twelve hours of daylight? Those who walk during the day do not stumble, because they see the light of this world. ¹⁰But those who walk at night stumble, because the light is not in them.' ¹¹After saying this, he told them, 'Our friend Lazarus has fallen asleep, but I am going there to awaken him.' ¹²The disciples said to him, 'Lord, if he has fallen asleep, he will be all right.' ¹³Jesus, however, had been speaking about his death, but they thought that he was referring merely to sleep. ¹⁴Then Jesus told them plainly, 'Lazarus is dead. ¹⁵For your sake I am glad I was not there, so that you may believe. But let us go to him.' ¹⁶Thomas, who was called the Twin,ᵍ said to his fellow-disciples, 'Let us also go, that we may die with him.'

Jesus the Resurrection and the Life

¹⁷When Jesus arrived, he found that Lazarusʰ had already been in the tomb for four days. ¹⁸Now Bethany was near Jerusalem, some two milesⁱ away, ¹⁹and many of the Jews had come to

e Gk *him*   f Gk *he*   g Gk *Didymus*   h Gk *he*   i Gk *fifteen stadia*

Martha and Mary to console them about their brother. ²⁰When Martha heard that Jesus was coming, she went and met him, while Mary stayed at home. ²¹Martha said to Jesus, 'Lord, if you had been here, my brother would not have died. ²²But even now I know that God will give you whatever you ask of him.' ²³Jesus said to her, 'Your brother will rise again.' ²⁴Martha said to him, 'I know that he will rise again in the resurrection on the last day.' ²⁵Jesus said to her, 'I am the resurrection and the life.ʲ Those who believe in me, even though they die, will live, ²⁶and everyone who lives and believes in me will never die. Do you believe this?' ²⁷She said to him, 'Yes, Lord, I believe that you are the Messiah,ᵏ the Son of God, the one coming into the world.'

Jesus Weeps

²⁸When she had said this, she went back and called her sister Mary, and told her privately, 'The Teacher is here and is calling for you.' ²⁹And when she heard it, she got up quickly and went to him. ³⁰Now Jesus had not yet come to the village, but was still at the place where Martha had met him. ³¹The Jews who were with her in the house, consoling her, saw Mary get up quickly and go out. They followed her because they thought that she was going to the tomb to weep there. ³²When Mary came where Jesus was and saw him, she knelt at his feet and said to him, 'Lord, if you had been here, my brother would not have died.' ³³When Jesus saw her weeping, and the Jews who came with her also weeping, he was greatly disturbed in spirit and deeply moved. ³⁴He said, 'Where have you laid him?' They said to him, 'Lord, come and see.' ³⁵Jesus began to weep. ³⁶So the Jews said, 'See how he loved him!' ³⁷But some of them said, 'Could not he who opened the eyes of the blind man have kept this man from dying?'

Jesus Raises Lazarus to Life

³⁸Then Jesus, again greatly disturbed, came to the tomb. It was a cave, and a stone was lying against it. ³⁹Jesus said, 'Take away the stone.' Martha, the sister of the dead man, said to him, 'Lord, already there is a stench because he has been dead for four days.' ⁴⁰Jesus said to her, 'Did I not tell you that if you believed, you

---

j Other ancient authorities lack *and the life*   k Or *the Christ* would see the glory of God?' ⁴¹So they took away the stone. And Jesus looked upwards and said, 'Father, I thank you for having heard me. ⁴²I knew that you always hear me, but I have said this for the sake of the crowd standing here, so that they may believe that you sent me.' ⁴³When he had said this, he cried with a loud voice, 'Lazarus, come out!' ⁴⁴The dead man came out, his hands and feet bound with strips of cloth, and his face wrapped in a cloth. Jesus said to them, 'Unbind him, and let him go.'

The Plot to Kill Jesus

⁴⁵Many of the Jews therefore, who had come with Mary and had seen what Jesus did, believed in him. ⁴⁶But some of them went to the Pharisees and told them what he had done. ⁴⁷So the chief priests and the Pharisees called a meeting of the council, and said, 'What are we to do? This man is performing many signs. ⁴⁸If we let him go on like this, everyone will believe in him, and the Romans will come and destroy both our holy place¹ and our nation.' ⁴⁹But one of them, Caiaphas, who was high priest that year, said to them, 'You know nothing at all! ⁵⁰You do not understand that it is better for you to have one man die for the people than to have the whole nation destroyed.' ⁵¹He did not say this on his own, but being high priest that year he prophesied that Jesus was about to die for the nation, ⁵²and not for the nation only, but to gather into one the dispersed children of God. ⁵³So from that day on they planned to put him to death.

⁵⁴Jesus therefore no longer walked about openly among the Jews, but went from there to a town called Ephraim in the region near the wilderness; and he remained there with the disciples.

⁵⁵Now the Passover of the Jews was near, and many went up from the country to Jerusalem before the Passover to purify themselves. ⁵⁶They were looking for Jesus and were asking one another as they stood in the temple, 'What do you think? Surely he will not come to the festival, will he?' ⁵⁷Now the chief priests and the Pharisees had given orders that anyone who knew where Jesus^m was should let them know, so that they might arrest him.

---

l Or *our temple*; Greek *our place*   m Gk *he*

Mary Anoints Jesus

12 Six days before the Passover Jesus came to Bethany, the home of Lazarus, whom he had raised from the dead. [2] There they gave a dinner for him. Martha served, and Lazarus was one of those at the table with him. [3] Mary took a pound of costly perfume made of pure nard, anointed Jesus' feet, and wiped them[n] with her hair. The house was filled with the fragrance of the perfume. [4] But Judas Iscariot, one of his disciples (the one who was about to betray him), said, [5] 'Why was this perfume not sold for three hundred denarii[o] and the money given to the poor?' [6] (He said this not because he cared about the poor, but because he was a thief; he kept the common purse and used to steal what was put into it.) [7] Jesus said, 'Leave her alone. She bought it[p] so that she might keep it for the day of my burial. [8] You always have the poor with you, but you do not always have me.'

The Plot to Kill Lazarus

[9] When the great crowd of the Jews learned that he was there, they came not only because of Jesus but also to see Lazarus, whom he had raised from the dead. [10] So the chief priests planned to put Lazarus to death as well, [11] since it was on account of him that many of the Jews were deserting and were believing in Jesus.

Jesus' Triumphal Entry into Jerusalem

[12] The next day the great crowd that had come to the festival heard that Jesus was coming to Jerusalem. [13] So they took branches of palm trees and went out to meet him, shouting,

'Hosanna!

Blessed is the one who comes in the name of the Lord—
the King of Israel!'

[14] Jesus found a young donkey and sat on it; as it is written:

[15] 'Do not be afraid, daughter of Zion.

Look, your king is coming,
sitting on a donkey's colt!'

[16] His disciples did not understand these things at first; but when Jesus was glorified, then they remembered that these things

---

n Gk *his feet*   o Three hundred denarii would be nearly a year's wages for a labourer
p Gk lacks *She bought it*

had been written of him and had been done to him. 17So the
crowd that had been with him when he called Lazarus out of
the tomb and raised him from the dead continued to testify.[q]
18It was also because they heard that he had performed this sign
that the crowd went to meet him. 19The Pharisees then said to
one another, 'You see, you can do nothing. Look, the world has
gone after him!'

Some Greeks Wish to See Jesus

20Now among those who went up to worship at the festival
were some Greeks. 21They came to Philip, who was from
Bethsaida in Galilee, and said to him, 'Sir, we wish to see Jesus.'
22Philip went and told Andrew; then Andrew and Philip went and
told Jesus. 23Jesus answered them, 'The hour has come for the
Son of Man to be glorified. 24Very truly, I tell you, unless a grain
of wheat falls into the earth and dies, it remains just a single
grain; but if it dies, it bears much fruit. 25Those who love their
life lose it, and those who hate their life in this world will keep
it for eternal life. 26Whoever serves me must follow me, and
where I am, there will my servant be also. Whoever serves me,
the Father will honour.

Jesus Speaks about His Death

27'Now my soul is troubled. And what should I say—"Father, save
me from this hour"? No, it is for this reason that I have come to
this hour. 28Father, glorify your name.' Then a voice came from
heaven, 'I have glorified it, and I will glorify it again.' 29The crowd
standing there heard it and said that it was thunder. Others said,
'An angel has spoken to him.' 30Jesus answered, 'This voice has
come for your sake, not for mine. 31Now is the judgement of
this world; now the ruler of this world will be driven out. 32And
I, when I am lifted up from the earth, will draw all people[r] to
myself.' 33He said this to indicate the kind of death he was to
die. 34The crowd answered him, 'We have heard from the law
that the Messiah[s] remains for ever. How can you say that the
Son of Man must be lifted up? Who is this Son of Man?' 35Jesus

---

q Other ancient authorities read *with him began to testify that he had called...from the dead*
r Other ancient authorities read *all things* s Or *the Christ*

said to them, 'The light is with you for a little longer. Walk while
you have the light, so that the darkness may not overtake you. If
you walk in the darkness, you do not know where you are going.
³⁶While you have the light, believe in the light, so that you may
become children of light.'

The Unbelief of the People

After Jesus had said this, he departed and hid from them.
³⁷Although he had performed so many signs in their presence,
they did not believe in him. ³⁸This was to fulfil the word spoken
by the prophet Isaiah:

'Lord, who has believed our message,
and to whom has the arm of the Lord been revealed?'
³⁹And so they could not believe, because Isaiah also said,
⁴⁰ 'He has blinded their eyes
and hardened their heart,
so that they might not look with their eyes,
and understand with their heart and turn—
and I would heal them.'
⁴¹Isaiah said this because[t] he saw his glory and spoke about him.
⁴²Nevertheless many, even of the authorities, believed in him. But
because of the Pharisees they did not confess it, for fear that
they would be put out of the synagogue; ⁴³for they loved human
glory more than the glory that comes from God.

Summary of Jesus' Teaching

⁴⁴Then Jesus cried aloud: 'Whoever believes in me believes
not in me but in him who sent me. ⁴⁵And whoever sees me sees
him who sent me. ⁴⁶I have come as light into the world, so that
everyone who believes in me should not remain in the darkness.
⁴⁷I do not judge anyone who hears my words and does not keep
them, for I came not to judge the world, but to save the world.
⁴⁸The one who rejects me and does not receive my word has
a judge; on the last day the word that I have spoken will serve
as judge, ⁴⁹for I have not spoken on my own, but the Father who
sent me has himself given me a commandment about what to
say and what to speak. ⁵⁰And I know that his commandment is

---

t Other ancient witnesses read *when*

eternal life. What I speak, therefore, I speak just as the Father has told me.'

Jesus Washes the Disciples' Feet

13 Now before the festival of the Passover, Jesus knew that his hour had come to depart from this world and go to the Father. Having loved his own who were in the world, he loved them to the end. ²The devil had already put it into the heart of Judas son of Simon Iscariot to betray him. And during supper ³Jesus, knowing that the Father had given all things into his hands, and that he had come from God and was going to God, ⁴got up from the table,ᵘ took off his outer robe, and tied a towel around himself. ⁵Then he poured water into a basin and began to wash the disciples' feet and to wipe them with the towel that was tied around him. ⁶He came to Simon Peter, who said to him, 'Lord, are you going to wash my feet?' ⁷Jesus answered, 'You do not know now what I am doing, but later you will understand.' ⁸Peter said to him, 'You will never wash my feet.' Jesus answered, 'Unless I wash you, you have no share with me.' ⁹Simon Peter said to him, 'Lord, not my feet only but also my hands and my head!' ¹⁰Jesus said to him, 'One who has bathed does not need to wash, except for the feet,ᵛ but is entirely clean. And youʷ are clean, though not all of you.' ¹¹For he knew who was to betray him; for this reason he said, 'Not all of you are clean.'

¹²After he had washed their feet, had put on his robe, and had returned to the table, he said to them, 'Do you know what I have done to you? ¹³You call me Teacher and Lord—and you are right, for that is what I am. ¹⁴So if I, your Lord and Teacher, have washed your feet, you also ought to wash one another's feet. ¹⁵For I have set you an example, that you also should do as I have done to you. ¹⁶Very truly, I tell you, servantsˣ are not greater than their master, nor are messengers greater than the one who sent them. ¹⁷If you know these things, you are blessed if you do them. ¹⁸I am not speaking of all of you; I know whom I have chosen. But it is to fulfil the scripture, "The one who ate my breadʸ has lifted his heel against me." ¹⁹I tell you this now,

---

u Gk *from supper*   v Other ancient authorities lack *except for the feet*   w The Greek word for *you* here is plural   x Gk *slaves*   y Other ancient authorities read *ate bread with me*

before it occurs, so that when it does occur, you may believe
that I am he.[z] [20]Very truly, I tell you, whoever receives one
whom I send receives me; and whoever receives me receives
him who sent me.'

Jesus Foretells His Betrayal

[21]After saying this Jesus was troubled in spirit, and declared,
'Very truly, I tell you, one of you will betray me.' [22]The disciples
looked at one another, uncertain of whom he was speaking.
[23]One of his disciples—the one whom Jesus loved—was reclining
next to him; [24]Simon Peter therefore motioned to him to ask
Jesus of whom he was speaking. [25]So while reclining next to
Jesus, he asked him, 'Lord, who is it?' [26]Jesus answered, 'It is the
one to whom I give this piece of bread when I have dipped it in
the dish.'[a] So when he had dipped the piece of bread, he gave
it to Judas son of Simon Iscariot.[b] [27]After he received the piece
of bread,[c] Satan entered into him. Jesus said to him, 'Do quickly
what you are going to do.' [28]Now no one at the table knew why
he said this to him. [29]Some thought that, because Judas had the
common purse, Jesus was telling him, 'Buy what we need for
the festival'; or, that he should give something to the poor. [30]So,
after receiving the piece of bread, he immediately went out. And
it was night.

The New Commandment

[31]When he had gone out, Jesus said, 'Now the Son of Man has
been glorified, and God has been glorified in him. [32]If God has
been glorified in him,[d] God will also glorify him in himself and
will glorify him at once. [33]Little children, I am with you only
a little longer. You will look for me; and as I said to the Jews so
now I say to you, "Where I am going, you cannot come." [34]I give
you a new commandment, that you love one another. Just as
I have loved you, you also should love one another. [35]By this
everyone will know that you are my disciples, if you have love
for one another.'

---

z Gk *I am* a Gk *dipped it* b Other ancient authorities read *Judas Iscariot son of Simon*;
others, *Judas son of Simon from Karyot* (Kerioth) c Gk *After the piece of bread* d Other
ancient authorities lack *If God has been glorified in him*

Jesus Foretells Peter's Denial

36 Simon Peter said to him, 'Lord, where are you going?' Jesus answered, 'Where I am going, you cannot follow me now; but you will follow afterwards.' 37 Peter said to him, 'Lord, why can I not follow you now? I will lay down my life for you.' 38 Jesus answered, 'Will you lay down your life for me? Very truly, I tell you, before the cock crows, you will have denied me three times.

Jesus the Way to the Father

14 'Do not let your hearts be troubled. Believe*e* in God, believe also in me. 2 In my Father's house there are many dwelling-places. If it were not so, would I have told you that I go to prepare a place for you?*f* 3 And if I go and prepare a place for you, I will come again and will take you to myself, so that where I am, there you may be also. 4 And you know the way to the place where I am going.'*g* 5 Thomas said to him, 'Lord, we do not know where you are going. How can we know the way?' 6 Jesus said to him, 'I am the way, and the truth, and the life. No one comes to the Father except through me. 7 If you know me, you will know*h* my Father also. From now on you do know him and have seen him.'

8 Philip said to him, 'Lord, show us the Father, and we will be satisfied.' 9 Jesus said to him, 'Have I been with you all this time, Philip, and you still do not know me? Whoever has seen me has seen the Father. How can you say, "Show us the Father"? 10 Do you not believe that I am in the Father and the Father is in me? The words that I say to you I do not speak on my own; but the Father who dwells in me does his works. 11 Believe me that I am in the Father and the Father is in me; but if you do not, then believe me because of the works themselves. 12 Very truly, I tell you, the one who believes in me will also do the works that I do and, in fact, will do greater works than these, because I am going to the Father. 13 I will do whatever you ask in my name, so that the Father may be glorified in the Son. 14 If in my name you ask me*i* for anything, I will do it.

---

e Or *You believe*   f Or *If it were not so, I would have told you; for I go to prepare a place for you*
g Other ancient authorities read *Where I am going you know, and the way you know*   h Other ancient authorities read *If you had known me, you would have known*   i Other ancient authorities lack *me*

The Promise of the Holy Spirit

¹⁵'If you love me, you will keep[j] my commandments. ¹⁶And I will ask the Father, and he will give you another Advocate,[k] to be with you for ever. ¹⁷This is the Spirit of truth, whom the world cannot receive, because it neither sees him nor knows him. You know him, because he abides with you, and he will be in[l] you.

¹⁸'I will not leave you orphaned; I am coming to you. ¹⁹In a little while the world will no longer see me, but you will see me; because I live, you also will live. ²⁰On that day you will know that I am in my Father, and you in me, and I in you. ²¹They who have my commandments and keep them are those who love me; and those who love me will be loved by my Father, and I will love them and reveal myself to them.' ²²Judas (not Iscariot) said to him, 'Lord, how is it that you will reveal yourself to us, and not to the world?' ²³Jesus answered him, 'Those who love me will keep my word, and my Father will love them, and we will come to them and make our home with them. ²⁴Whoever does not love me does not keep my words; and the word that you hear is not mine, but is from the Father who sent me.

²⁵'I have said these things to you while I am still with you. ²⁶But the Advocate,[m] the Holy Spirit, whom the Father will send in my name, will teach you everything, and remind you of all that I have said to you. ²⁷Peace I leave with you; my peace I give to you. I do not give to you as the world gives. Do not let your hearts be troubled, and do not let them be afraid. ²⁸You heard me say to you, "I am going away, and I am coming to you." If you loved me, you would rejoice that I am going to the Father, because the Father is greater than I. ²⁹And now I have told you this before it occurs, so that when it does occur, you may believe. ³⁰I will no longer talk much with you, for the ruler of this world is coming. He has no power over me; ³¹but I do as the Father has commanded me, so that the world may know that I love the Father. Rise, let us be on our way.

Jesus the True Vine

15 'I am the true vine, and my Father is the vine-grower. ²He removes every branch in me that bears no fruit. Every

---

j Other ancient authorities read *me, keep*   k Or *Helper*   l Or *among*   m Or *Helper*

branch that bears fruit he prunes[n] to make it bear more fruit. [3]You have already been cleansed[n] by the word that I have spoken to you. [4]Abide in me as I abide in you. Just as the branch cannot bear fruit by itself unless it abides in the vine, neither can you unless you abide in me. [5]I am the vine, you are the branches. Those who abide in me and I in them bear much fruit, because apart from me you can do nothing. [6]Whoever does not abide in me is thrown away like a branch and withers; such branches are gathered, thrown into the fire, and burned. [7]If you abide in me, and my words abide in you, ask for whatever you wish, and it will be done for you. [8]My Father is glorified by this, that you bear much fruit and become[o] my disciples. [9]As the Father has loved me, so I have loved you; abide in my love. [10]If you keep my commandments, you will abide in my love, just as I have kept my Father's commandments and abide in his love. [11]I have said these things to you so that my joy may be in you, and that your joy may be complete.

[12]'This is my commandment, that you love one another as I have loved you. [13]No one has greater love than this, to lay down one's life for one's friends. [14]You are my friends if you do what I command you. [15]I do not call you servants[p] any longer, because the servant[q] does not know what the master is doing; but I have called you friends, because I have made known to you everything that I have heard from my Father. [16]You did not choose me but I chose you. And I appointed you to go and bear fruit, fruit that will last, so that the Father will give you whatever you ask him in my name. [17]I am giving you these commands so that you may love one another.

The World's Hatred

[18]'If the world hates you, be aware that it hated me before it hated you. [19]If you belonged to the world,[r] the world would love you as its own. Because you do not belong to the world, but I have chosen you out of the world—therefore the world hates you. [20]Remember the word that I said to you, "Servants[s] are not greater than their master." If they persecuted me, they will

---

n The same Greek root refers to pruning and cleansing   o Or be   p Gk slaves
q Gk slave   r Gk were of the world   s Gk Slaves

persecute you; if they kept my word, they will keep yours also.
²¹But they will do all these things to you on account of my name,
because they do not know him who sent me. ²²If I had not come
and spoken to them, they would not have sin; but now they have
no excuse for their sin. ²³Whoever hates me hates my Father also.
²⁴If I had not done among them the works that no one else did,
they would not have sin. But now they have seen and hated both
me and my Father. ²⁵It was to fulfil the word that is written in
their law, "They hated me without a cause."

²⁶'When the Advocate^t comes, whom I will send to you from
the Father, the Spirit of truth who comes from the Father, he will
testify on my behalf. ²⁷You also are to testify because you have
been with me from the beginning.

16 'I have said these things to you to keep you from
stumbling. ²They will put you out of the synagogues.
Indeed, an hour is coming when those who kill you will think
that by doing so they are offering worship to God. ³And they
will do this because they have not known the Father or me. ⁴But
I have said these things to you so that when their hour comes
you may remember that I told you about them.

The Work of the Spirit

'I did not say these things to you from the beginning, because
I was with you. ⁵But now I am going to him who sent me; yet
none of you asks me, "Where are you going?" ⁶But because
I have said these things to you, sorrow has filled your hearts.
⁷Nevertheless, I tell you the truth: it is to your advantage that
I go away, for if I do not go away, the Advocate^u will not come
to you; but if I go, I will send him to you. ⁸And when he comes,
he will prove the world wrong about^v sin and righteousness
and judgement: ⁹about sin, because they do not believe in me;
¹⁰about righteousness, because I am going to the Father and you
will see me no longer; ¹¹about judgement, because the ruler of
this world has been condemned.

¹²'I still have many things to say to you, but you cannot bear
them now. ¹³When the Spirit of truth comes, he will guide you
into all the truth; for he will not speak on his own, but will speak

---

t Or *Helper*   u Or *Helper*   v Or *convict the world of* whatever he hears, and he will declare to you the things that are to come. ¹⁴He will glorify me, because he will take what is mine and declare it to you. ¹⁵All that the Father has is mine. For this reason I said that he will take what is mine and declare it to you.

Sorrow Will Turn into Joy

¹⁶'A little while, and you will no longer see me, and again a little while, and you will see me.' ¹⁷Then some of his disciples said to one another, 'What does he mean by saying to us, "A little while, and you will no longer see me, and again a little while, and you will see me"; and "Because I am going to the Father"?' ¹⁸They said, 'What does he mean by this "a little while"? We do not know what he is talking about.' ¹⁹Jesus knew that they wanted to ask him, so he said to them, 'Are you discussing among yourselves what I meant when I said, "A little while, and you will no longer see me, and again a little while, and you will see me"? ²⁰Very truly, I tell you, you will weep and mourn, but the world will rejoice; you will have pain, but your pain will turn into joy. ²¹When a woman is in labour, she has pain, because her hour has come. But when her child is born, she no longer remembers the anguish because of the joy of having brought a human being into the world. ²²So you have pain now; but I will see you again, and your hearts will rejoice, and no one will take your joy from you. ²³On that day you will ask nothing of me.ʷ Very truly, I tell you, if you ask anything of the Father in my name, he will give it to you.ˣ ²⁴Until now you have not asked for anything in my name. Ask and you will receive, so that your joy may be complete.

Peace for the Disciples

²⁵'I have said these things to you in figures of speech. The hour is coming when I will no longer speak to you in figures, but will tell you plainly of the Father. ²⁶On that day you will ask in my name. I do not say to you that I will ask the Father on your behalf; ²⁷for the Father himself loves you, because you have loved me and have believed that I came from God.ʸ ²⁸I came from the Father and have come into the world; again, I am leaving the world and am going to the Father.'

---

w Or *will ask me no question*   x Other ancient authorities read *Father, he will give it to you in my name*   y Other ancient authorities read *the Father*

²⁹His disciples said, 'Yes, now you are speaking plainly, not in any figure of speech! ³⁰Now we know that you know all things, and do not need to have anyone question you; by this we believe that you came from God.' ³¹Jesus answered them, 'Do you now believe? ³²The hour is coming, indeed it has come, when you will be scattered, each one to his home, and you will leave me alone. Yet I am not alone because the Father is with me. ³³I have said this to you, so that in me you may have peace. In the world you face persecution. But take courage; I have conquered the world!'

Jesus Prays for His Disciples

17 After Jesus had spoken these words, he looked up to heaven and said, 'Father, the hour has come; glorify your Son so that the Son may glorify you, ²since you have given him authority over all people,ᶻ to give eternal life to all whom you have given him. ³And this is eternal life, that they may know you, the only true God, and Jesus Christ whom you have sent. ⁴I glorified you on earth by finishing the work that you gave me to do. ⁵So now, Father, glorify me in your own presence with the glory that I had in your presence before the world existed.

⁶'I have made your name known to those whom you gave me from the world. They were yours, and you gave them to me, and they have kept your word. ⁷Now they know that everything you have given me is from you; ⁸for the words that you gave to me I have given to them, and they have received them and know in truth that I came from you; and they have believed that you sent me. ⁹I am asking on their behalf; I am not asking on behalf of the world, but on behalf of those whom you gave me, because they are yours. ¹⁰All mine are yours, and yours are mine; and I have been glorified in them. ¹¹And now I am no longer in the world, but they are in the world, and I am coming to you. Holy Father, protect them in your name that you have given me, so that they may be one, as we are one. ¹²While I was with them, I protected them in your name thatᵃ you have given me. I guarded them, and not one of them was lost except the one destined to be lost,ᵇ so that the scripture might be fulfilled. ¹³But now I am coming

---

z Gk *flesh*   a Other ancient authorities read *protected in your name those whom*
b Gk *except the son of destruction*

to you, and I speak these things in the world so that they may have my joy made complete in themselves.[c] [14]I have given them your word, and the world has hated them because they do not belong to the world, just as I do not belong to the world. [15]I am not asking you to take them out of the world, but I ask you to protect them from the evil one.[d] [16]They do not belong to the world, just as I do not belong to the world. [17]Sanctify them in the truth; your word is truth. [18]As you have sent me into the world, so I have sent them into the world. [19]And for their sakes I sanctify myself, so that they also may be sanctified in truth.

[20]'I ask not only on behalf of these, but also on behalf of those who will believe in me through their word, [21]that they may all be one. As you, Father, are in me and I am in you, may they also be in us,[e] so that the world may believe that you have sent me. [22]The glory that you have given me I have given them, so that they may be one, as we are one, [23]I in them and you in me, that they may become completely one, so that the world may know that you have sent me and have loved them even as you have loved me. [24]Father, I desire that those also, whom you have given me, may be with me where I am, to see my glory, which you have given me because you loved me before the foundation of the world.

[25]'Righteous Father, the world does not know you, but I know you; and these know that you have sent me. [26]I made your name known to them, and I will make it known, so that the love with which you have loved me may be in them, and I in them.'

The Betrayal and Arrest of Jesus

18 After Jesus had spoken these words, he went out with his disciples across the Kidron valley to a place where there was a garden, which he and his disciples entered. [2]Now Judas, who betrayed him, also knew the place, because Jesus often met there with his disciples. [3]So Judas brought a detachment of soldiers together with police from the chief priests and the Pharisees, and they came there with lanterns and torches and weapons. [4]Then Jesus, knowing all that was to happen to him, came forward and asked them, 'For whom are you looking?'

---

c Or *among themselves*   d Or *from evil*   e Other ancient authorities read *be one in us*

⁵They answered, 'Jesus of Nazareth.'ᶠ Jesus replied, 'I am he.'ᵍ Judas, who betrayed him, was standing with them. ⁶When Jesusʰ said to them, 'I am he',ⁱ they stepped back and fell to the ground. ⁷Again he asked them, 'For whom are you looking?' And they said, 'Jesus of Nazareth.'ʲ ⁸Jesus answered, 'I told you that I am he.ᵏ So if you are looking for me, let these men go.' ⁹This was to fulfil the word that he had spoken, 'I did not lose a single one of those whom you gave me.' ¹⁰Then Simon Peter, who had a sword, drew it, struck the high priest's slave, and cut off his right ear. The slave's name was Malchus. ¹¹Jesus said to Peter, 'Put your sword back into its sheath. Am I not to drink the cup that the Father has given me?'

Jesus before the High Priest

¹²So the soldiers, their officer, and the Jewish police arrested Jesus and bound him. ¹³First they took him to Annas, who was the father-in-law of Caiaphas, the high priest that year. ¹⁴Caiaphas was the one who had advised the Jews that it was better to have one person die for the people.

Peter Denies Jesus

¹⁵Simon Peter and another disciple followed Jesus. Since that disciple was known to the high priest, he went with Jesus into the courtyard of the high priest, ¹⁶but Peter was standing outside at the gate. So the other disciple, who was known to the high priest, went out, spoke to the woman who guarded the gate, and brought Peter in. ¹⁷The woman said to Peter, 'You are not also one of this man's disciples, are you?' He said, 'I am not.' ¹⁸Now the slaves and the police had made a charcoal fire because it was cold, and they were standing round it and warming themselves. Peter also was standing with them and warming himself.

The High Priest Questions Jesus

¹⁹Then the high priest questioned Jesus about his disciples and about his teaching. ²⁰Jesus answered, 'I have spoken openly to the world; I have always taught in synagogues and in the temple, where all the Jews come together. I have said nothing in secret.

---

f Gk *the Nazorean*   g Gk *I am*   h Gk *he*   i Gk *I am*   j Gk *the Nazorean*   k Gk *I am*

²¹Why do you ask me? Ask those who heard what I said to them; they know what I said.' ²²When he had said this, one of the police standing nearby struck Jesus on the face, saying, 'Is that how you answer the high priest?' ²³Jesus answered, 'If I have spoken wrongly, testify to the wrong. But if I have spoken rightly, why do you strike me?' ²⁴Then Annas sent him bound to Caiaphas the high priest.

Peter Denies Jesus Again

²⁵Now Simon Peter was standing and warming himself. They asked him, 'You are not also one of his disciples, are you?' He denied it and said, 'I am not.' ²⁶One of the slaves of the high priest, a relative of the man whose ear Peter had cut off, asked, 'Did I not see you in the garden with him?' ²⁷Again Peter denied it, and at that moment the cock crowed.

Jesus before Pilate

²⁸Then they took Jesus from Caiaphas to Pilate's headquarters.ᴵ It was early in the morning. They themselves did not enter the headquarters,ᴵ so as to avoid ritual defilement and to be able to eat the Passover. ²⁹So Pilate went out to them and said, 'What accusation do you bring against this man?' ³⁰They answered, 'If this man were not a criminal, we would not have handed him over to you.' ³¹Pilate said to them, 'Take him yourselves and judge him according to your law.' The Jews replied, 'We are not permitted to put anyone to death.' ³²(This was to fulfil what Jesus had said when he indicated the kind of death he was to die.)

³³Then Pilate entered the headquartersᴵ again, summoned Jesus, and asked him, 'Are you the King of the Jews?' ³⁴Jesus answered, 'Do you ask this on your own, or did others tell you about me?' ³⁵Pilate replied, 'I am not a Jew, am I? Your own nation and the chief priests have handed you over to me. What have you done?' ³⁶Jesus answered, 'My kingdom is not from this world. If my kingdom were from this world, my followers would be fighting to keep me from being handed over to the Jews. But as it is, my kingdom is not from here.' ³⁷Pilate asked him, 'So you are a king?' Jesus answered, 'You say that I am a king. For this I was

---

1 Gk *the praetorium*

born, and for this I came into the world, to testify to the truth. Everyone who belongs to the truth listens to my voice.' [38] Pilate asked him, 'What is truth?'

Jesus Sentenced to Death

After he had said this, he went out to the Jews again and told them, 'I find no case against him. [39] But you have a custom that I release someone for you at the Passover. Do you want me to release for you the King of the Jews?' [40] They shouted in reply, 'Not this man, but Barabbas!' Now Barabbas was a bandit.

19 Then Pilate took Jesus and had him flogged. [2] And the soldiers wove a crown of thorns and put it on his head, and they dressed him in a purple robe. [3] They kept coming up to him, saying, 'Hail, King of the Jews!' and striking him on the face. [4] Pilate went out again and said to them, 'Look, I am bringing him out to you to let you know that I find no case against him.' [5] So Jesus came out, wearing the crown of thorns and the purple robe. Pilate said to them, 'Here is the man!' [6] When the chief priests and the police saw him, they shouted, 'Crucify him! Crucify him!' Pilate said to them, 'Take him yourselves and crucify him; I find no case against him.' [7] The Jews answered him, 'We have a law, and according to that law he ought to die because he has claimed to be the Son of God.'

[8] Now when Pilate heard this, he was more afraid than ever. [9] He entered his headquarters[m] again and asked Jesus, 'Where are you from?' But Jesus gave him no answer. [10] Pilate therefore said to him, 'Do you refuse to speak to me? Do you not know that I have power to release you, and power to crucify you?' [11] Jesus answered him, 'You would have no power over me unless it had been given you from above; therefore the one who handed me over to you is guilty of a greater sin.' [12] From then on Pilate tried to release him, but the Jews cried out, 'If you release this man, you are no friend of the emperor. Everyone who claims to be a king sets himself against the emperor.'

[13] When Pilate heard these words, he brought Jesus outside and sat[n] on the judge's bench at a place called The Stone Pavement, or in Hebrew[o] Gabbatha. [14] Now it was the day of Preparation for

---

m Gk *the praetorium*   n Or *seated him*   o That is, *Aramaic*

the Passover; and it was about noon. He said to the Jews, 'Here is your King!' [15]They cried out, 'Away with him! Away with him! Crucify him!' Pilate asked them, 'Shall I crucify your King?' The chief priests answered, 'We have no king but the emperor.' [16]Then he handed him over to them to be crucified.

The Crucifixion of Jesus

So they took Jesus; [17]and carrying the cross by himself, he went out to what is called The Place of the Skull, which in Hebrew[o] is called Golgotha. [18]There they crucified him, and with him two others, one on either side, with Jesus between them. [19]Pilate also had an inscription written and put on the cross. It read, 'Jesus of Nazareth,[p] the King of the Jews.' [20]Many of the Jews read this inscription, because the place where Jesus was crucified was near the city; and it was written in Hebrew,[q] in Latin, and in Greek. [21]Then the chief priests of the Jews said to Pilate, 'Do not write, "The King of the Jews", but, "This man said, I am King of the Jews." ' [22]Pilate answered, 'What I have written I have written.' [23]When the soldiers had crucified Jesus, they took his clothes and divided them into four parts, one for each soldier. They also took his tunic; now the tunic was seamless, woven in one piece from the top. [24]So they said to one another, 'Let us not tear it, but cast lots for it to see who will get it.' This was to fulfil what the scripture says,

'They divided my clothes among themselves,
and for my clothing they cast lots.'

[25]And that is what the soldiers did.

Meanwhile, standing near the cross of Jesus were his mother, and his mother's sister, Mary the wife of Clopas, and Mary Magdalene. [26]When Jesus saw his mother and the disciple whom he loved standing beside her, he said to his mother, 'Woman, here is your son.' [27]Then he said to the disciple, 'Here is your mother.' And from that hour the disciple took her into his own home.

[28]After this, when Jesus knew that all was now finished, he said (in order to fulfil the scripture), 'I am thirsty.' [29]A jar full of sour wine was standing there. So they put a sponge full of the wine on a branch of hyssop and held it to his mouth. [30]When Jesus

---

o That is, *Aramaic*   p Gk *the Nazorean*   q That is, *Aramaic*

had received the wine, he said, 'It is finished.' Then he bowed his head and gave up his spirit.

Jesus' Side Is Pierced

³¹Since it was the day of Preparation, the Jews did not want the bodies left on the cross during the sabbath, especially because that sabbath was a day of great solemnity. So they asked Pilate to have the legs of the crucified men broken and the bodies removed. ³²Then the soldiers came and broke the legs of the first and of the other who had been crucified with him. ³³But when they came to Jesus and saw that he was already dead, they did not break his legs. ³⁴Instead, one of the soldiers pierced his side with a spear, and at once blood and water came out. ³⁵(He who saw this has testified so that you also may believe. His testimony is true, and he knowsʳ that he tells the truth.) ³⁶These things occurred so that the scripture might be fulfilled, 'None of his bones shall be broken.' ³⁷And again another passage of scripture says, 'They will look on the one whom they have pierced.'

The Burial of Jesus

³⁸After these things, Joseph of Arimathea, who was a disciple of Jesus, though a secret one because of his fear of the Jews, asked Pilate to let him take away the body of Jesus. Pilate gave him permission; so he came and removed his body. ³⁹Nicodemus, who had at first come to Jesus by night, also came, bringing a mixture of myrrh and aloes, weighing about a hundred pounds. ⁴⁰They took the body of Jesus and wrapped it with the spices in linen cloths, according to the burial custom of the Jews. ⁴¹Now there was a garden in the place where he was crucified, and in the garden there was a new tomb in which no one had ever been laid. ⁴²And so, because it was the Jewish day of Preparation, and the tomb was nearby, they laid Jesus there.

The Resurrection of Jesus

20 Early on the first day of the week, while it was still dark, Mary Magdalene came to the tomb and saw that the stone had been removed from the tomb. ²So she ran and went to Simon

---

r Or *there is one who knows*

Peter and the other disciple, the one whom Jesus loved, and said to them, 'They have taken the Lord out of the tomb, and we do not know where they have laid him.' ³Then Peter and the other disciple set out and went towards the tomb. ⁴The two were running together, but the other disciple outran Peter and reached the tomb first. ⁵He bent down to look in and saw the linen wrappings lying there, but he did not go in. ⁶Then Simon Peter came, following him, and went into the tomb. He saw the linen wrappings lying there, ⁷and the cloth that had been on Jesus' head, not lying with the linen wrappings but rolled up in a place by itself. ⁸Then the other disciple, who reached the tomb first, also went in, and he saw and believed; ⁹for as yet they did not understand the scripture, that he must rise from the dead. ¹⁰Then the disciples returned to their homes.

Jesus Appears to Mary Magdalene

¹¹But Mary stood weeping outside the tomb. As she wept, she bent over to look^s into the tomb; ¹²and she saw two angels in white, sitting where the body of Jesus had been lying, one at the head and the other at the feet. ¹³They said to her, 'Woman, why are you weeping?' She said to them, 'They have taken away my Lord, and I do not know where they have laid him.' ¹⁴When she had said this, she turned round and saw Jesus standing there, but she did not know that it was Jesus. ¹⁵Jesus said to her, 'Woman, why are you weeping? For whom are you looking?' Supposing him to be the gardener, she said to him, 'Sir, if you have carried him away, tell me where you have laid him, and I will take him away.' ¹⁶Jesus said to her, 'Mary!' She turned and said to him in Hebrew,^{t} 'Rabbouni!' (which means Teacher). ¹⁷Jesus said to her, 'Do not hold on to me, because I have not yet ascended to the Father. But go to my brothers and say to them, "I am ascending to my Father and your Father, to my God and your God." ' ¹⁸Mary Magdalene went and announced to the disciples, 'I have seen the Lord'; and she told them that he had said these things to her.

Jesus Appears to the Disciples

¹⁹When it was evening on that day, the first day of the week, and the doors of the house where the disciples had met were

s Gk lacks *to look*   t That is, *Aramaic*

locked for fear of the Jews, Jesus came and stood among them and said, 'Peace be with you.' ²⁰After he said this, he showed them his hands and his side. Then the disciples rejoiced when they saw the Lord. ²¹Jesus said to them again, 'Peace be with you. As the Father has sent me, so I send you.' ²²When he had said this, he breathed on them and said to them, 'Receive the Holy Spirit. ²³If you forgive the sins of any, they are forgiven them; if you retain the sins of any, they are retained.'

Jesus and Thomas

²⁴But Thomas (who was called the Twin ᵘ), one of the twelve, was not with them when Jesus came. ²⁵So the other disciples told him, 'We have seen the Lord.' But he said to them, 'Unless I see the mark of the nails in his hands, and put my finger in the mark of the nails and my hand in his side, I will not believe.'

²⁶A week later his disciples were again in the house, and Thomas was with them. Although the doors were shut, Jesus came and stood among them and said, 'Peace be with you.' ²⁷Then he said to Thomas, 'Put your finger here and see my hands. Reach out your hand and put it in my side. Do not doubt but believe.' ²⁸Thomas answered him, 'My Lord and my God!' ²⁹Jesus said to him, 'Have you believed because you have seen me? Blessed are those who have not seen and yet have come to believe.'

The Purpose of This Book

³⁰Now Jesus did many other signs in the presence of his disciples, which are not written in this book. ³¹But these are written so that you may come to believe ᵛ that Jesus is the Messiah, ʷ the Son of God, and that through believing you may have life in his name.

Jesus Appears to Seven Disciples

21 After these things Jesus showed himself again to the disciples by the Sea of Tiberias; and he showed himself in this way. ²Gathered there together were Simon Peter, Thomas called the Twin, ˣ Nathanael of Cana in Galilee, the sons of

---

u Gk *Didymus*   v Other ancient authorities read *may continue to believe*   w Or *the Christ*
x Gk *Didymus*

Zebedee, and two others of his disciples. ³Simon Peter said to them, 'I am going fishing.' They said to him, 'We will go with you.' They went out and got into the boat, but that night they caught nothing.

⁴Just after daybreak, Jesus stood on the beach; but the disciples did not know that it was Jesus. ⁵Jesus said to them, 'Children, you have no fish, have you?' They answered him, 'No.' ⁶He said to them, 'Cast the net to the right side of the boat, and you will find some.' So they cast it, and now they were not able to haul it in because there were so many fish. ⁷That disciple whom Jesus loved said to Peter, 'It is the Lord!' When Simon Peter heard that it was the Lord, he put on some clothes, for he was naked, and jumped into the lake. ⁸But the other disciples came in the boat, dragging the net full of fish, for they were not far from the land, only about a hundred yards^y off.

⁹When they had gone ashore, they saw a charcoal fire there, with fish on it, and bread. ¹⁰Jesus said to them, 'Bring some of the fish that you have just caught.' ¹¹So Simon Peter went aboard and hauled the net ashore, full of large fish, a hundred and fifty-three of them; and though there were so many, the net was not torn. ¹²Jesus said to them, 'Come and have breakfast.' Now none of the disciples dared to ask him, 'Who are you?' because they knew it was the Lord. ¹³Jesus came and took the bread and gave it to them, and did the same with the fish. ¹⁴This was now the third time that Jesus appeared to the disciples after he was raised from the dead.

Jesus and Peter

¹⁵When they had finished breakfast, Jesus said to Simon Peter, 'Simon son of John, do you love me more than these?' He said to him, 'Yes, Lord; you know that I love you.' Jesus said to him, 'Feed my lambs.' ¹⁶A second time he said to him, 'Simon son of John, do you love me?' He said to him, 'Yes, Lord; you know that I love you.' Jesus said to him, 'Tend my sheep.' ¹⁷He said to him the third time, 'Simon son of John, do you love me?' Peter felt hurt because he said to him the third time, 'Do you love me?' And he said to him, 'Lord, you know everything; you know that

---

y Gk *two hundred cubits*

I love you.' Jesus said to him, 'Feed my sheep. ¹⁸Very truly, I tell you, when you were younger, you used to fasten your own belt and to go wherever you wished. But when you grow old, you will stretch out your hands, and someone else will fasten a belt around you and take you where you do not wish to go.' ¹⁹(He said this to indicate the kind of death by which he would glorify God.) After this he said to him, 'Follow me.'

Jesus and the Beloved Disciple

²⁰Peter turned and saw the disciple whom Jesus loved following them; he was the one who had reclined next to Jesus at the supper and had said, 'Lord, who is it that is going to betray you?' ²¹When Peter saw him, he said to Jesus, 'Lord, what about him?' ²²Jesus said to him, 'If it is my will that he remain until I come, what is that to you? Follow me!' ²³So the rumour spread in the community[z] that this disciple would not die. Yet Jesus did not say to him that he would not die, but, 'If it is my will that he remain until I come, what is that to you?'[a]

²⁴This is the disciple who is testifying to these things and has written them, and we know that his testimony is true. ²⁵But there are also many other things that Jesus did; if every one of them were written down, I suppose that the world itself could not contain the books that would be written.

z Gk among the brothers   a Other ancient authorities lack *what is that to you*